W9-BZW-465

Every Day by the Sun

Every Day by the Sun

A MEMOIR OF THE FAULKNERS
OF MISSISSIPPI

DEAN FAULKNER WELLS

CROWN PUBLISHERS ◉ NEW YORK

FAULKNER FAMILY

CROWN and the Crown colophon are registered trademarks of
Random House, Inc.

Parts of the Christmas story on pages 102–5 first appeared in *Mississippi
Magazine*, December 1987.

Library of Congress Cataloging-in-Publication Data
Wells, Dean Faulkner.
    Every day by the sun: a memoir of the Faulkners of Mississippi / by Dean
Faulkner Wells.—1st ed.
        p.   cm.
    Includes index.
1. Faulkner family.   2. Wells, Dean Faulkner.   3. Wells, Dean
Faulkner—Family.   4. Faulkner, William, 1897-1962.   5. Faulkner,
William, 1897-1962—Family.   6. Mississippi—Biography.   I. Title.
    CT274.F377W45 2011
    920.0762—dc22   2010031684

ISBN 978-0-307-59104-3
eISBN 978-0-307-59106-7

Printed in the United States of America

Book design by Lauren Dong
Title page photograph © Buddy Mays/CORBIS
Jacket design by Jennifer O'Connor
Jacket photographs: © Kevin Fleming/CORBIS (house), courtesy of the author (portraits)

10 9 8 7 6 5 4 3 2 1

First Edition

Larry

Dean never needed a watch. He lived every day of his life by the sun.

—FAMILY MEMBER SPEAKING OF DEAN SWIFT FAULKNER

Contents

Every Day by the Sun

Faulkner Family Tree

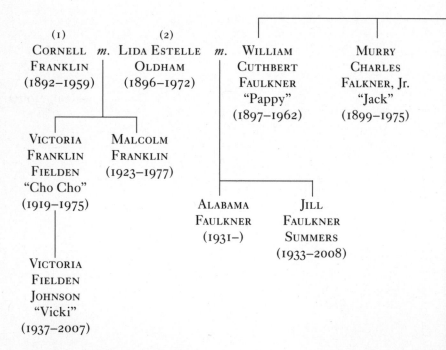

| (1) CORNELL FRANKLIN (1892–1959) | *m.* | (2) LIDA ESTELLE OLDHAM (1896–1972) | *m.* | WILLIAM CUTHBERT FAULKNER "Pappy" (1897–1962) | MURRY CHARLES FALKNER, Jr. "Jack" (1899–1975) |

VICTORIA FRANKLIN FIELDEN "Cho Cho" (1919–1975)

MALCOLM FRANKLIN (1923–1977)

ALABAMA FAULKNER (1931–)

JILL FAULKNER SUMMERS (1933–2008)

VICTORIA FIELDEN JOHNSON "Vicki" (1937–2007)

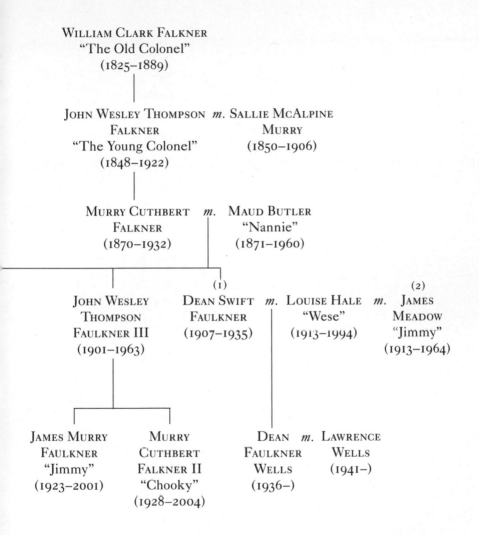

WILLIAM CLARK FALKNER
"The Old Colonel"
(1825–1889)

JOHN WESLEY THOMPSON *m.* SALLIE McALPINE
FALKNER   MURRY
"The Young Colonel"   (1850–1906)
(1848–1922)

MURRY CUTHBERT *m.* MAUD BUTLER
FALKNER   "Nannie"
(1870–1932)   (1871–1960)

(1)   (2)
JOHN WESLEY   DEAN SWIFT *m.* LOUISE HALE *m.* JAMES
THOMPSON   FAULKNER   "Wese"   MEADOW
FAULKNER III   (1907–1935)   (1913–1994)   "Jimmy"
(1901–1963)   (1913–1964)

JAMES MURRY   MURRY   DEAN *m.* LAWRENCE
FAULKNER   CUTHBERT   FAULKNER   WELLS
"Jimmy"   FALKNER II   WELLS   (1941–)
(1923–2001)   "Chooky"   (1936–)
                  (1928–2004)

Butler Family Tree

MAUD BUTLER *m.* MURRY C. FALKNER
(1871–1960)   (1870–1932)

WILLIAM CUTHBERT
MURRY CHARLES
JOHN WESLEY THOMPSON
DEAN SWIFT

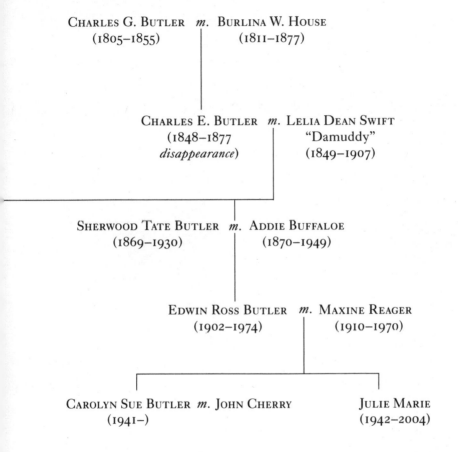

CHARLES G. BUTLER   *m.*   BURLINA W. HOUSE
(1805–1855)   (1811–1877)

CHARLES E. BUTLER   *m.*   LELIA DEAN SWIFT
(1848–1877   "Damuddy"
disappearance)   (1849–1907)

SHERWOOD TATE BUTLER   *m.*   ADDIE BUFFALOE
(1869–1930)   (1870–1949)

EDWIN ROSS BUTLER   *m.*   MAXINE REAGER
(1902–1974)   (1910–1970)

CAROLYN SUE BUTLER   *m.*   JOHN CHERRY   JULIE MARIE
(1941–)   (1942–2004)

Prologue

T HE BEST AND THE WORST THING THAT COULD HAVE HAP-
pened to me took place on November 10, 1935, four
months before I was born, when my father, a barnstorming pilot,
was killed in a plane crash at the age of twenty-eight. The best,
because it placed me at the center of the Faulkner family; the
worst, because I would never know my father.

He was Dean Swift Faulkner, the youngest of the four
Faulkner brothers of Mississippi: William, the future Nobel
Prize winner in literature; Jack, an FBI agent; and John, a painter
and writer. All four were pilots. Dean was the baby of his generation as I am in mine. His death defined my position in the family.
I became more than just another granddaughter or niece. I was
the last link to my father, and since he was gone, the people who
loved him so dearly cared for me in his stead; they did the best
they could for me. Due to an accident of birth I belonged to
all of them, but it was Dean's oldest brother, William, who felt
the heaviest responsibility for me. He encouraged Dean to learn
to fly, paid for his lessons, gave him a Waco C cabin cruiser—
William's own plane—and with it a job at Mid-South Airways in
Memphis, Tennessee.

After Dean's death, William suffered from grief and guilt I
imagine almost every day of his life. He attempted to assuage
the pain by offering me security, both emotional and financial,

whenever he could. It was as if William made a vow to Dean that November afternoon when he saw his unrecognizable body in the wreckage of the plane: He would tend to me in Dean's place. He fulfilled his promise, and I grew up calling him "Pappy."

Cherished by my family as an extension of my father, I have had to struggle to find my identity. My search for who I am started when I began to research my father's life. His influence on me could not have been stronger had he lived. And as Pappy's fame grew, of course we were all touched by it.

In 2010, I became the oldest surviving Faulkner in the Murry Falkner branch of the family. My father's first cousin, Dorothy "Dot" Falkner Dodson, daughter of Murry's brother, John, died January 23, 2010. We were the only remaining family members with firsthand memories of the long dead people who shaped and supported the man who is arguably the finest American writer of the twentieth century. Now I am, one might say, the last primary source—and I don't like anything about it. By the time I reached seventy, I expected to be transformed into Miss Habersham, Aunt Jenny, Granny Millard, or, if I was lucky, Dilsey. I believed with all my heart that to grow older was to grow wiser. I am living proof that this aint so. (Note that throughout I'm using Pappy's preferred "aint," without the apostrophe.)

My relatives were private people, building walls not only to shield themselves from outsiders but from one another. This vaunted Faulkner privacy, which has been interpreted as anything from crippling shyness to arrogance to paranoia, may have evolved as a safety hatch in light of our eccentric and sometimes outrageous behavior.

Over the generations my family can claim nearly every psychological aberration: narcissism and nymphomania, alcoholism and anorexia, agoraphobia, manic depression, paranoid schizophrenia. There have been thieves, adulterers, sociopaths, killers, racists, liars, and folks suffering from panic attacks and real bad tempers, though to the best of my knowledge we've never had a barn burner or a preacher.

The only place we can be found in relative harmony is St. Peter's Cemetery in Oxford, Mississippi. Yet there we can't even agree on how to spell our name. It appears as "FALKNER" on several headstones; in the next plot "FAULKNER"; in the main family plot both "FALKNER" and "FAULKNER," buried next to one another; and one grave marker reads "FA(U)LKNER." It is obvious that though there were not many of us to begin with, we've never been a close-knit family. We are prone to "falling-outs," quick to anger, and slow to forgive. Whereas most families come together at holidays or anniversaries, ours rarely has, at least not in my generation. With the exception of our immediate kin, we've been derelict in keeping up family ties.

Pappy tried. On New Year's Eve in the 1950s, he liked to host small gatherings for family and friends at his home, Rowan Oak. Dressed to the nines, we met shortly before midnight in the library, where magnums of champagne were chilling in wine coolers, and crystal champagne glasses were arranged on silver trays. As the hour approached, Pappy moved about the room and welcomed his guests. When our glasses were filled he would nod at one of the young men standing near the overhead light switch. Then he would take his place in front of the fire. When the lights were out and the room was still, with firelight dancing against the windowpanes, Pappy would lift his glass and give his traditional New Year's toast, unchanged from year to year. "Here's to the younger generation," he would say. "May you learn from the mistakes of your elders."

I'm still learning.

1

My Father's Death

I T NEVER OCCURRED TO ME THAT IT COULD HAVE BEEN PILOT error, that the plane crash that killed four young men—including the pilot, my father—could have been his fault. He had been taught to fly by the best. He had a commercial pilot's license and hundreds of hours of flight time and complete confidence in himself. When I began to search for answers, his fellow pilots told me that he was a natural, a pilot's pilot, that there was no aircraft that Dean couldn't fly, that his instincts for flying were almost mystical. The crash, the old barnstormers insisted, was caused by factors beyond his control. It could not have been Dean's fault.

He loved performing in air shows, and several days before his last one, in November 1935, he flew to Pontotoc, a small town in north Mississippi, where he was scheduled to put on an Armistice Day exhibition. He flew the Waco C cabin cruiser, a gift from William, a fire-engine-red biplane with tan leather seats and ashtrays on the armrests. An elegant aircraft, it seated four in comfort.

As usual, Dean had written all the promotional copy for the air show, had flyers printed, and flew over the town making low passes to drop the leaflets. Down they fluttered like confetti onto streets, trees, and rooftops. It was supper time on a Friday. At the sound of the plane's engine, people ran outside, children first, clapping their hands in excitement, pointing at the sky, their parents close behind, all caught up in the moment, plucking the flyers out of the air.

MAMMOTH ARMISTICE DAY AIR PAGEANT

Two days—Nov. 10–11, Two O'Clock.
Featuring Dean Faulkner and Navy Sowell.
THRILLING EXHIBITION OF STUNT FLYING
AND AERIAL ACROBATICS.
Death-defying parachute jumps by Navy Sowell.
See Pontotoc from the air. Long rides, one dollar.
Landing field west of Pontotoc.
In case of inclement weather show will be held
the following week.

Barnstorming shows were circuses, carnivals, vaudeville shows, and county fairs rolled into one. As a plane would thunder over, spectators would gather in a field to watch female wing walkers make their way from the cockpit to the struts, as sure and as precise as ballet dancers. Jumpers with parachutes clutched to their chests would plunge out of the planes, feeding the chute out to catch air as they plummeted toward earth. The real stars, however, were the daring young men in their flying machines. Reeve Lindbergh once wrote me that her father thought of the early aviators as members of a select fraternity, "the brotherhood of the air," drawn together by the love and danger of flight.

Dean had flown into Pontotoc from Memphis on Friday. He was at work early Saturday morning taking up fifty or sixty passengers before stunt flying in the afternoon: figure eights and loop-the-loops and heart-stopping stalls. One of his passengers that morning was a young farmer, Bud Warren, who had never flown before. As soon as the plane landed, Bud knew he was coming back the next day with two of his cousins. He wanted them to see their farms from the air. Bud Warren had had a real good time.

Sunday, November 10, 1935, was just right for flying. Dean went out early that morning to check on the weather. He rubbed his bare feet in the moist grass, licked his finger, and held it up against the wind. Perfect.

He was at the landing field west of Pontotoc by ten o'clock dressed in khakis, a white shirt, boots, a leather helmet with goggles, and a white silk scarf around his neck. He began, as he had on Saturday, taking passengers for rides, charging a dollar for ten or fifteen minutes in the air. Dean's wife, Louise, arrived unexpectedly around one o'clock, having driven down from Memphis. He was delighted to see her. They chatted briefly before he went back to work. Louise was five months pregnant with me and had recently been grounded by her doctor until she came to term. She had logged so many hours, Dean teased, that she could have been a pilot herself.

The line for rides was a long one, and it was nearly one thirty when Bud Warren, who had been waiting patiently, came forward with his cousins Henry and Lamon "Red" Graham. Dean recognized Bud from the day before. "Come on," he said. "Let's go see those farms."

Bud and Henry settled themselves into the back seats. Red, probably because he was a student pilot with several hours of flying time, sat up front with Dean. As they taxied down the field to get ready for takeoff, Dean returned Louise's wave. The red Waco took off into the sun.

Louise stood by the airfield eating an apple, wishing she were flying. As she waited for the plane, her sister, Clara, and brother-in-law, Roger Caldwell, showed up. Louise sat in the front seat of their car, chatting through the open door with Navy Sowell, the parachutist who was to make a jump that day. A young man delivered a ham sandwich that Dean had ordered from a café. Louise paid him and said, "Just hold on to it and take it out to the plane. He'll be hungry when he lands." Thirty or forty minutes passed. Someone in the crowd remarked, "Those Grahams are getting a first-class ride." Dean must have been rewarding them, Louise reasoned, for having waited so long. Then another onlooker: *"I bet they've crashed."* It was past two. The crowd was restless, complaining that the show should have started. Louise began to worry.

Louise, Clara, Roger, and Navy drove down a narrow gravel road where Dean's plane had last been seen. A pickup truck came barreling toward them. Passengers stood in the truck bed, shouting, "We saw it. We saw it go down. Over there just past that stand of pines. In the pasture. The plane's buried in the ground."

Navy and Roger ran across the field, leaving the car doors open. Louise struggled against Clara to get out. The men vanished into the pine thicket. When they reappeared moments later Clara could read the agony in their faces. They had found the Waco. Dean and his three passengers were dead.

Louise collapsed. Roger held her as Navy turned the car around and headed back to Pontotoc. News of the crash had reached the airfield by the time they returned. Spectators raced toward their cars. Two of Dean's friends and fellow pilots, Murry Spain and C. D. Lemmons, were waiting. They took Louise to C.D.'s home, where Lemmons's first phone call was to his family doctor to come take care of Louise. The second was to 546 in Oxford—William Faulkner's number.

When the telephone rang at Rowan Oak, William was outside in his yard putting up a trellis for a grape arbor. His wife,

Estelle, called him inside and handed him the phone. His features went smooth with shock. "How far from Thaxton? At what time? Was he alone?" He turned to Estelle. "Dean was killed in a crash at Thaxton." He began to place calls, first to Judge John Falkner, his uncle, asking him to get the operator to block calls to 15, the telephone number of his mother, Maud Butler Falkner. He phoned his brothers, Jack and John, and told them, "Come home. Mother will need us." Then he called the police. Thinking Louise was in Memphis, he asked them to set up a roadblock to detain her in Byhalia, Mississippi, and bring her to Oxford. "She must not be allowed to go to Thaxton." He was soon on his way to his mother's house.

One of Dean's fellow pilots had just heard the news. He had flown with Dean the week before and could not believe he was dead. He picked up the receiver and asked the operator to connect him to 15. After a long pause, the operator explained that she had orders not to put through any calls, but "just this once—"

Maud was waiting on her front steps when William pulled into her driveway. She gripped her handbag and gloves, rigid with grief. William reached out and she took his hand. They stood together in silence. Then he helped her into the car. They drove to Pontotoc without a word passing between them. Highway 6 was filled with traffic as Dean's friends raced to the scene of the crash. William drove to C. D. Lemmons's house and went inside. Maud stayed in the car, a small, erect figure.

Louise was in bed, groggy from a sedative the doctor had given her. William and C.D. helped her to the car, and C.D. tucked a blanket over her lap. She sat in the backseat, staring out the window. Then they began the drive back to Oxford. Maud spoke only once. "Did I ever do anything to make him unhappy?"

At Maud's home they were met by family members. Clara

helped put Louise to bed in Dean's old room. Before dark, Maud's second son, Jack Falkner, an FBI agent in North Carolina, would fly home in his yellow and black Aeronca. Her third son, John, was delayed in Lambert, Mississippi, when his crop duster nosed over on takeoff. He was now driving to Oxford with his family. The Falkners were banding together.

William drove by himself to the crash site at Thaxton. He found men working with blowtorches and hacksaws, racing against darkness to remove Dean's body from the wreckage. The Waco had been almost completely destroyed, its nose buried deep. It had gone down in an open spot in a wooded area about ten miles from the Pontotoc airfield. Under a towering oak, the bodies of the Graham cousins and Bud Warren lay on a flatbed truck. They had been hastily covered with bedsheets. William went to the plane and looked inside. The impact had driven the engine through the cockpit and smashed it into the passengers. When William saw what the crash had done to his brother, one of the Graham kinsmen overheard him say, "Hell, Dean, is that you?"

At five o'clock that afternoon, after the bodies had been taken to the funeral home in Pontotoc, a crowd was still standing around the plane, many of them Dean's fellow pilots, staring at the crash site in disbelief. Part of the red fabric covering the top left wing had ripped away.

On Armistice Day, November 11, 1935, the story of the crash appeared on the front page of the *Memphis Press-Scimitar*. The article stated that "an unofficial investigation disclosed that the control was on the right side and the wheel in the lap of Red Graham [which] would indicate that the student-pilot had taken control." The story ran with pictures of the Waco and of Dean's pilot's license photograph. He was twenty-eight; Red Graham was twenty-four, Henry Graham and Bud Warren were both twenty-one. Red, Henry, and Bud were buried the day after the crash in Sand Springs Cemetery, "the cemetery near where the wing fabric fluttered to earth." Finding fault for the crash is beyond mortal consideration.

2

Second Coming

OXFORD IN THE 1930S WAS A SLEEPY LITTLE ONE-HORSE town in the hills of north Mississippi, seat of Lafayette County (pronounced La*fay*ette by locals), and home to the University of Mississippi (Ole Miss). The town doubled in population every fall with a vital influx of youth and energy. The courthouse dominated the square, big and white in the center of an island of grass and old oak trees, its two stories and clock tower making it the tallest structure in town. Four clock faces pointed in each direction, and chimes rang the hour. Benches beneath the trees were occupied by farmers in overalls who whittled, talked, and played dominoes when the weather was right.

Town streets were laid out in an orderly grid with the courthouse at the hub, and the main street, Lamar Boulevard, connecting north and south. A Confederate statue, so common to Mississippi towns, faced south.

On Saturdays, farmers from out in the county came to town in mule-drawn wagons filled with seasonal produce to sell on the circle surrounding the courthouse. The pace was easy and slow even on days when Ole Miss had a home football game.

Each Christmas the square was transformed into a magical place when long strands of brightly colored electric lights were mounted on the courthouse cupola and stretched across the streets to the roofs of surrounding buildings. The square at night resembled a giant carousel, an enchanted place.

———

DURING THEIR BRIEF year together, Dean and my mother had lived in Memphis with Vernon Omlie, Dean's mentor and partner at Mid-South Airways. One painful afternoon in late November, Louise and William drove to Memphis and collected her belongings and Dean's. They said good-bye to a weeping Exxie Hardiman, Omlie's housekeeper, who had taken Dean under her wing and later welcomed Louise with open arms, nicknaming her "Baby Lou." Every Christmas, my mother received a letter from Exxie recalling the good times. They were addressed:

> *Baby Lou Faulkner*
> *South Lamar*
> *Oxford, Mississippi*

Louise moved in with Maud and settled into Dean's room to await my birth.

Maud's house was a buff brick structure located a few blocks south of the square. The courthouse clock could be seen from the dining room window. It was a British-style "captain's cottage" that she had designed herself with a gabled roof, a porthole-shaped window in the center gable, and a wraparound front gallery with French windows and a green canvas awning. A captain's lantern hung by the front door. Each morning Maud would roll down the awning to keep the sunlight off the parlor furniture. In winter the house was heated by a cantankerous coal furnace that she stoked by hand, and in summer it was cooled by large, black oscillating floor fans. The house was a few blocks from the local cotton gin, and in season it rumbled day and night. By late October the window screens were white with cotton lint.

Maud's home showed her love of detail: high ceilings, hardwood floors, a formal dining room, a spacious parlor with a fireplace, three compact bedrooms, and two baths ideally suited for her, her husband, Murry, and Dean, when he still lived at home. Much of the furniture had belonged to Murry's grandfather, William Clark Falkner, some of which he brought back from Mexico after the war of 1846: primitively carved, heavy oak chairs and tables, mirrors, and sideboard.

Dean's bedroom had a private entrance off the gallery. After Murry's death in 1932, Maud and Dean lived together until September 1934, when he married Louise and moved to Memphis. Two maiden ladies, Miss Frances Ward and Miss Judy Reed, rented the front bedroom for twenty-five dollars a month (the same rate Maud charged writer Elizabeth Spencer fifteen years later). Then on November 10, 1935, the crash brought Louise to her.

Maud's other sons were married with families of their own. Jack lived in North Carolina and was an FBI agent who traveled the world, and John lived in Lambert, Mississippi, farming and crop dusting. One year John sent his sons, Jimmy, fourteen, and Chooky, eleven, to live with Maud and attend school in Oxford. They slept on cots in the dining room. William and his wife, Estelle, lived in Oxford, but at the time of my birth he was in Hollywood working as a screenwriter. A month before I was born, he sent my mother a one-line telegram: "What will we do if it's a girl?" After Maud telephoned and left the news of my birth, he wrote to my mother: "You take care of the girl until I can get there and do it," a vow he honored for the rest of his life. The first step was having himself declared my legal guardian shortly after my birth.

STUDIOS
BEVERLY HILLS, CALIFORNIA

March 27th, 1936.

Dear Louise:-

Grand news. I know everything is going well.
You take good care of the girl until I can get there
and do it.

Sincerely,

Bill

Mrs. Louise Faulkner
Oxford,
Miss.

I was born in Oxford just before daylight on Sunday, March 22, 1936. Spring had come early that year. The redbuds and dogwoods were in full bloom as Maud took Louise for a long afternoon drive in her yellow Buick coupe with a rumble seat, which she loved dearly. They had driven far out in the county on gravel roads. It was twilight when they pulled back into Maud's driveway. Before dark she telephoned her family doctor, Gene Bramlett. "Gene, this is Maud. Meet us at the hospital now. Louise is having our baby."

Being born in a Mississippi hospital during the Depression was apparently a luxury. Two babies were delivered in Oxford's Bramlett Hospital in 1936. I was one of them, and William

Lewis, Jr., son of the co-owner of Neilson's Department Store, born exactly one month before I was, was the other.

There has never been a Poor Little Fatherless Child as spoiled as I. For the first five years, I thought life was perfect. My uncle William believed that a girl would be secure psychologically if she felt safe between the ages of two and five. (I certainly qualified.) My mother and I alternated between Maud's home in Oxford, and that of my Hale grandparents in the country, with occasional interludes at Rowan Oak. They were all havens of order and stability.

I never called anyone "Mother" or "Father," or "Mom" or "Dad," and certainly not "Mommy" or "Daddy," though my Hale grandparents, Pearl Brown and Elijah Sanford, were "Mama" and "Papa," which I thought were their real names. Maud was always "Nannie," and William was "Pappy." Their attempts to get me to say "Mother Louise" failed. The best I could do was "Mowese," which I gradually shortened to "Wese." The name on my birth certificate was Dean Faulkner. Nannie called me "Lamb." Papa Hale called me "Little Feller." Everybody else called me "Dean Baby."

When I was just six months old, Wese went to work as a part-time secretary. Caroline Barr, whom we called Mammy Callie, and who had nursed all four Faulkner boys and Jill, Pappy's daughter, walked the half mile from Rowan Oak to Nannie's every morning before dawn to supervise my care. In winter and summer she wore layers of clothing topped by a frilly long apron stiff with enough starch to stand by itself, and a matching white lace cap. She was so tiny that when Pappy picked her up after she collapsed shortly before her death, he could not believe how light she was, smaller than his mother, who stood a mere four feet eight inches and weighed eighty-nine pounds. Pappy held her funeral in the front parlor at Rowan Oak, and in 1940 he dedicated *Go Down, Moses* to her:

TO MAMMY

CAROLINE BARR

Mississippi
[1840–1940]

Who was born in slavery and who
gave to my family a fidelity without
stint or calculation of recompense
and to my childhood an immeasur-
able devotion and love

Her tombstone in St. Peter's Cemetery bears the inscription "Her white children bless her."

At Nannie's house, Mammy would sit in a child-sized wooden rocking chair with a cane seat and no armrests to prevent bumping a baby's head. Pappy had it made especially for her. It was placed next to the fireplace in the front parlor, where she dipped snuff as she held me and spat into the furnace register. In winter the stench of drying snuff was overpowering. An argument arose between Nannie and Mammy over whether snuff dipping was permitted in the parlor. If Nannie wanted her to attend me— and she did, though certainly not for any physical contribution, considering that Mammy at her advanced age could hold me only when someone placed me in her lap—she would have to take Mammy, snuff and all.

A young woman named Jerry was my regular nurse. She came every weekday at eight and stayed until five. Her one duty: *Keep Dean Baby happy.* To Jerry, a happy baby was a good baby, and good babies who were mostly seen and not heard had good schedules. Early to bed was an integral part of Jerry's routine. Before she left for the day, I ate an early supper and then went happily into the bathtub, where she sang my favorite song: "Froggy Went a-Courting." And if we had had an exceptionally good day she would recite "The Little Orphan Annie." I could hardly wait to hear her say "The goblins will get you if you don't watch out."

Then, thoroughly scrubbed, in a clean fresh nightgown, I was handed over to Nannie or Wese for a bedtime story such as "The King's Stilts." When I was old enough, Pappy had a pair of fire-engine-red stilts made for me with "DEAN" painted on them in large black letters. Then I said my "Now I Lay Me" prayers on my knees and stalled as long as I could over my list of "God blesses" from every family member down to every dog I could think of. By six o'clock I was in bed. Rarely did I see the sun go down.

Jerry taught me wonderful things: how to stand on my head, to say the alphabet backward (which I can still do), and to mind my manners. I learned not to be a scaredy-cat sissy-britches cry-baby tattletale Goody Two-shoes. The yessums and no'ms, please-sirs and thank-you-ma'ams are still with me—and with my children—thanks to Jerry's attention-getting devices, such as "I'll snatch you bald-headed," and "I'll yank a knot in you," and most of all, "Just because you don't get caught telling a lie don't mean you were telling the truth."

Nannie also had a cook, Lily, who arrived at the house by nine o'clock to have dinner ready at noon, the main meal of the day. The laundry was picked up on Monday and delivered on Thursday. A handyman, Henry Jones, lived just two blocks across the street from us. He could fix anything that broke. Every Friday, Mr. Ray drove in from the county to deliver a dozen eggs and a pound of butter. On our doorstep at dawn every other day appeared two quarts of milk in glass bottles that revealed cream at the top, along with a pint of heavy cream, which Nannie hand-whipped for desserts. She ran a tight ship with some very good help. We lived well in spite of the Depression.

Meals were served in the dining room because to Nannie the kitchen was a workplace. In block letters she painted "DONT COMPLAIN DONT EXPLAIN" over the stove, her adaptation of a phrase made famous by Wallis Simpson, Duchess of Windsor. When she ate alone, Nannie took all of her meals in the dining room, where she kept her easel by the window to catch the morning light. A slight odor of turpentine infused the air.

At every meal she would entertain me with a story we called "The Boat." I don't know when she made it up, but it was a significant part of our daily ritual, a meal-to-meal serial of adventure and danger during the First World War. At supper she painted a different scene on the bottom of my glass using tempera paint on the outside. I was able to see these pictures only if I drank all my milk. Our "boat" looked very much like the *Titanic*, but the heroic characters were based on our family and friends. Whenever Pappy ate with us he would take over the storytelling. His torpedoes barely missed the bow (and Jimmy and Chooky and me), and more than once the machine guns of his Messerschmitts raked the deck. We abandoned ship only to be miraculously rescued at breakfast the next morning.

I lived with Nannie, but I thought of Rowan Oak as home, too. Pappy had bought the antebellum house with four acres of land for six thousand dollars. It had been built in 1848 by Colonel Robert R. Sheegog and was designed by the architect William Turner. A traditional Greek Revival–style home, it had two stories, high ceilings, and two large parlors on either side of a central hallway. The facade featured a second-floor balcony behind four white columns, all framed by a cedar-lined walk. The first impression was of quiet grandeur, but in 1930 when Pappy, his wife, Estelle, and her two children from a previous marriage moved in, the house was falling apart from years of neglect. There was no electricity and no running water; squirrels and mice were completely at home on the second floor. Pappy and Aunt Estelle had their work cut out for them. The shell of a house needed everything from a new foundation to a new roof, wallpaper, wiring, plumbing, painting, and screens for windows. Pappy rolled up his sleeves and went to work, doing many repairs himself. Even in its dilapidated state, the house—with its grounds and long, curving driveway—evoked his great-grandfather's estate at Ripley. He named it "Rowan Oak," after the Scottish legend that a rowan tree bough nailed over a barn threshold would ward off evil spirits, keep the cow's milk from going bad, and—most important—guard and protect the privacy of all who lived there.

Behind Rowan Oak was a small cabin, and after Mammy Callie's death in 1940, Chrissie and Andrew Price moved into it. Chrissie and her daughter, Estelle, helped run the house, while Andrew tended the grounds and horses. At Rowan Oak, I learned that "dinner" meant the *evening* meal and candlelight. Aunt Estelle was an excellent cook. She made exotic curries and chutney dishes and set an elegant table with meals served by houseboys on delicate china, with silver goblets, silver bread and butter plates, and finger bowls on hand-embroidered linen place mats. In season there was a centerpiece of fresh-cut flowers. Pappy presided over this table with a quiet dignity and pleasure.

He was a stickler for good manners and taught my cousins Jill and Vicki and me how to behave at table: We were not to sit down until Aunt Estelle was seated. The grown-ups were given a choice before the first course was served: to smoke at table or drink wine with the meal. He would not allow anyone to do both. Smoking dulled the palate. The wine could not be appreciated. He would circle the table, wine bottle in hand, and each adult had to make a choice. He designated smokers by turning their empty wine glasses upside down so there could be no recanting the decision. We were to serve ourselves from dishes presented by the houseboy left to right. We were not to begin to eat until Aunt Estelle took the first bite (just in case the food was poisoned, he said). We were not allowed to leave the table until permission to be excused had been asked of, and granted by, our host.

The year I was born, the Prince of Wales was to be crowned Edward VIII, King of England. In his honor the Gorham Company released a new flat sterling silver pattern called "King Edward." Nannie's sister-in-law Holland Pierce Falkner (whom we children called "Auntee") and Nannie promptly ordered my first place setting of sterling flatware. By the time I was married twenty-two years later, twelve place settings were nearly complete—the king's abdication notwithstanding.

Every two or three months, Wese would drive me out to Mama and Papa Hale's farm, where Papa had built a wood-frame house on land he inherited from his father. While Mama and their three children stayed in the nearby town of Ecru in Union County, Papa and some hired hands sawed wood, baked bricks, framed and roofed, put in window panes, whitewashed the house and picket fence, and dug a well. They added a front porch with a swing and rocking chairs, and—best of all—a screened sleeping porch in the back.

As Wese and I drove east on Highway 30, time fell away. The farm, without electricity or plumbing, seemed to exist in a bygone era. There was no running water, no telephone or radio or refrigerator or electric fans. Not even a coal furnace or stove. The house was heated by fireplaces and the kitchen by a cast-iron wood-burning stove. A box of kindling sat next to it. At night the house was lit by kerosene lamps.

Mama Hale was up before dawn every morning, stoking the kitchen stove. She made ham and eggs (if the hens were laying), biscuits with white gravy, her blackberry jelly or Papa's homemade molasses. We had fresh milk, if the cows were giving and hadn't grazed on bitterweed. Otherwise Mama opened a small tin of Carnation Evaporated. There was an icebox—a large wooden cabinet with the bottom half insulated to hold a fifty-pound block of ice. Food that needed refrigerating was stored above. The ice truck would show up intermittently during the summer. Most of the time we did without. Water was drawn from the well behind the house. It was always cold.

My best friend in town was a little towheaded boy, Carl Downing, who lived two doors down from Nannie and who charged me a penny to ride my tricycle in front of his house till Nannie caught him at it. My best friend in the country was B. C. Jones, a handsome and funny African American boy a year older than I, who lived with his parents just down the road.

B.C.'s father sharecropped with Papa and ran the sawmill, worked the fields, slaughtered the hogs, cured the meat, and made the sorghum. Every Saturday his mother helped Mama Hale wash clothes in a cast-iron pot over a fire in the yard. B.C. and I would follow her around as she hung the wash out to dry. We tried to do everything the grown-ups did—hoeing, chopping and picking cotton, weeding Mama's garden, and generally getting in the way.

Life on the farm was orderly. Cows had to be milked, chickens fed, pigs slopped. Every Saturday afternoon, Papa would put B.C. and me in the back of his pickup for the five-minute ride to George Adams's store. He'd bring us a Baby Ruth to share while he talked weather and crops with our neighbors. If he could find some children to play with us, he'd stay for a game of checkers. On Sunday morning, Papa, Mama, and I were at Philadelphia Baptist Church by nine o'clock, squeaky clean.

B.C.'s main job was to "take care of Dean Baby"—along with my dog, Spot. Though Pappy and Aunt Estelle had several dogs at Rowan Oak, they weren't mine. Nannie hated dogs and would not have one in her house. Spot stayed in the country and waited for me. As the sun went down, I would say good-bye to B.C. and go inside. Mama would light the kerosene lamps, one in the living room and one to walk around with. We ate a cold supper left over from noon, then played Rook or Chinese checkers until everyone was yawning. Papa and Mama Hale allowed me to stay up past my bedtime. Nights were still and silent except for katydids and tree frogs. It was my favorite place on earth.

Occasionally the comfortable rhythms were disturbed. During the Depression many homeless, hopeless men walked the country roads. Some stopped at our house and begged a meal or offered to work for food. Mama fed all of them. B.C. and I would watch them approach the house. They made us feel sad but they never scared us. Gypsies were another matter.

Late on a Saturday afternoon, Papa came home from George Adams's store and told Mama that a band of gypsies had been seen camped on Cypress Creek only a mile or two away. "How many?" Mama said. We were shelling beans on the porch. Her voice shook. B.C. and I moved closer to each other on the swing.

"Probably two families," Papa said. "They have two wagons, a horse and a donkey, five or six men and women and a few little ones. They'll be coming this way before dark."

B.C. and I were terrified. We had never seen Papa so serious and could not have imagined that anything or anyone could scare Mama Hale. This was the woman who drove a surrey over a flooded bridge to take her five-year-old daughter to the doctor.

This time, however, she was afraid. "Gypsies steal children," B.C. whispered. The dogs crept under the house.

"I think we better hide now," I said. I was halfway around the house when I heard the jingling of the bells and an accordion playing. There they were at the top of the hill. The caravans were covered in designs of vivid colors. The gypsies wore bright red vests, green scarves, and blue sashes trimmed in gold. The men wore big gold earrings. Papa went to meet them. I noticed that he stretched to his full height of six feet, four inches.

"What can we do for you?" he said. B.C. and I couldn't understand the heavily accented reply. After a moment, Papa turned to Mama. "Pearl, they're hungry. They'll work. They sharpen knives and do chores. Or we can trade. They have jewelry and spools of thread."

"Trade!" Mama said. "Go get them a ham. I'll take a spool of silk thread." When Papa came back from the smokehouse Mama was holding a small spool of green thread. Then the gypsies were gone, vanishing as if by magic.

Darkness was setting in. Papa said, "Little Feller, let's walk B.C. home." Hand in hand, we went down the path, B.C. on one side of Papa, me on the other, holding on tight.

One night I was awakened by the dogs barking and chickens squawking. Papa took his shotgun and went outside. I ran to Mama's room. "Fox in the henhouse," she said, and put me back to bed. Another night I awoke to a bell tolling. Each farm had a large iron bell in the yard close to the house, and each one had a distinctive tone so that the urgent tolling in the middle of the night was identifiable and frightening. "Trouble at the Waiteses'," Papa said. Someone needed help, and all who heard the bell got dressed and went to their aid.

—

IN DECEMBER 1941 my mother married Jimmy Meadow, a news-paperman. I had been sent out in the country to stay with Mama and Papa while the newlyweds were on their honeymoon.

My mother and Jimmy returned late at night. Papa had long since gone to bed. I refused to sleep, and Mama and I waited up for them. She held me in her lap in a rocking chair in front of the fire. The kerosene lamps were out. The house was dark except for firelight.

We heard the car coming a mile away, as it turned off the highway onto the Hales' dirt road. We watched the headlight beams glancing off the treetops while the car came closer and closer, stopping just outside the picket fence. I ran to the window and watched my mother and stepfather coming across the yard. Then I hid behind Mama. While we waited, I had been idly playing with the big pearl buttons on her nightgown. They were cool to the touch and pretty. Now, when Mama picked me up to hand me to Wese and *Jimmy*—no longer the Wese that I had known and had had all to myself—I instantly and forever hated all buttons.

Late the next afternoon, Monday, December 8, 1941, we drove into town. I had overheard some of the whispered grown-up talk all day Sunday and had seen Mama shake her head at Papa whenever he started to ask Jimmy a question. I'd even heard her say, "Hush, Sanford, you'll scare the baby." Now I sat in the backseat clutching Janie Walker, my doll. There was a light frost and I was glad the car had a heater. Even so, I should have been up front with Wese. Then Jimmy turned on the radio. At first there was static, then I heard a clear, resonant voice say, "This is a date that will live in infamy." I didn't know what infamy was, but I agreed with the man. I did not know who or what a president was, but this voice spoke to me when he said that our country was at war. This sounded too good to be true. We'd probably all get shot or blown up and die and I wouldn't have to go and live with Wese and Jimmy.

We settled in Clarksdale, some sixty miles west of Oxford. We lived in a small apartment building on the second floor. Janie Walker was my only link to Oxford. I had packed her clothes in her doll suitcase when I left Nannie's. Within months my identity was gone. Dean Baby Faulkner was gone. Jimmy adopted me and I became Dean Meadow and would be for twelve long years. It's too easy to blame my mother. She always said, "I did it for you. You needed a father." She could not have spoken truer words.

Poor Jimmy. He had married a beautiful young widow, a tragic figure, a lovely woman who needed him—and with her came the worst piece of would-be-royal baggage in Mississippi. Later we moved into a nice white house on a nice tree-lined street. Jimmy bought me a bicycle and taught me how to ride it. He bought me a fox terrier puppy that I named "Little Bit," who became an integral part of my life for the next thirteen years. I taught Little Bit how to ride in the basket of my bicycle. We were a sight to behold. One Saturday afternoon when Jimmy and I were walking home from the picture show, he taught me to recite the Twenty-third Psalm, betting me a quarter that I couldn't learn it by the time we got home.

JIMMY: "The Lord is my shepherd. I shall not want."
ME: "The Lord is my shepherd. I shall not want."
JIMMY: "He leadeth me beside the still waters."
ME: "He leadeth me beside the still waters."

We stopped at the school playground to swing. The lesson went on. By the time we got home I could recite the psalm all the way to *I shall dwell in the house of the Lord forever,* which to my five-year-old ears sounded like a real good place to be. I kept that quarter a long time.

From Jimmy I also learned what the smell of whiskey on a man's breath could mean. I learned to run fast when things got ugly and then to feel fearful and guilty about running away. He may have been a fine journalist, but he was also a world-class drunk. The first night that Jimmy hit Wese, I packed my suitcase, then I packed Janie's. I picked her up and we left. It was very late. Wese and Jimmy had finally gone to sleep. I made it down two flights of stairs, out the front door, and two blocks down the street. There was no place to go. I sat on the curb in the dark until I stopped crying. Then I turned back to the only home I knew. *Where did I belong? Where were my people? Who was I?*

3
Ancestors

MAUD BUTLER FALKNER, MATRIARCH OF THE FALKNER FAMily and my beloved grandmother, was one of those people I thought were just born old. She was sixty-four when I came along. Recently the *Oxford Eagle* ran a picture of her taken by an unidentified photographer in the mid-1890s. There she sits in all her lace and ruffles, puffed sleeves falling below her elbows, a wide sash at her corseted waist, upswept hair, a small, delicate, lovely, dark-eyed figure with a childlike countenance, slightly sad, innocent and shy, and very, very young.

This is not the woman I thought I knew. Growing up I became aware of her private nature, of the distance she kept between herself and the rest of the world—and her family—but I had no idea of the extent to which she had isolated herself. For instance, we never celebrated her birthday because no one knew the date. Though I had always understood that I was named for my father, I did not know until I was a grown woman, long after Maud's death, that my father had been named for his maternal grandmother, Lelia Dean Swift Butler.

The day that Maud married Murry Falkner in the fall of 1896 in Oxford, Mississippi, she gave up being a Butler and became a Falkner. It was as if she wished to eradicate everything pertaining to the Butlers, or so I've been told. Yet there are a few family members and Faulkner biographers who credit the Butlers for the genius of William Faulkner.

I did not know that Maud's mother and brother were buried in St. Peter's Cemetery within a stone's throw of all the old Falkners (and now of Maud herself). I was not aware that she had a brother or that they grew up in Oxford. The house where she spent her childhood still stands on what is now Jefferson Avenue. A Victorian cottage with a touch of gingerbread surrounding the porch, of light brown clapboard construction with heavy oak double doors and a backyard large enough to hold her father's pigs, cow, and mule, it is situated a few blocks northeast of the square within shouting distance of the L. Q. C. Lamar house. The Butler and Lamar children were playmates. I like to think of her as a happy little girl sitting in the front porch swing, waiting for her father to come home for supper.

Maud's family arrived in Oxford long before the Falkners. According to Joel Williamson's *William Faulkner and Southern History*, Charles G. Butler and his wife, Burlina, Maud's grandparents, were living in Oxford in the early 1830s while the Falkners were still in Ripley, Mississippi. They were among the earliest settlers in Lafayette County. Charles G., an influential Baptist and prosperous property owner, was the first county sheriff and surveyor. He laid out the grid for the new city of Oxford. He and Burlina owned twenty-five acres of land, including lots on the courthouse square where, in 1840, they built a hotel named the Oxford Inn that "became the centerpiece of the Butler family's prosperity."

I had no idea, growing up, that my Butler great-great-grandparents owned more property in Oxford than the Falkners. Their real estate holdings approached $12,000, "placing them comfortably among the well-to-do people in the county." There were six children in the family. The youngest son, Charles Edward, was to be Maud's father. They called him "Charlie." I never heard his name mentioned.

After Charles G. died in 1855, Burlina, "a woman of impressive managerial skills," was able to double her husband's real estate holdings. A successful businesswoman and a "slaveholder of significant proportions," she, along with her sons William and Henry, owned real estate holdings worth some $95,000, nearly twice that of the Falkner fortune.

Then the Butlers fell on hard times. During the war, General A. G. "Whiskey" Smith burned Oxford to the ground. Burlina, according to Williamson, "escaped from her burning hotel with nothing more than the clothes on her back." Until then, the Butlers and Falkners had led parallel lives, comfortable and financially secure. They also shared a penchant for violence, which was a source of pride for the Falkners, shame for the Butlers.

Very little is known about any Faulkner ancestors before the "Old Colonel," William Clark Falkner, for whom William was named. He was larger than life with an extraordinary career: lawyer; veteran of two wars, Mexican and Civil; owner of extensive land holdings in Ripley, Mississippi; builder of the first railroad in north Mississippi; and published writer, best known for *The White Rose of Memphis* and *Rapid Ramblings in Europe*. He served as the prototype for several of William's aristocratic characters, such as Colonel John Sartoris and Major de Spain. In many ways William emulated his great-grandfather by living as a gentleman farmer with horses and dogs on an antebellum estate, and by writing, of course.

The Old Colonel was the most violent of the Falkners. It was generally known in north Mississippi that his "Bowie knife and pistols [were] consistently about his person." In May 1849, one Robert Hindman made the fatal mistake of calling Falkner "a damned liar," then pointing a revolver at him. As the two men struggled for the pistol, it misfired three times. Falkner drew his knife and stabbed Hindman through the heart, killing him instantly. The inscription on Hindman's original tombstone read "Murdered at Ripley, Miss. By Wm. C. Falkner May 8, 1849." The Old Colonel was tried and acquitted. "Murdered" was changed to "killed."

Two years later, the Old Colonel shot and killed a friend of the Hindman family, Erasmus W. Morris. Again, an argument had led to violence. Falkner pulled his pistol and fired at Morris's head, killing him instantly. Once again he was tried for murder and acquitted.

Then Colonel Falkner and Thomas Hindman, Jr., the brother of the murdered—or killed—Robert Hindman, drew up an agreement to fight a duel in Arkansas, where it would be easier for the survivor to avoid prosecution. The agreement read: "Each man is to have two revolvers, take stands fifty yards apart, and *advance and fire as he pleases*" (italics mine), which is the strangest dueling procedure I've ever heard of. Fortunately, a mutual friend intervened and the duel never took place.

On November 5, 1889, Colonel Falkner was shot dead on the public square in Ripley by his former business partner, Richard Thurmond. The two had run against each other for a seat in the state legislature, which Falkner won by a landslide. Presumably embittered by the loss, Thurmond came looking for Falkner. The local newspaper reported that "Thurmond used a .44 caliber pistol to do the work." Thurmond was indicted for manslaughter and was released on his own recognizance after he posted a $10,000 bail. His trial was postponed for a year. When the jury came in after a short deliberation, the verdict was "Not guilty." Guilty verdicts were obviously hard to come by in those days.

A statue of the Old Colonel, which he himself commissioned in Italian marble at a cost of $2,022 (paid for by his heirs), stands today in the Ripley cemetery—in Williamson's words: "Eight feet in height and one quarter larger than life. It rests atop a fourteen foot pedestal. . . . The right forearm thrusts forward from the elbow, hand open, palm up" as though "explaining earnestly, patiently, things that can be made clear to thoughtful persons."

When I was a girl and a not-so-thoughtful person, I organized a midnight ride to Ripley to offer my respects to the Old Colonel. All was quiet in the cemetery. The moonlight was bright enough for us to read the inscription on the tombstone.

COL. WILLIAM FALKNER
BORN
JULY 6, 1825
DIED
Nov. 6, 1889

It took a few moments and a little help from my friends for me to climb his statue. They handed me a cold Budweiser already opened. I carefully placed it in his palm.

The violent streak passed over the next generation only to be inherited by Murry Falkner, the Old Colonel's grandson and William's father. According to Williamson, Murry "in an overly aggressive attempt to defend the honor" of a young woman (not Maud) "got into a fight with a local man with a dangerous reputation." Murry won the fight, but the next day the man found him in a drugstore on the square and shot Murry "from behind with a twelve-gauge shotgun. . . . Then, while Murry lay on the floor, pointed a pistol at his face and shot him in the mouth." His mother, Sallie Murry Falkner, rushed to the scene as soon as she heard about the shooting. She used asafetida to induce vomiting. Murry threw up the bullet, the story goes, and his life was saved. A miracle.

Growing up I heard about Falkners good and bad, but the

Butlers were seldom mentioned. I knew, for instance, that my father's generation called the Young Colonel and his wife "Grandfather and Grandmother Falkner." Murry was referred to as "Big Dad." My cousins Jimmy and Chooky called their uncle William "Brother Will," though my cousin Jill and stepcousins Cho Cho, Malcolm, and Vicki—and I, of course—called him "Pappy." Maud was "Sis Maud" to her in-laws, "Granny" to Vicki and Jill, and "Nannie" to Jimmy, Chooky, and me. This confusing array of nicknames demonstrates once again the Falkner propensity for failing to agree about almost anything. And yet only one such name survived in the *Butler* family: "Damuddy" was her grandchildren's pet name for Lelia Dean Swift Butler, Maud's mother.

There were, as I was to discover, reasons for this omission.

Charlie Butler—Maud's father—and Murry's father, John Wesley Thompson Falkner, were contemporaries, both born in 1848. In 1885, J.W.T. moved his family to Oxford, set up a law practice, and later became the founding president of the First National Bank. At the same time, the war and its aftermath had taken a serious toll on the Butlers. Before he was twenty, Charlie became head of the family. His father and two older brothers were dead. On July 31, 1868, Charlie and Lelia Dean Swift applied for a marriage license in Lafayette County. They were married on August 2.

Little is known about Lelia Dean Swift. It was said that she came to Oxford from Arkansas, that she had studied sculpture and painting, that she was a staunch Southern Baptist, and that she had been offered a scholarship to study art in Italy, which she declined because by that time she had two children: Sherwood, born in 1869, and Maud, born in 1871.

Maud rarely spoke of her mother, but when she did it was with admiration for her talent. All of Oxford, it seemed, knew of Lelia's ability to carve a pound of butter into a swan, or chisel dolls from blocks of ice. She was considered an intelligent, talented woman, yet, as far as I know, only one of her paintings survives.

In 1875, Charlie Butler had to borrow money to support his family, but the next year his circumstances improved vastly. He was appointed town marshal by the mayor and board of aldermen, a position he would hold for nearly twelve years. According to Williamson, as town policeman, a job similar to that of his father, Oxford's first sheriff, Charlie's duties included the arrest of "anyone drunk or committing a nuisance, or exhibiting a deadly weapon or using profane or obscene language or acting disorderly or violating any ordinance of this town."

In addition to keeping the peace, Williamson continues, Charlie served as tax collector. His salary was $50 a month and 5 percent of all taxes collected. In 1876, city taxes totaled $3,000 and Charlie earned $150, a sum that quadrupled over the next few years as Oxford grew. Charlie was also responsible for enforcing quarantines during epidemics, for "disinfecting privies with lime, and the never-ending, exasperating chore of rounding up livestock that had escaped into the streets. He was paid 50 cents for catching a pig, 25 cents for keeping it, 25 cents for removing a dead dog."

Charlie filled an office later called "town manager," and with it his duties grew. His "place in the Oxford community seemed very secure. . . . He was seen as an energetic and engaging young man . . . who moved about town doing its business effectively and efficiently." He joined the Masonic Order in 1878.

Charlie's downfall started in 1881, when he came up $2,000 short in reported tax revenues. The board of aldermen showed leniency, however, and allowed him sizable deductions for expenses. He ended up paying the city $138.05.

The next problem was far more serious. On May 17, 1883, the *Oxford Eagle* reported that Charlie had killed Sam Thompson, the editor of the newspaper. On the day of the shooting, court was in session and Charlie was acting as bailiff. It was his job to summon defendants to court. He called for a man named Sullivan. At that moment Sam Thompson, also waiting to be summoned, was slumped on a bench outside the courthouse, very drunk. Each time Charlie called Sullivan's name, Thompson answered, *"Here!"* Then he staggered about, pretending to be the bailiff, calling his own name.

Thompson was facing trial "for abduction of a female and unlawful cohabitation." This was no news to Oxford. Everyone knew that Thompson was keeping a teenage mistress, Eudora Watkins. She lived with an African American woman who worked in Thompson's household and, according to rumor, served "sexual purposes." Eudora herself was under indictment for carrying a deadly weapon.

When Sullivan passed Thompson on his way into court, Thompson cursed him, "applying to him . . . a very gross epithet." Charlie attempted to arrest Thompson, who at first went peaceably. Then he refused to go any farther. In the ensuing scuffle, Thompson grabbed Charlie's "coat sleeve, lapel or throat," and Charlie shouted for help. A man appeared within seconds; everyone inside the courthouse heard the shouting and commotion. The three men became locked in a deadly embrace. Charlie drew his revolver and said, "Thompson, if you don't let me go, I'll kill you." Then he lowered the gun and pointed it at the ground and repeated, "Turn me loose or I will kill you."

"Shoot, you barn-burning son of a bitch!" Thompson yelled. And so Charlie did. Thompson was dead, a bullet through his heart. Charlie surrendered, was indicted for manslaughter, and released on $2,500 bail pending the next court session. No one knows why Thompson accused Charlie of arson. As Williamson writes, barn burning, "the crime of sneaks and cowards," was not one of Charlie's failings. At his trial in May 1884, Charlie Butler was found not guilty of manslaughter, the consensus being that "if there was any man who needed killing in Lafayette County . . . it was Sam Thompson."

Throughout the next year Charlie continued to serve as marshal and tax collector. Since taxes had been raised to support a new school, a considerable amount of money was flowing through his hands. Then the board of aldermen hired attorney J. W. T. Falkner to audit the books. He found a great deal of tax revenue missing. No one knew exactly how much, since Charlie had been keeping the accounts. Before Christmas 1887, Charlie Butler disappeared. He took his leave on a westbound train with an estimated three to five thousand dollars in embezzled city tax revenues and a beautiful octoroon, a seamstress in the Jacob Thompson household. Jacob Thompson was a prominent lawyer and politician who served as secretary of the Interior from 1857 to 1861. They vanished without a trace, never to be seen or heard from again—or so the Falkner version of the story goes.

Four inches of snow fell on Lafayette County that December. Oxford must have looked like a Christmas card. I ache for Maud, who turned sixteen that November. She never (in my lifetime) put up a Christmas tree, no red and green candles in the dining room, no wreath on the front door. There was no Christmas celebration for Maud in 1887 or thereafter. I had always thought Dean's death caused her to ignore the holiday. Now I know better.

I've learned much more about Charlie's disappearance thanks to a newly discovered cousin, Carolyn Butler Cherry. We share Charlie, for better or for worse, as a great-grandfather: Charlie's son, Sherwood, was Carolyn's grandfather; Charlie's daughter, Maud, was my grandmother. (Charlie was William Faulkner's grandfather.) I was raised in the Faulkner family, where

Charlie's infamous departure was never discussed. Carolyn grew up in the Butler family, where the consensus was that Charlie had no intention of abandoning his wife and children, was planning to come back home someday, and was possibly killed by a prisoner he was transporting.

The source of this information, previously unpublished and appearing here for the first time with Carolyn's permission, is a letter passed down in the Butler family. It is handwritten by Charlie and dated November 19, 1887:

Topeka Kansas 11–19/87

My Dear Lelia,

   I did not stop in either St Louis or Kansas. I was up all night last night & feel real well this morning. I will only be here a few minutes, so I will have to make this short—but I will write you a long letter as soon as I stop. I never saw any body that I even know before I left—Cairo. I wanted to stop and see Barry Glick in Kansas City but did not stop will see when I come back through there. Much love and kisses for your self and children.

Lovingly,
Charlie

According to Carolyn, the Butler family has long believed that Charlie, acting as a deputy sheriff, was in the process of transporting a prisoner from Topeka, Kansas, to Holly Springs, Mississippi. He and the unnamed prisoner disappeared and were never heard from again. Sometime after the disappearance in November 1887, Lelia Butler received an envelope marked "United States Senate/Official or Department Business/FREE" postage. It was addressed to Mrs. L. D. Butler of Oxford, Mississippi. The envelope contained an unused ticket, number D437, on the Kansas City, Memphis and Birmingham Railroad. The ticket was issued in Memphis on November 13, 1887. The passenger is identified as "Charles Butler + one." It was good from Memphis to Holly Springs. The account listed was I.C.R.R. and it was good for one trip only, until November 31 [*sic*], 1887. This reservation for two seats was sent to her apparently because it had been paid for in advance but had not been used.

Another document that was passed down in the Butler family is a telegram dated "December 188?" from Topeka, Kansas, addressed to "G. T. O'Haver Supt of Police Mps." The message reads simply "No such warrant applied for." It is signed "E. B. Allen, Secy State."

A month after Charlie disappeared, Lelia must have contacted authorities to investigate whether he was indeed assigned to bring back a prisoner from Kansas. The Memphis superintendent of police, G. T. O'Haver, contacted Topeka on her behalf, and this telegram indicates that no prisoner transfer warrant was applied for, by Charlie or anyone else.

It is possible that Charlie told Lelia that he was going to To-peka to escort a prisoner back to Mississippi. The letter does not mention his mission, which implies that Lelia might have known why he was in Topeka.

Carolyn observed that "the tone of the letter does not appear to be from a man who was about to disappear, leaving a wife and two children." I agree, but if there was no warrant or prisoner, Charlie's letter becomes suspect. Why was he in Topeka? At best, the letter seems to be a poignant farewell to his wife and children. One senses the desperation of a man on the run, missing his family and racked by guilt, yet at the same time trying to cover his tracks and provide a plausible explanation for his disappearance. The promised follow-up letter ("a long letter as soon as I stop") never arrived.

With his experience in law enforcement, Charlie would have known that reserving a train ticket for two was routine planning for transporting a prisoner. At a stopover in Memphis, before boarding the train to Kansas (via Cairo, Illinois) he reserved two return tickets from Memphis to Holly Springs for "Charlie Butler + one." Two days later he posted a letter from Topeka and disappeared forever.

Carolyn grew up believing that the prisoner Charlie allegedly was transporting from Topeka robbed and killed him. She accepted that his letter to Lelia was sincere and that he intended to return to Oxford and take his punishment. She grew up hoping for the best, whereas I grew up knowing nothing about the Butlers.

However, I now believe Charles E. Butler may have surfaced in Fort Smith, Arkansas. In 1899, a "G. S. Butler" was sworn in as a U.S. deputy marshal at Fort Smith. Was this Charles E. Butler's alias? Charles may have substituted his father's and son's initials for his own. His father's middle initial was G and his son was named Sherwood.

It is logical that Charlie would have returned to law enforcement. If so, Fort Smith was the place to do it. The Federal Court for the Western District of Arkansas was based there. Judge Isaac C. Parker, known as the "hanging judge," presided over the court, which had jurisdiction over the Indian territories and many lawmen on its payroll.

It is intriguing that the deputy marshal's oath of office signed

"G. S. Butler" contains a signature similar to Charlie's handwriting. He had a distinctive way of writing a capital B with a loop before it. This loop can be seen in both the G. S. Butler signature and the name "Barry" in line eleven of Charlie's November 19 letter to his wife.

G. S. Butler was a man of mystery who left behind no personal data, no birth or burial records. He is not listed on any census in Fort Smith, Arkansas, or the surrounding counties. Who was he? Was he Charles E. Butler?

When Charlie left Oxford with the town's tax receipts, a seamstress in the household of Jacob Thompson disappeared at the same time. It was said that they ran away together. The 1880 census listed two mulatto servants in the Thompson household, Laura Poindexter, twenty-five, born in Kentucky in 1855, and her daughter, Lou, six, born in Tennessee in 1874. At the time of the census, Jacob Thompson lived in Memphis, but he had retired by 1887 and had a home in Oxford when Laura ran away (presumably taking her daughter with her). It is possible that Laura Poindexter was the "beautiful octoroon" who disappeared with Charlie Butler. We will probably never know.

The situation is as complicated as a William Faulkner short story: After Maud's father ran away with tax receipts, her future father-in-law, J. W. T. Falkner, in his capacity as city attorney, prosecuted Charlie Butler in absentia. Obviously, Maud and Murry were so much in love that they did not allow the tensions between their parents to affect them. Almost to the day nine years later they were married, and from then on neither her father's crime nor his *name* was discussed by the Falkners.* William would not have learned about his Butler grandfather at home. Perhaps one of his schoolmates said, one day at recess, "Hey, Bill, I hear your granddaddy ran off with the town's money."

In January 1888, Charlie was voted out of office, in absentia, at a special meeting of the board of aldermen held "for the

---

*In the summer of 2008 I asked my father's cousin Dot Falkner Dodson, Murry's niece, what she had heard about Charlie. She was shocked that I would bring up the subject and was cautious and politic in her reply. She said that she'd always wondered if I "knew about it." Charlie's disappearance was still a taboo subject among the Falkners, more than a century after the fact!

purpose of hearing report of committee to audit Books of C.E. Butler, absconding marshall."

At the time of Charlie's flight, Lelia was thirty-eight years old. Their marriage had been above reproach. Charlie was considered an earnest, hardworking provider. Although Lelia herself remained a mystery, refusing to discuss her past with anyone, the couple was well connected socially. The problem, as Joel Williamson diplomatically observes, was that Charlie and Lelia "did not get along." Lelia did not have any more children after Sherwood and Maud. The absence of doctors' records of miscarriages or stillbirths would suggest that after Maud's birth there was little or no sexual relationship between Lelia and Charlie.

Charlie did not leave his family penniless. The house was in Lelia's name, and in 1889, the 148 acres that Charlie had inherited from his parents were auctioned off on the courthouse steps. Meanwhile, Maud attended the Industrial Institute and College for the Education of White Girls in Columbus, Mississippi. In 1890, she and Lelia were living in Texarkana, Arkansas, where Maud worked as a secretary. She and her mother visited Sherwood often in Oxford. Maud renewed friendships with her childhood friends, among them Holland Falkner and her brother Murry.

Murry and Maud were married in the Methodist parsonage on November 8, 1896, quietly, without any family members present. They left for their new home in New Albany, Mississippi, the next morning. Lelia did not attend the ceremony because of her hard feelings toward Murry's father. For years afterward, whenever she wrote to her daughter, the letters were addressed:

Miss Maud Butler
in care of
Mr. Murry Falkner

No wonder Maud never talked about her family.

Lelia died leaving little tangible evidence of her existence, no letters or books, no pieces of jewelry or furniture. I have one painting, fourteen-by-twenty-two-inch, oil on canvas, of three ears of Indian corn with large husks, tied together against an azure background. The painting has no date. The signature is in white block letters in the lower right-hand corner: "Lelia Dean Butler." The painting is so old and dry that the oils have flaked off, leaving splotches of bare canvas. I found it rolled up on the top shelf of a linen closet when I moved into my grandmother's house in 1970. Now it hangs in our living room in an ornate antique gilt frame.

Above Lelia's *Indian Corn* hangs a painting by Maud, an oil on canvas approximately the same size, unframed. It is a near-life-size portrait of a beautiful copper-skinned African American girl, just the head and shoulders, dressed in green with a small green cap on her close-cropped black hair, a gaudy red and green drape behind her. Her large black eyes stare solemnly out at you. The painting is signed in the lower left-hand corner "MFalkner," Maud's standard signature. Printed on the back of the canvas in her distinctive hand is the title, *Dulcie*. The portrait is undated but I know that Dulcie modeled for Maud's art class at Oxford's Mary Buie Museum in the 1940s. I also know that Maud would never have displayed *Dulcie* in the living room or anywhere else.

When I asked my grandmother to help me join the DAR— having failed miserably as a Girl Scout I thought I might fare better as a Daughter of the American Revolution—she made her attitude toward her ancestors quite clear. "Lamb," she said, "I don't know whether my ancestors were hanging by their heads or their tails and I don't intend to find out. Not even for you."

4

My Father's World

We arrived at Oxford after dark and were met at the station by our grandmother and grandfather Falkner. We descended from the coach . . . covered with soot, cinders and sweat . . . speechless with wonder; never had we seen so many people, so many horses and carriages, and so much movement everywhere. And the lights—arc lights! As we drove to Grandfather's house by way of the town square we noticed the fine board sidewalks which extended the whole way. . . . People were walking along them and it was already past nine at night. We could hardly wait to see these wonderful sights by daylight.

—JACK FALKNER, 1902

WHEN J. W. T. FALKNER MOVED HIS HOUSEHOLD FROM RIP-ley, Mississippi, the Old Colonel's home base, to Oxford, he bought property on South Street within sight of the court-house. In 1899, he built one of the largest houses in town, a three-story white elephant the family called "the Big Place." The lot had originally belonged to Maud Butler Falkner's grand-father in the 1830s. For years the house stood in the center of the large lot facing east; then it was moved to the northwest corner, facing north. The Falkners celebrated the turn of the century in the third-floor ballroom.

Even as J.W.T. flourished, however, his older son Murry suffered major setbacks. His dream had been to operate his grandfather's short-run railroad, the Gulf & Ship Island, a narrow-gauge line connecting Ripley, Tennessee, and Pontotoc, Mississippi. It was affectionately known as the "Doodlebug Line." With little interest in attending college, Murry had thrown himself wholeheartedly into the operation of "his" railroad. He loved every job on the train and enthusiastically served as fire tender, engineer, and conductor. If he couldn't live in the West and be a cowboy, this was the next best thing.

He and Maud settled halfway between either terminus in New Albany, where their first three sons, William, Jack, and John, were born. Murry was content with his railroad career and growing family until J.W.T., without warning or explanation, sold the Gulf & Ship Island out from under him. Penniless, unschooled, and desperate, his railroad dreams gone forever, Murry moved his family to Oxford and operated businesses financed by his father, first a freight line and livery stable, and later a hardware store. But his boys were happy. Oxford was quite a change from rural New Albany. They were used to going to bed with the chickens and had never seen streets lit up at night.

They moved into a big two-story cottage south of the square, trimmed with gingerbread latticework, with large front and back yards. They needed the extra room since Lelia had come to live with them. Maud, however, needed even more help with her three boys than Lelia could provide. Caroline Barr, a small African American woman in her sixties, was the solution. She had worked for the Young Colonel in Ripley and moved to Oxford with him when her own children were grown. She settled into the cabin behind Maud and Murry's home and soon became a second mother to the boys. They called her "Mammy Callie." She moved into the cabin behind Rowan Oak when William bought the place in 1930, and lived there until she died.

William, Jack, and John took to their new surroundings and made their presence known in Oxford. The saying went, "If you pick on a Falkner you'll have to whip all three." With William as their undisputed leader, or as Jack put it, "crew chief in word and deed," the brothers roamed the streets on their ponies. According to Jack they had "played the same games, eaten at the same table and generally read the same books. In short, the day-to-day life of one had been the same as that of the other." They honored a code of conduct instilled in them by Maud and Mammy: "Rise when a lady entered a room . . . lie only when it would be of great value to another . . . take pride in family and country . . . [be part of] a closely knit and self-sustaining family unit" until inevitably "each would go his separate way to do what he had the capacity to do and to refrain from doing what he had the capacity to withstand."

Before Dean was born, the Falkner brothers' infatuation with flying began. One day a balloonist appeared in Oxford. With or without the mayor's consent, he dug a fire pit on the square and started a fire. With the aid of his assistant he slowly inflated his hot-air balloon with smoke from burning tires. A crowd soon gathered, including the Falkner brothers. The thick smoke blackened their faces. The balloonist drank whiskey from a jug, and when the balloon was ready to lift off he jumped on the swing (no gondola but only a wooden plank suspended by ropes) and was *airborne.* William and his brothers were transfixed by the miracle of flight. The canvas balloon, trailing smoke and with its drunken, blackened rider clinging to the ropes, cleared the two-story buildings south of the square and rose as high as two hundred feet above ground. A little breeze nudged it gently southward. The boys chased the smoking craft down South

Street. Within seconds, the hot air cooling, the balloon began to descend. The dangling balloonist had no clue where he would land. The Falkner boys were ecstatic when the balloon came to rest on their grandfather's property and the canopy collapsed. They ran pell-mell around the house only to find Mammy Callie brandishing a scantling at the "crazy man" whose smoking wreck lay on top of the henhouse. As alarmed chickens flapped about them, William explained to Mammy Callie that the airborne intruder meant no harm and in fact was probably the greatest living person in Mississippi, if not the world.

William was the overlord of all neighborhood wars, safaris, circuses, and entertainments. One day he decided to build an airplane in the toolshed. When Jack and John, and cousin Sallie Murry, could think of no objections, they collected odd planks, nails and sacking, and began to hammer and saw.

When the rickety fuselage with a wing and a tail looked airworthy to William, he instructed his exhausted crew to drag it to the edge of a ravine. Then he mounted the pilot's seat and told them to push. With a great heave the brothers Falkner and Sallie Murry launched the wooden crate—which only in the mind of its creator resembled an airplane—and down he slid into the "bottomless abyss." He emerged seconds later to thank his crew and supporters, telling them not to worry. They'd get it right next time. His only regret was that he bore no marks or scratches to bolster his claim that he was "the first man (or child) to become airborne in Mississippi—well, almost."

The boys were thriving in Oxford—yet 1906–7 were difficult years for Maud. Her mother-in-law, Sallie Murry Falkner, died in December, and six months later her mother, Lelia, "Damuddy," was dead of cancer after a long, painful struggle during which Maud and Mammy tended to her, carefully hiding from the boys her addiction to laudanum. Maud was pregnant with her fourth child.

Shortly after her mother's funeral, Maud moved her family into the Big Place so that her own home could be fumigated to eliminate the medicinal smells and memories of laudanum, dirty linens, and death. As Jack Falkner described his mother, she was "the eternal enemy of dirt and disarray in any form."

The fourth son of Murry and Maud was born two and a half months later on August 15, 1907, two days before his father's thirty-seventh birthday. "He's my birthday present," Murry told Maud. "Let's name him Henry."

William Henry Falkner was the oldest son of the Old Colonel William Clark Falkner and Lizzie Vance (his second wife). Henry was a "handsome ne'er do well . . . a gambler, a womanizer," and pretty much worthless. When a crippled jeweler found out that Henry had taken up with his wife, he shot and killed him. When the Old Colonel was informed of the shooting, he is said to have responded, "That's all right. I'm afraid I would have had to do it myself, anyway."

Maud's response to Murry's suggestion that they name her baby Henry was *Over my dead body.*

They named the child Dean Swift Falkner in honor of Maud's mother, Lelia Dean Swift. Maud was thirty-six years old and her childbearing days were done. Dean was the darling of the family, a present for his father and brothers, William, ten, Jack, eight, and John, six—a gift that brought them joy all of his life.

In a formal portrait of my father as a little boy, Dean bears a striking resemblance to William's description of John Sartoris as a child in the novel *Sartoris:* "The steady eyes looked quietly back . . . and from the whole face among its tawny curls, with its smooth skin and child's mouth, there shone a warm radiance something sweet and merry and wild." In this warm radiance William sensed the free spirit of his youngest brother, the boy he loved, the man upon whom he would later rely.

When Dean started the first grade, Maud noticed that Mammy disappeared every morning shortly after he left for school, only to reappear in the afternoon once he came home. It did not take her long to figure out that Dean, at seven, and Mammy in her seventies, were both attending school; Dean on the inside, Mammy outside sitting under a shade tree and visiting with passersby until school let out. She took two ham biscuits wrapped in a linen napkin in her apron pocket for lunch.

Maud could not stop Mammy from following Dean until Mammy was satisfied that he could take care of himself. One afternoon he got into a playground fight with a bully two years older. Mammy proudly reported to Miss Maud, "My Deanie come out on top."

The Falkner boys loved their ponies but also came by their love of cars naturally. Their grandfather J.W.T. owned one of the first cars in Lafayette County, a yellow Buick roadster. He and his driver were a regular sight on the unpaved streets of Oxford, spooking horses and frightening women, children, and dogs.

As the story goes, J.W.T. began celebrating his acquisition even as his driver, Chess Carothers, was learning how to steer an automobile. J.W.T. sat in the rear seat and drank whiskey while Carothers taught himself how to crank the engine and operate the clutch and gears. Away they went, Carothers quickly gaining confidence as he circled the courthouse, then drove back and forth from the square to the university campus. When J.W.T. ran out of whiskey he instructed Carothers to turn around and head for home. Carothers said he would be glad to as soon as he figured out how to stop the car. "The Lord is with us!" J.W.T. declared from the backseat.

"Well, he's taking an awful chance," said Carothers.

Dean's love affair with automobiles can be seen in an undated entry in his school notebook:

a Jeffrey four is the Best auto in the world.
We have an Overland and we work on it all
the time. A Overland is not any count A cole 8
is a good auto if I could have my choose I
would take a Jeffrey It can go every where I
want a Jeffrey and a cole I wish my mother had
a cole 8 and Jack had the kind of auto that he
wanted and dad had the pretties horse in the world

A Jeffrey Four was a "runabout" sports coupe, whereas a Cole Eight was a luxurious sedan and thus, in his eyes, most appropriate for his mother. Dean knew his father well and "the pretties horse in the world" suited Murry's temperament and attitude. He was a nineteenth-century man all his life. An excellent horseman, he rode twenty miles or more every day until his health failed, calling the rides "the best hangover cure known to mankind."

In 1914, the Falkner brothers witnessed the first airplane landing in Oxford. Dean heard the plane fly over and ran to the First National Bank, where William was working as a clerk—a job his grandfather had given him and which he despised. "Billy, there's a plane!" Dean whispered excitedly. The two of them slipped outside and rode double on Dean's bicycle as the plane circled over a pasture north of town. It had rained recently and the field was muddy. As Dean and William watched with other spectators, the biplane landed and quickly became bogged down in the mud. William took off his shoes and trudged across the field after his barefoot brother. They marveled at the flying machine. To their delight the aircraft was stranded for a week until the ground was dry enough to take off. Dean went to see it every day and ran his hands over engine, propeller, and fuselage until he knew them by heart.

That was the year that William quit high school, then

reenrolled to play quarterback on the football team, then dropped out again when a broken nose ended both his football and academic careers. Years later he would take pride in referring to himself as the "world's oldest living eighth grader."

Murry ruled his sons as tightly as his father had ruled him. None of them except William gave him much trouble. To William's contemporaries, "Mister Murry" seemed reserved and uncompromising. Everybody in town knew the story about William borrowing his father's car to take Dean for a ride. Perhaps to entertain his brother, William started to pass a car. The cranky old gentleman at the wheel recognized the Falkner brothers and speeded up. The race was on. William put the pedal to the metal. For a few exciting moments the two cars raced up South Street. William roared by the other car, no doubt to Dean's delight, and circled the square in triumph. When they returned home, they found that the irate motorist had reported William's reckless driving. Murry accepted the man's story at face value despite William's insistence that he "was not racing any more than the other man was!" He never drove his father's car again.

Dean was Murry's favorite, but none of the brothers resented this preferential treatment, perhaps because Maud showered affection on all four. In return, they worshipped her, especially William, confident that *he* was *her* favorite. Dean was probably the only son who loved *and* understood his father. As Jack would observe, "Murry shared a companionship with Dean that seemed closer than any he had enjoyed with the others."

All four boys were caught up in the excitement of the First World War. At seven, Dean imitated his teenage brothers as they pored over the morning paper, laid out maps of the continent in front of the fireplace, and traced the lines of battle. Dean pretended to understand both the geography and the battle reports. They spent hours drawing planes with exotic names such as Albatros, Sopwith Camel, Fokker. They hated the kaiser but respected pilots who won the Blue Max. They were fascinated with the ten-month-long Battle of Verdun, following its lines daily. (After the war William told Jack that he "trudged the length and breadth of the battle ground" while on a walking tour of France.) During a recruitment drive, the army shipped a tank to Oxford by train. When it arrived at the depot, the Falkner boys were at the front of the crowd watching the tank being unloaded and racing alongside as it was driven to the square.

Around 1917, William fell in love with Estelle Oldham, one of the belles of Oxford. Her parents took a dim view of the romance, however, and were determined to break it up. The Oldhams did not approve of Falkners in general, much less one with literary ambitions, nor did the Falkners approve of them. Major Oldham was the postmaster, which in Mississippi was a high-paying Republican-appointed position. Maud and Murry derided Oldham's honorary title, "Major," conveniently forgetting that Murry's father, J.W.T., was known as the "Young Colonel." The closest either came to a battlefield was probably a tour of Shiloh, ninety-five miles northeast of Oxford. The two families lived a block apart, and Major Oldham walked by the Falkner home on his way to work. I can still hear the disdain in my grandmother's voice when she spoke about "that man in the double-breasted suit with a red carnation in his lapel, strutting past our house every morning on his way uptown to do nothing, at which he was very, very good!"

In early summer of 1918, the Oldhams arranged for Estelle to marry Cornell Franklin, a rising young attorney in Columbus, Mississippi. William, frustrated and embarrassed, his hopes dashed, left Oxford, intending to join the Royal Air Force in Canada and prove himself equal in war to his brother Jack. He may have chosen the RAF because of its glamour, or perhaps he figured that the RAF would be less likely to reject him on account of his short stature. He claimed to be five foot eight. (I think five foot five was closer.) While waiting for his application to be processed he went to New Haven, Connecticut, and briefly worked at the Winchester Arms Company.

He stayed in touch with his family, sending Dean two sketches from New Haven.

The first, marked "FOR DEAN," is a rough sketch on typing paper of a football player with small shoulders and a prominent nose—Dean's nose rivaled, even surpassed, his brother William's, broken or not—carrying the football tucked under his right arm, his left arm extended to stiff-arm a tackler who is slicing his legs out from under him.

The second drawing, more detailed, also pencil on typing paper, is entitled "The Hand Organ." It is a street scene of an

Italian organ-grinder, complete with mustache and goatee. The figure is off-center, looking toward a crowd that has gathered to watch an off-stage monkey. Only the backs of the people can be seen. In the center is an animal cage, and in the distance, tall buildings with smoke stacks. The drawing is bordered by two distinct figures. To the left, a boy with hands cupped around his mouth as if to call to someone. On the right, another boy has climbed a street lamp to see over the crowd. William obviously was projecting his little brother into the sketches.

William reported to RAF duty at Toronto on July 9, 1918. As a cadet he threw himself into the training and became "one of the chaps." He sent Dean sketches of himself standing by the barracks and other drawings of warplanes and cadets.

Jack had already joined the U.S. Marines Corps and gone to Quantico, Virginia, for basic training, while John was working in a power plant at Muscle Shoals, Alabama. Jack would later see action in France. At eleven years of age, Dean was the only son left at home. That fall, the family eagerly awaited news of the war. Jack's letters from France came every week. When the letters abruptly stopped, Maud was beside herself. Dean was worried sick. Murry went to pieces.

A businessman in Oxford, it was rumored, had "bought" his own son out of the army. Every morning at eight o'clock, to Murry's disgust, this man paraded about the square waving an American flag. One morning, Murry opened his hardware store just as the draft evader passed by. Already distraught at not hearing from Jack, Murry became furious. He grabbed a singletree—a wooden yoke for harnessing mules—and started for the man, shouting, "I'll kill that son of a bitch." Fortunately, two employees held him back. Jack, they would later learn, had been wounded at the Argonne Forest, though not critically.

Although Murry obviously cared deeply for Jack, his natural

reserve caused him to hold back his feelings. Jack wrote in his memoir, *The Falkners of Mississippi*, "As I look back over the years I realize how little I actually came to know him, and, perhaps, even less to understand him. He was not an easy man to know. . . . His capacity for affection was limited, but I'm sure that to such extent as it allowed he loved us all."

The war ended before William completed RAF flight training. He had failed to receive either a pilot's wings or a commission. News of the war's end reached town before the peace agreement was signed. Dean and his friends and their parents rushed to the square, beating on buckets and pots, celebrating victory over the Huns. The impromptu parade had just reached the Ole Miss campus when word arrived that the Germans had not signed the armistice. Deflated and disappointed, the celebrants took their pots and tin pails and went home. Dean glumly reported to his mother that the war "was not over after all." Two days later, the official signing of the armistice was received with little or no fanfare. Oxford had worn itself out on November 10. The good news for the Falkners, however, was that their three oldest sons would soon be coming home.

In December 1918, Dean, along with his parents, welcomed John home from Muscle Shoals, Jack from France, and William from Canada. The Falkner house resounded with young voices, energy, and hope. Jack would later observe that they "came together again . . . for several memorable and sometimes uproarious years." In addition to this happy homecoming, the family had something else to celebrate. Murry had been appointed assistant secretary (business manager) at the University of Mississippi. A house on the campus would be provided for them in one year's time.

5
Count No 'Count

ALL DEAN WANTED FOR HIS TWELFTH BIRTHDAY, AUGUST 15, 1919, was a Boy Scout uniform so that he could look like William, who returned from Canada in a dashing RAF uniform. In spite of the heat, he put on his Scout uniform the day it arrived. Although it was as stiff as a hair shirt, Dean kept it on all day and marched around the house and yard. Soon, he and William were seen walking on the square, Dean in his Scout outfit and William in his RAF uniform with silver RAF wings, a swagger stick, and trim little mustache. Neither Dean nor anyone else knew that William had bought the wings in a Toronto pawnshop. The war having ended before he finished flight training, he commissioned himself and came home to Oxford a WWI veteran. In 1980, his biographer Joseph Blotner, upon seeing the silver wings up close for the first time, identified them as insignia of the British Royal Flying Corps, not of the Royal Air Force in Canada. The RFC had flown the majority of combat missions and had more prestige and military luster. William, with the luxury to choose, had purchased a set of RFC wings.

William had fun dressing up and teasing the townsmen who ridiculed his literary ambitions and aloof manner. He sometimes walked with a cane and claimed to have a silver plate in his head implanted by surgeons after his plane was shot down in France.

Other times, he sported a natty British bowler, spats, and a walking stick. The wags called him "Count No 'Count."

The fact is, William never got too old to enjoy dressing up. The more he aged, the more handsome he became. With his white hair, beautifully shaped head, aquiline nose, and small ears, he was stunning and he knew it. He bore himself like a five-star general and could carry off any style of dress with the insouciance of a male model.*

In 1919, Murry assumed the duties of the secretary at the University of Mississippi. The Falkners lived in a house previously occupied by the Delta Psi fraternity. Located on a bluff overlooking the railroad tracks, "it was a charming house," recalled Ben Wasson, William's friend and classmate from Greenville, Mississippi, and later his literary agent, "like a miniature Walt Disney castle with a tower room and stained glass windows." A three-story redbrick dwelling with a wide porch, it stood on its own large lot on the edge of the main campus. The backyard was big enough for William and Dean to set up a tennis court. The whole family enjoyed the house and its location, especially Maud. Provided by the university, it was rent-free.

For a short while, William and Dean were the only brothers living at home. Ben Wasson spent many hours in the Falkner home and observed William's fondness for his youngest brother. He remembered Dean as "a little wren darting in and out of the room, constantly asking his brother for help with his lessons or,

---

*Some of my favorite pictures of him are those taken at West Point, by Henri Cartier-Bresson, in a gray suit, black bowler hat, and with a folded umbrella, his back as ramrod straight as any cadet. His son-in-law, Paul Summers, himself a former cadet, had arranged the West Point visit and accompanied him, which I think accounts for the stunning photographs. He was in a good mood.

perhaps, how a particular Boy Scout knot should be tied. Bill was always amicable." Ben and William engaged in literary discussions that apparently irritated Murry. "Obviously, Murry thought Bill and I were nuts. He was not at all interested in what we were doing. He was not a literary man. Maud, however, was interested in poetry and writing."

At twenty-two, William was reading voraciously and trying to find his identity as a writer. He was less interested in completing coursework than in serving as prop man for the student drama group, the Marionettes. He sketched illustrations for the Ole Miss yearbook. Murry, whose favorite writer was Zane Grey, neither understood nor approved of these artistic leanings. On one occasion he walked in on William showing Maud a newly completed poem, turned on his heel, and left.

William became a scoutmaster and took Dean and his friends hiking and camping in pup tents. Sometimes they would hike three miles to Thacker Mountain, cook supper, then hike back in the dark following the railroad tracks. One evening, they heard a freight train coming. When it slowed down for a sharp bend, William let the boys hop an empty boxcar and ride back to Oxford. It was an unforgettable moment. After the camping trip, William wrote the letter on the next page to Dean.

A few months later, however, the scoutmaster-storyteller was dismissed after one of the boys' fathers, a strict teetotaler, circulated rumors of William's drinking. (One of the original Scouts told me, years later, "Bill set a good example and would never have taken a drink on a camping trip.")

In 1920, William quit taking classes at Ole Miss and became assistant postmaster at the university. His father, of course, had arranged this entrée into federal employ. Murry's feelings of satisfaction soon faded, however: Faculty members complained that the mail was not being delivered to their post office

My dear young friend:----

        Will you kindly have the kindness
to kindly try to remember if you and I didnt carry Lee
Baggett's tent out to his house in our white mule the same
afternoon we taken mr eD daVIdson'S tent back?

        If we did, try to recall whom we
returned it to, and if it warn't us, see Mr Bill Hune and
ask him what he done with it. Seems to me I remember seeing that tent on top of his ¢ord that day----or maybe it was
Bill Henry Hutchinson's face I seen.

        1 b3en P*acti)cin- on m7 TypxwZiter
e'vever?y day andd 7 h(ve tpken afwe lexxon§ andd onw 7 a5
grtt7ng prtte ¢lrrr¿k ¿oOD.

        Remember me to the old lady, tell
her wecmet oncet in Omahaw or one of them Indian places.
Maybe Indiana, and for she not to take no wooden knickles.

        (Subscribed to and swore before me,
a Noterary Publick for the countey of Lafayettette, this
the bbbhb half past eight of March, r s v p 2519.

You can jest hand her the quarter. I already give her mine.

                      B.f

boxes. They had observed Assistant Postmaster Falkner reading books or sketching, smoking his pipe—anything but what
he was being paid to do. It was a known fact that William tossed
all but first-class mail in the trash and ignored patrons rapping
on the counter. The outraged professors were reduced to sorting
through the trash for their mail. "I refuse," William cheerfully

explained to Ben Wasson, "to be at the beck and call of every SOB with the price of a two-cent stamp."*

The rebel postmaster continued to live with his parents. Long after Maud and Murry had gone to bed, he and Dean would sit up talking and listening for the whistle of the nine thirty southbound out of Memphis. Trains passed through at all hours within a stone's throw of the former Delta Psi house. William and Dean knew every engineer by name and could recognize his touch on the whistle. Those were the days of porters, redcaps, and meals in the dining car served on white linen with real cutlery, fresh flowers, and finger bowls. William and Dean were great-grandsons of the founder of a railroad and probably wished (as much as I) that the Falkners still owned a railroad.

Eight trains were scheduled each day, four of them passenger trains. Walking home from school in the afternoon, Dean could hear the three o'clock heading north and would race to join schoolboys gathered by the tracks. A particular engineer loved children and often would stop and allow two or three lucky boys to climb aboard for a short ride to the depot.

On Sunday afternoons, the arrival of the three o'clock northbound was a special occasion, a social gathering. Town and gown would gather at the Shack, a café and boardinghouse across the street from the train depot. In their Sunday best, the locals waited for the train, then rushed to see who was getting on or off. The depot would be surrounded by horse-drawn cabs, hacks, and phaetons from Oxford's three livery stations, waiting to take passengers to their destinations.

---

*How it would have amused the former postal employee that in 1987 the U.S. Postal Service issued a William Faulkner stamp, though he probably would have declined an invitation to the official ceremony honoring him. Ironically, he married the Oxford postmaster's daughter.

William and Ben Wasson rarely missed a Sunday afternoon. They were as caught up in the excitement and drama as Dean and his schoolmates, especially the arrival of Pullman diners with people framed in the windows, eating and drinking so casually and elegantly. "We wondered where they were going," Wasson recalled, "and we longed to go with them."

On March 3, 1922, Murry's father died. In all probability his death did not affect Dean greatly, since he had only had casual exposure to the Young Colonel. By the time Dean was old enough to be influenced by J.W.T., his grandfather was deaf and approaching senility. William, however, was much saddened. He remembered his grandfather telling stories of the Civil War, passed down from the Old Colonel. One of his favorites was how Colonel Falkner, who had resigned his army commission, made the family fortune by smuggling black-market goods into Memphis. He would pack sugar, flour, coffee, and tobacco on mules and send his "loyal retainer," as the Falkner family referred to the colonel's slave, across Union army lines. If picked up, he was to pose as a runaway. Pappy liked to say that the Falkner family understood the true purpose of war—to make money.

One Sunday afternoon Dean and William were attending an ice cream social at the First Methodist Church. William leaned over and whispered that he had borrowed a car (though certainly not his father's Buick). Would Dean like to go to Memphis? Within minutes they were on their way. Both brothers knew their grandfather's tale of traveling the "Reivers' Road" that passed through College Hill, north of Oxford. There was a family of reivers—thieves—who flooded the road and charged J.W.T. a fee for pulling him out after his car got stuck.

Arriving in Memphis, William took his twelve-year-old brother to the red-light district on Mulberry Street, where he parked in front of Miss Reba's, a deceptively staid two-story house on this quiet, tree-lined street. Dean went into the parlor with William and was introduced to the "lady of the house." He was allowed to stay until all the girls came in, and then he was sent outside. He played jacks on the sidewalk until his brother emerged. They rode back to Oxford over the clay hills of Mississippi singing Methodist hymns all the way.

———

ABOUT THE TIME that William withdrew from Ole Miss, he self-published his first serious attempt at writing, a play called *Marionettes*. He hand-printed the one-act play and illustrated it with pen-and-ink drawings of bare-breasted women. Then he stapled the little book together and pasted it to a cover. He made six copies, which he and Ben Wasson circulated among their Sigma Alpha Epsilon fraternity brothers. Wasson would later write: "My copy was passed among the students and there was a wild scramble to see it, since word had gotten around that the 'Count' had written and illustrated a salacious book containing 'hot' illustrations. The text of the book was undoubtedly influenced by Oscar Wilde's play *Salome* and the illustrations by Aubrey Beardsley. . . . The final full-page illustration in *Marionettes* was felt to be by those who saw it a real 'eye popper' inasmuch as it showed Marietta, the heroine of the piece, depicted with two nude breasts in a full forward view which was, as one student said, 'titillating.' " Ben and William sold five copies for $5 each so that the author could "buy some corn whiskey." (In 1975, one of these books sold for $30,000 at auction in New York.)

On summer afternoons William and Dean would walk down Mill Street to Calloway's Pool, change their clothes in one of the wooden bathhouses, and spend a pleasant four or five hours swimming. Dean was an expert swimmer and diver. The Olympic-sized concrete pool had a swing. One of his favorite stunts was to stand on the swing and pump until he was going as high as he could go. Then, timing it exactly, he would let go of the rope and dive off the swing into the water. It was a perfect dive every time, or so it was said.

Dean learned to tolerate his brother's penchant for drinking and partying with his college friends. Oxford was dry in 1921, though crated liquor could be shipped by railway express. This was how fraternities obtained whiskey even though it was against the law. One day in late November, Dean and some friends were crossing a footbridge by the tracks. They spotted an empty whiskey crate. One of them began joking about the crate being an early Christmas package. "I think it's addressed to William Falkner," the friend said. There was an awkward pause. Dean shrugged it off. "It's none of your business, but you're probably right," he said.

6

Two Brothers

IN 1924, WILLIAM WAS EAGER IF NOT DESPERATE TO SEE HIS work in print before he turned thirty. He feared dying in his late twenties. He and his friend and mentor, attorney Phil Stone of Oxford, agreed to share the expense of self-publishing *The Marble Faun*, a slender book of poetry. The publisher was a New York firm, the Four Seas Company, who agreed to print five hundred copies at a cost of $400—half to be paid in advance and half after the books were delivered. When the books arrived, he and Stone peddled them on campus and in town, and within a short time had sold seventy-five copies. Stone ordered another fifty to be shipped to him. The book was priced at $1.50, a lot more words for the price than the $5, handmade *Marionettes*, but *The Marble Faun* didn't have pictures.

William had written his own biographical sketch for the book: "Born in Mississippi in 1897. Great-grandson of Colonel W.C. Faulkner. [He added the *u* to match the new spelling of his surname.] C.S.A., author of *The White Rose of Memphis, Rapid Ramblings in Europe*, etc. Boyhood and youth were spent in Mississippi, since then has been (1) under-graduate (2) house painter (3) tramp, day laborer, dish washer in various New England cities (4) clerk in Lord and Taylor's book shop in New York City (5) bank and postal clerk. Served during the war in the British Royal Air Force. A member of Sigma Alpha Epsilon fraternity.

Present temporary address Oxford, Mississippi. *The Marble Faun* was written in 1919."

Shortly after the book was published, Phil Stone and Judge John Falkner, William's uncle, happened to meet on the square. "There's a black sheep in everybody's family and Billy's ours. Not worth a cent," said the judge. Stone rushed to his friend's defense. "You're wrong about Bill. . . . There'll be people coming to Oxford on account of Bill who would never have heard of the place except for Bill and what he writes."*

Unsure about the success of his first book, but excited at seeing his work in print, William left for New Orleans, where he lived in a cramped apartment on Pirate's Alley in the French Quarter. Here he met Sherwood Anderson and William Spratling, wrote articles for the *Times-Picayune*, and enjoyed the "Bohemian life" in the company of writers and artists. Early that summer he

---

*I'm glad Phil Stone never knew how right he was. He would not believe the changes Oxford has suffered in part due to Pappy's fame: We were "discovered" just before the turn of the twenty-first century, when several national publications listed Oxford as one of the top one hundred small towns to retire in—or just die in—rising to the top fifty, and then the top ten. Oxford was deemed the epitome of traditional southern charm, with swings on porches, hundred-year-old oak trees lining streets, picket fences, flower beds in every front yard, and its own literary icon. The developers discovered Pappy was salable—though I doubt if one in ten of second-home Oxonians has read him or intends to. When *USA Today* listed Oxford as one of the top five retirement communities in the country, the rush was on. Developers couldn't get their cookie-cutter subdivisions built fast enough. Some nine hundred units were erected, with something for everybody: McMansions and million-dollar condos for the rich, real rich, and wannabe rich. The fine old houses that Pappy had known vanished into dust and rubble overnight, their big old trees with them. His prediction that the Snopeses would conquer was all too true. Meanwhile, his likeness cast in bronze by sculptor Bill Beckwith sits on a bench in front of city hall, available 24/7 to every tourist with a three-dollar throwaway camera who wants to have his picture taken with a Nobel Prize winner—old what's-his-name. One Christmas, some fool put a Santa Claus hat on him.

moved into the vacation home of the Stone family at Pascagoula, where he worked on his first novel, *Soldiers' Pay*, typing on a concrete picnic table within sight of the ocean.

He found time, however, to date a beautiful and sophisticated girl named Helen Baird, and fell in love with her. They roamed the coast and William showed her his favorite haunts in the French Quarter. He wrote a sonnet sequence that he dedicated to her, and like *Marionettes*, hand-printed it and saddle-stitched the folded pages in the center; he then glued the endpapers to a cloth cover. He called it *Helen: A Courtship*. (The handmade volume is now part of the Tulane University Library collection.) One of its themes was the traditional sonnet conceit that one loved most intensely when one's affections were spurned. In attaining his goal, the would-be lover ironically lost interest in the beloved. This would prove prophetic in a way. In August, Dean drove Maud to the coast to visit William, only to find him in the throes of breaking up with Helen. She had decided to marry another man, perhaps sensing that one day her poet would pack up his sonnets and leave.

In July 1925, William set sail for Europe. Landing in Italy, he made his way to Paris, where he took up residence near the Luxembourg Gardens. He spent hours feeding the pigeons, watching children sail toy boats in the fountain, and revising short stories and narratives that would later form parts of his novels *Sanctuary* and *The Sound and the Fury*. Dean and Maud couldn't wait for his letters from Paris. He wrote his much-loved Aunt Bama,* "I have just finished the most beautiful short story in the world. So beautiful that when I finished it I went to look at myself in a mirror. And I thought, Did that ugly ratty-looking

---

*His great-aunt Mrs. Alabama McLean, the youngest child of the Old Colonel.

face, that mixture of childishness and unreliability and sublime vanity, imagine that? But I did. And the hand doesn't hold blood to improve on it."

He was referring to material he would use in *Sanctuary:* "On the street old men wore overcoats, and in the Luxembourg Gardens as Temple and her father passed the women sat knitting in shawls and even the men playing croquet played in coats and capes, and in the sad gloom of the chestnut trees the dry click of balls, the random shouts of children, had that quality of autumn, gallant and evanescent and forlorn."

During a walking tour of the French countryside, he sent his father, Murry, a postcard about British hunting parties: "Swell looking Lords and dukes spinning along in carts behind trotting horses. They go out hunting in red coats, and ride right over you if you don't dodge." He also sent Dean an illustrated postcard depicting a hunt—*"Le Cerf hallali sous Bois"*—the stag at the finish. "What do you think of a country like this?" he wrote his brother. "But you can't kill a deer like this here unless you got a red swallow-tail coat."

William was back home before Christmas, a man of the world, an artist shaped and matured, as were his contemporaries James Joyce and Ernest Hemingway, by a Paris apprenticeship. He attended Dean's high school graduation in the spring of 1926 about the same time that he cashed his first royalty check for *Soldiers' Pay.* Estelle had come home from Shanghai with her children, Cho Cho and Malcolm. They spent several weeks in Oxford with her parents, the Oldhams, and created quite a stir with the children's Japanese amah. Estelle was unhappy and thinking of divorcing Cornell Franklin. William began seeing her again. That fall, Dean was kicked off the Ole Miss football team for being "too small." He had played quarterback for Oxford High School, as William had, but Dean also hoped to play for the Ole Miss Red and Blue. At five feet eight inches and 135 pounds, Dean was not meant for the brutal college game. I don't know if his father pushed him to play, but no doubt Murry's lifelong interest in sports had something to do with it.

Dean's introduction to higher education barely altered his daily routine. He still lived with Murry and Maud in the former Delta Psi fraternity house. He walked to class, just as he had walked to high school, and came home for lunch every day. His attitude toward academics had not changed, either.

My father attended the University of Mississippi for one reason only, to play baseball, yet he didn't make the Ole Miss varsity baseball team until he was a fifth-year senior. There was no such thing as redshirting in those days, but somehow an extra year of eligibility was "found" for him, as well as the occasional gift of a passing grade. The angels of innocence, the gods of childhood, were still smiling on Dean even as he entered his twenties. For William, as he approached his thirtieth birthday, the fear of failure and burden of genius lay heavy upon him. And yet he was about to enter the most productive period of any writer in all of American letters.

By 1927, William, who'd been living in New Orleans, had taken Sherwood Anderson's advice to return to Oxford and write about "that postage stamp of native soil" that he knew best, the people, places, and traditions with which he had grown up. He was to find so much material waiting in his hometown that he "would never live long enough to exhaust it." He moved back into the Delta Psi house, where in warm weather he and Dean slept on the screened porch on the third floor to escape the heat, listening to the night trains. Dean's grades were weak, but his college life was as enjoyable as anything else he had ever done.

He was playing baseball, had pledged SAE, the same fraternity to which William had belonged, and was a man about campus.

William's favorite holiday from the typewriter was playing golf with Dean on the university course. They played barefoot, and according to Dean's special rules, using a single club that each chose for the other. Once Dean took a .22 rifle onto the golf course, shot par with a nine-iron, and bagged his limit of squirrels, or so the story goes. William began calling him "Whiz."

In 1927 William completed *Flags in the Dust,* the first novel set in his fictional Yoknapatawpha County. In it he introduced the aristocratic and doomed Sartoris family. William and Phil Stone both felt this novel would reach a wider audience than his war novels, *Soldier's Pay* and *Mosquitoes,* both published by Boni & Liveright.

To William's shock and dismay, Horace Liveright rejected the manuscript, writing that it lacked "plot, dimension and projection." William was outraged, perhaps not as much at the criticism, which he could accept, as at his publisher's failure to recognize his grand design, his sweeping vision of the South.

"It's too bad you dont like Flags in the Dust . . . ," he responded. "I'd like you to fire it on back to me, as I shall try it on someone else. I still believe it is the book which will make my name for me as a writer."

William went to New York determined to get out of his contract with Liveright, and *Flags in the Dust* was eventually published by Harcourt, Brace under the title *Sartoris.*

In the summer of 1928, William was at work on his most ambitious novel yet, *The Sound and the Fury.* Dean, meanwhile, spent much of his time oversleeping on his summer job as a cement truck driver. Oxford was going to have its first paved street, "Depot Street," which ran from the train station to the square.

That fall, a turning point came for William when Estelle was divorced from Cornell Franklin and moved back to Oxford. Their courtship began again in earnest, and in June 1929 they were married at College Hill and moved into an upstairs apartment in an antebellum home along with Cho Cho and Malcolm. They were only two blocks from the Big Place.

Estelle was a very different woman from the carefree social butterfly she had been at the time of her first marriage. Her life in the Far East had been one of elegance and indulgence—or overindulgence—and with this came a sense of desperation and despair that the life she wanted would somehow always be just beyond her grasp. Franklin could give her financial security, but not the happiness she thought she deserved, and in all probability neither could William Faulkner. Her children, Cho Cho and Malcolm, would always be financially well cared for, thanks to their father's secure position, but she faced a lifetime, she thought, of eating with borrowed silver on borrowed dining room tables and chairs. "One could endure being broke," she said, "but never poor."

For most of her life Estelle was the victim of her own addictions: drugs and alcohol. She was a fragile woman, graceful but very thin with a tiny waist accented by her tightly belted, full-skirted dresses. Her legs looked barely strong enough to support her; she tottered on her high heels; her arms seemed too weak to raise a cup of her beloved chicory coffee to her lips. She was a heavy smoker with nervous fingers and glittery eyes—pretty eyes distorted by the thick lens of her eyeglasses. Photographs of her remind me of Wallis Simpson: a woman very well turned out, chic, a little sad. Her credo was much like Simpson's "You can never be too rich or too thin." Over the years she sometimes drank so heavily that on occasion she, like Pappy, had to be hospitalized; but in the summer of 1955 she became a member of Alcoholics Anonymous and gave up alcohol for the rest of her life.

In an earlier period she had been more gypsy moth than butterfly, and she flew too close to the flame. She and William had spent their honeymoon in Pascagoula on the Mississippi Gulf Coast. Rumors persist about Estelle's suicide attempts. The most frequently cited occurred after a dinner party during their honeymoon, when wine and whiskey flowed. Late in the evening, Estelle, dressed in an elegant silk dinner gown, walked to the beach alone while William watched from the gallery. "She's going to drown herself," he shouted. One of the dinner guests sprinted across the lawn into the shallow water, grabbed her just before she waded into the channel, and dragged her, struggling against him, onto the sand. Why didn't her husband try to rescue her?

Her favorite novel, she often said, was *Anna Karenina*.

In October 1929, *The Sound and the Fury* was published by Jonathan Cape and Harrison Smith. In the novel, William drew from memory as he often did in his fiction. The idiot Benjy was based on a child he had known when he was growing up. The boy lived with his parents in a white two-story home surrounded by ancient magnolia trees, only a few blocks from the Big Place, an easy walk for Maud and her eldest son. Maud and the boy's mother were friends, both avid readers, and their sons were close to each other in age, if nothing else. During their frequent visits, while the two women chatted, William, with infinite patience, entertained the severely retarded boy by helping him tear stacks of newspapers into long strips. Intent on their work, they sat cross-legged on the parlor rug, side by side, for hours.

On pretty days they might play in the yard, which was guarded by a six-foot wrought-iron fence to ensure that the child could not wander off and to protect him from intruders. The gate was always locked. A servant used a key to admit callers.

In spite of the family's precautions, one day when the boy was in his teens, he brought matches into the shed where stacks of his beloved newspapers were stored. A fire raged up and "Benjy" burned to death.*

William's publishers printed 1,729 copies of *The Sound and the Fury* priced at $2.50 apiece. Although many reviews were positive, the first edition did not sell out for almost a year and a half. The *New York Herald Tribune* reviewer wrote, "I believe simply and sincerely that this is a great book." The *New York Times* was equally emphatic in its praise, and the *Saturday Review of Literature* noted Faulkner's "power and tenderness," adding, "This is a man to watch." Unfortunately, good reviews did not translate into quick sales. William earned 10 percent, or twenty-five cents per book, less his agent's 10 percent commission.

In the fall of 1929, in order to support his family, William was forced to go to work as night foreman at the university power plant. He began his twelve-hour shift at 6 p.m., carrying a large supply of "Fidelity onion-skin, legal-size blank white sheets" rolled up in a rubber band.

According to Blotner, "On October 25, 1929 . . . [at the powerhouse] he took one of these sheets, unscrewed the cap from his fountain pen, and wrote at the top in blue ink, 'As I Lay Dying.' Then he underlined it twice and wrote the date in the upper right-hand corner."

William claimed he "shoveled coal from the bunker into a wheelbarrow and wheeled it and dumped it where the fireman could put it into the boiler. About eleven o'clock the people would be going to bed, and so it did not take much steam. And

---

*Many years later, when Nannie loaned me her copy of *The Sound and the Fury*, she offered excellent advice: "All you need do is think like an idiot, Lamb, and you will understand the novel. Trust the man who wrote the book."

so we could rest, the fireman and I." While the fireman nodded off in his chair, William wrote on the back of a wheelbarrow he had turned upside down, listening to "the deep, constant humming noise" of the dynamo. By 4 a.m., he had finished a chapter in time "to clean the fires and get up steam again." But evidently William's main job was just to be there, to oversee the two African Americans who did the work, and sometimes an Ole Miss football player who used the shoveling to get in shape. Estelle observed, "He would go to work after dinner immaculate, and return before breakfast, still immaculate."

On the last page of the completed manuscript he wrote, "page 107, Oxford, Miss./11 December, 1929." Forty-seven days had elapsed since he had started.

As I Lay Dying was published by Jonathan Cape and Harrison Smith on October 6, 1930. William dedicated it to Harrison Smith. The first print run was 2,522.

The early New York critics were hardly sympathetic. The *Herald Tribune* claimed that some passages "were absolutely unhinged from the point of view of the character whose mind they expose." Other reviewers found "the Bundrens . . . almost as strange as Martians." Southern reviewers, however, were far more generous, but unfortunately this did not translate into sales.

His family remained loyal. When Maud's friends asked "what Bill meant" in such-and-such book, or whether he was "really earning a living by doing nothing but writing," she would tighten her mouth, as only she could, and stonewall. She did not have to defend "her Billy" for the ups and downs of a precarious career any more than she had to defend Dean for his bad grades.

Dean, however, was outspoken in his brother's defense. When his friends claimed they could not understand *The Sound and the Fury,* or *As I Lay Dying,* he would smile and say, with utter confidence, "One of them may be the great American novel."

The fact that he made this pronouncement while racing turtles at the SAE house did nothing to lessen his sincerity. He was his brother's number one fan, and nothing would change that.

———

WHEN WILLIAM PURCHASED the "old Bailey place" on Garfield Avenue (now Old Taylor Road), he named the antebellum house and its thirteen acres "Rowan Oak." It was his way of declaring *This is my private place.* To keep up payments and buy materials for repairs, he churned out short stories at a furious pace, submitting thirty-seven in one year, but selling only six.

In midsummer of 1930, the *Saturday Evening Post* accepted "Red Leaves," a short story whose subject differed from his other Yoknapatawpha sagas. It dealt with the Chickasaw Indians' tribal custom of burying their chiefs with their dogs, horses, and a slave—in this case a body servant not ready to die. The *Post* paid him $750. Rowan Oak could now have electricity and Estelle a new stove.

Times were not easy for the newlyweds. William could not afford to hire carpenters to repair Rowan Oak, so Dean regularly brought fraternity brothers to help work on the house. They put on a new roof, rewired and expanded electrical circuits, and, thanks to "Red Leaves," put in new fixtures, ceiling lamps, pipes, and plumbing.

In spite of their financial difficulties, Estelle and William were eagerly looking forward to the birth of their first child in March 1931. So were Cho Cho and Malcolm.

Estelle's doctor, John Culley, was an excellent physician but a man with whom William did not get along. His wife, Nina, was Estelle's best friend. Dr. Culley was extremely concerned about Estelle because of the difficult deliveries of both of her children. In addition, she was weakened by anemia and weighed less than one hundred pounds. He warned her to be careful and prescribed iron and calcium pills for her.

Christmas at Rowan Oak with both their families in attendance was happy but exhausting for Estelle. She woke William late at night on January 10 and told him the baby was coming. At first he did not believe her, but he called Dr. Culley and asked him to meet them at the hospital. She gave birth the next day to a small, perfectly formed baby girl. They named her Alabama, in honor of William's Aunt Bama. He wanted his wife and child at home, believing that since there was no incubator at Dr. Culley's hospital, they would be cared for just as well at Rowan Oak with a trained nurse for Alabama and a practical nurse for Estelle, who was too sick to care for the infant. Dr. Culley noticed that the baby had problems with her digestive tract. By the end of the week, this dilemma became life threatening. She was tiny and weak and could not retain any milk.

William was frantic. He tried everything, first hiring a wet nurse, then begging Dean to find a goat. Maybe the baby could digest goat milk. Within hours Dean brought one to Rowan Oak. The brothers took turns milking it and carrying the precious milk to the house. Nothing had prepared William for this terrible, grinding fear. The practical nurse tried to feed the milk to Alabama; then William tried, then Dean. She could not keep it down.

Dr. Culley suggested an incubator and William, desperate to get his hands on one but not trusting himself to drive, asked Dean to take him to Memphis. They drove in the middle of the road at top speed, passing every vehicle. They got an incubator and brought it back to Oxford—only to find the infant fading before their eyes. Dean sat up with William and Estelle all night. The next day, January 20, Alabama died. The Faulkners mourned as one. A private service was held at Rowan Oak and

William read from the Bible. Dean drove to the cemetery while his brother cradled the tiny casket in his lap and wept. The rest of the family followed in two cars. It was bitter cold. At the gravesite, as his only granddaughter was laid to rest, Murry said a prayer that has been described as eloquent. William's grief staggered him. Soon after Alabama's death he donated an incubator to a second hospital in Oxford to be used free of charge by anyone in need.

——

ABOUT A MONTH after Alabama's death, Murry lost his job at the university. He had been a devout supporter of Mississippi governor Theodore Bilbo, to whom he owed the appointment. Now Bilbo had been defeated and thrown out of office in disgrace, and Murry was being replaced. The *Oxford Eagle* reported diplomatically: "Mr. M.C. Falkner, who has been Secretary and Business Manager of the University for the past twelve years, has announced that he will not be an applicant for the position again. His reasons are that there is too much work attached to the position, and also that he is growing too old to keep up with it. No statement has been made about his future plans." For the remainder of that year, Murry continued to work at the university in the diminished capacity of assistant secretary. The Falkner family moved out of the Delta Psi house and into the Big Place. That summer Murry contracted for the construction of a house on the same lot as his father's home. Maud chose the design and supervised its building and completion.

Murry readily adapted to retirement, riding six miles every morning to and from Campground Road, a dirt road lined by tall pines, one of the few flat stretches in the red clay hills of Lafayette County. He ate dinner at noon sharp. If the meal was not on the table when he entered the dining room, he turned on his heel and left the house. Maud and Mammy were of one mind about such behavior. It was disgusting. He spent the afternoons cutting out pictures of dogs and horses and pasting them into the lined pages of old railroad ledgers, while sitting in his favorite chair and listening to "Beautiful Dreamer" played over and over on the Victrola.

Dean's last college baseball home game was in May 1931. Murry, who was Dean's number one fan, was in the stands bellowing encouragement. In his usual bullheaded way, without waiting for athletic department approval, he had designed the first Ole Miss baseball letter and ordered a batch to hand out at

an M-Club meeting. (Forget about *The Sound and the Fury* and *As I Lay Dying;* his youngest son was about to become an Ole Miss letterman!) Ole Miss was playing Louisiana State University, whose Tigers were leading by three runs in the bottom of the ninth. In a storybook finish, Ole Miss had loaded the bases with two out. It was Dean's turn at bat. Murry was so excited he came out of the stands. As Dean left the on-deck circle, Murry shouted, "Son, hit a home run and I'll give you the car."

Dean stepped confidently into the batter's box, even as his teammates in the Ole Miss dugout swooned in panic. "Your dad couldn't hit a bull in the ass with a bass fiddle," his teammate Tad Smith later told me. Murry, gripping the fence, watched Dean take two strikes. Then came a slow curve and Dean connected. The hit was a high floater that just cleared the left-field fence. Amid cheers and glory, Dean rounded third base to see Murry standing on home plate, the keys to the family Buick in his hand. Mighty Casey had not struck out!

Over time I have convinced myself that William was there. He would have known that this was his brother's moment, that the dreams of the majors really came down to this one at-bat. The victory—Ole Miss 4, LSU 3—was Dean's immortality.

That day in 1931 the sun shone on my father as he trotted to home plate with his teammates slapping him on the back and accepted the keys to the car—and in the long, hot summer that followed he ran the wheels off that Buick, with Tad Smith riding shotgun, touring the cotton-patch ballparks of Lafayette County. They hired themselves out as ringers at two dollars per game. (Tad Smith would become athletic director at the University of Mississippi, whose basketball coliseum is affectionately known as "the Tad Pad.") It was his one and only tour as a semipro and the closest he got to his dream of playing professional baseball. He wore the convertible out, going as far as thirty miles to Holly Springs and forty-five to Tupelo and ninety to Corinth. Day in and day out, he drove it until the canvas top was in rags, the motor sputtered, and finally the Buick sat down in the road and died.

I'm not sure if my father actually graduated from Ole Miss, though Maud saved a program from the 1931 graduation exercises and Dean Swift Falkner is listed among the graduates in the College of Liberal Arts. It's quite possible that strings were pulled and he was allowed to graduate without fulfilling all of his course requirements.

Regardless, I am sure he was pleased with his baseball team photo in the 1931 yearbook, *Ole Miss*. He is in batting stance, looking happy, rugged, and several years older than the rest of the players. Unlike previous dedications, such as "To the University Greys," "To Our Mothers," or "To Our Fathers," accompanied by appropriately sedate pictures, the 1931 yearbook contained a pictorial "dedication": a photograph of an airplane on its cover, and on the end sheet, a two-page pictorial history of changes in transportation, from a covered wagon to the horse and buggy, train, automobile, and airplane. Times were changing and changing fast.

———

Frustrated by his lack of income, William was planning to write a novel "purely for money," a detective thriller as salacious and gritty as those of best-selling authors Ellery Queen and Dashiell Hammett. He had observed the girls of Ole Miss in their short flapper dresses and heavy makeup, flirts and coquettes that he compared to "golden butterflies." Maybe he would take such licentious behavior to its logical conclusion. Maybe a sorority girl would go too far in her flirtations and attract the Memphis underworld. Maybe she would be kidnapped and become an altar of sex in the white slave trade. He would call her "Temple," and he would name the novel *Sanctuary*. When it was published in 1931, a reviewer called him "the corncob man."

One day when Maud was playing bridge, a woman at the table asked what they were all dying to know. *Maud, why did Bill write that book?* She looked up from her cards and said, "My Billy writes what he has to." She played out the rubber and left, never to play bridge in that foursome again.

In February, the reviews of *Sanctuary* came out. The *New York Times Book Review* critique was entitled "Dostoyevsky's Shadow in the Deep South." (William wrote his agent asking who in the hell was this Dostoyevsky? If he had any of the Russian's books, send them on to Mississippi.) Throughout the spring, summer, and into the fall, praise for *Sanctuary* and its author continued. From the *Nation:* "By this book alone Faulkner took his place in the first rank of younger American novelists." Other periodicals called William a "prodigious genius," and *Sanctuary* "a great novel," an "extraordinary" piece of work.

But not everyone in the literary world saw it as the best of all possible novels. Newspapers closer to home were decidedly negative. The *Memphis Evening Appeal* called *Sanctuary* "an inhuman monstrosity of a book that leaves one with the impression of having been vomited bodily from the sensual cruelty of its page." A reviewer for the *New Orleans Times Picayune* wrote that "he was probably America's best living novelist" but that he was "very likely becoming a scandal in his native state."

In spite of provincial naysayers, a literary lion had been born. In October 1931, William was invited by Ellen Glasgow to the University of Virginia for a southern writers' conference. Then he went to New York, where Estelle joined him for a glittering but debilitating seven-week stay. There was too much of everything.

Dean had agreed to look after Rowan Oak in the meantime. He moved into the house and within a few days started a marathon poker game that lasted two weeks. The gambling den was in William's upstairs bedroom. The boys shoved his double bed up against the windows and set a round breakfast table in the middle of the room. When William and Estelle returned, Dean moved back into his room at Maud and Murry's new house on South Lamar.

Everyone was home for the holidays. Shortly after Christmas, William wrote Bennett Cerf, the cofounder of Random House, "Xmas was quiet here. Estelle and the children are with her mother in town and so I am alone in the house. I passed Christmas with a three foot back log on the fire, and a bowl of eggnog and a pipe and Tom Jones."

—

WILLIAM'S LIFE AT the beginning of 1932 would test every ounce of faith in his talent and hope for success. He finished *Light in August* in early spring. Family lore has it that his relationship with Estelle had deteriorated so badly that one afternoon as he drove with her to the square, she threw his just-completed manuscript out the car window. He parked at the curbside and went about methodically picking up the invaluable sheets of paper. Estelle did not help him.

They were again in desperate financial straits; they had no credit; they were overdrawn at the bank. At one point, William took out the following ad in the *Commercial Appeal* and *Oxford Eagle:* "I will not be responsible for any debt incurred or bills made, or notes or checks signed by Mrs. William Faulkner or Mrs. Estelle Oldham Faulkner."

To nudge Faulkner into paying his bill at Neilson's Department Store, Will Lewis, Sr., requested that he sign some post-dated checks. William wrote back, "I'm not going to sign these checks anymore than I ever signed the checks and notes you have filled out and sent to me in the past. Attached is my own check for ten. I will send more on the account when I can. I make no promise as to when that will be. . . . If this dont suit you, the only alternative I can think of is, in the old Miltonic phrase, sue and be damned. . . . You may even get an autographed book. That will be worth a damn sight more than my autograph on a check dated ten months from now."*

Hollywood came galloping to the rescue. When Metro-Goldwyn-Mayer offered William a screenwriting contract worth five hundred dollars a week, he borrowed three dollars from his uncle John to pay Western Union to wire his acceptance. He was to begin work on May 7, 1932. MGM sent him a prepaid ticket and a small advance. He was not happy about leaving Oxford but he had no choice. When he left for Los Angeles, he asked Dean to watch over Rowan Oak and to care for Estelle and the children. Each brother worried about the other. William was concerned about Dean's lack of direction, while Dean worried that the screenwriting job, while a necessity, would interfere with William's fiction writing.

Sometime after graduation, Dean became determined to try his own hand at writing. He asked William for advice and instruction. Though Maud saved hundreds of pages of Dean's handwritten (occasionally typewritten) stories, none are dated. On several of them William made corrections. He must have told Dean that the first step in learning to write was to build a vocabulary. To that end, he sat down and wrote a list of sixty-four words, picking them out of the air.

---

*Lewis, a man learned and wise, framed the letter. For some time it decorated the office wall at Neilson's Department Store.

unabashed
peering
lounging
combative
brandishing
Gambit
Futilely
condescended
rigidity
permeated
repose
cumbersome
diffidently
responsive
ascendency
exasperating
suffused
unfathomable
epicenity body (sexless body)
somnolent
misanthropic
contemplative
Latent
portentous
a pagan cata falque
embryonic
explicable
aspiring
accursed
sophisticated
reminiscences
condescend
imminent
belligerent
affable
devastated
Fervent
disinclination
amnoyance
profoundly
astonishing
bemused
banshee

fortitude
heritage
evocation
tranquill
anonymous
avatars
hypnosis
infinitesimal
merge
chowsly
trivial
augmenting
semblance
palpable
aura
somnolence
sparse
candid
inert
expiration
brusque

The last word, *brusque*, hints that someone's patience was wearing thin. The list was printed in William's hand up to the word *bemused*. From then on, beginning with *banshee*, the list is written in cursive (Dean's hand). Perhaps this was when Dean decided—as he sat beside William taking dictation, stumped by the spelling of unknown words, words as mysterious and sad as the whistle of an Illinois Central freight train—that he would become not a writer but a painter.

All three of William's brothers tried their hands at writing. John published *Men Working, Dollar Cotton*, and a Gold Medal paperback series called *Uncle Good's Girls*. Jack wrote short stories—many, many short stories—which he submitted to only one magazine: *Collier's*. When *Collier's* rejected each and every one, he never made a submission to any other magazine. The year *Collier's* folded so did Jack's writing career.

Possibly because of Murry's nagging that he learn a trade, Dean took a correspondence art course offered by *Modern Illustrating*. The talent he had inherited from Maud and her mother, Lelia Dean Swift, can be seen in the advertisements he drew as art assignments. He had a gifted hand and eye, as did William and John. Maud saved many of his drawings, as well as the art lesson books. Almost all of the sketches Dean did on his own were of female subjects. He worked in pen and ink, pastels and pencil.

Added to Dean's doubts about the future was his concern for his father's health. Murry had not been well. His back bothered him, and the doctors thought it might be the result of an old injury. He drank heavily. One evening shortly after he and Maud had moved into the new house, Murry, well into his cups, lurched into the parlor, settled himself in his favorite chair, and started to turn on the Victrola when he heard the unmistakable sound of a record breaking. He stood up, threw the chair cushion to the floor, and stared at the padding in the chair. On it lay his recording of "Beautiful Dreamer," deep cracks in the black disc. Only one person could have, or would have, placed the record in his chair. Murry did not take another drink—ever.

Early in August 1932, his health seemed to improve, and he took up his familiar habit of sitting with Maud on the front gallery in the late afternoon. On Saturday, August 6, Jack arrived for an unexpected visit. Murry and Maud were delighted to see him. They talked for a while, then retired. That night Murry suffered a heart attack and died in his sleep. He was not quite sixty-two. The next morning, Dean telephoned John in the Mississippi delta and William in Los Angeles. The Falkner family began to gather.

On Monday, August 8, 1932, a funeral service was held in the new house, conducted by the Methodist minister. It was short and private, with few flowers and no music. Murry's casket was placed on a bier in the parlor in front of the double French doors that opened onto the gallery. He was buried in St. Peter's Cemetery beside his father, the Young Colonel. Dean was crippled by grief. William had arrived from California and as the eldest male Faulkner had taken over as head of the clan. It was his responsibility to provide financial and emotional security not just for Maud and Dean but for the family. He served as executor of Murry's will. Maud was to inherit the estate until her remarriage or death, then Murry's sons were to divide the property among themselves. The will stated "Remember at all times that you are Brothers, and deal justly by each other." It ended "My signature is known, and no witness is needed."

As a relief and distraction from grief, William invited Dean and Maud to accompany him when he returned to Los Angeles. Late in the fall of 1932, they made a three-week trip to the West Coast. Estelle was pregnant and could not travel. William showed them Hollywood, no doubt taking them to his favorite restaurant, Musso and Frank, and introducing them to Culver City. For the most part William found the dull, anonymous work of screenwriting to be defeating, and he longed to return to writing narrative fiction in his own distinctive voice and style. William's salary was near the bottom of director Howard Hawks's pay scale. But this steady income during the Depression allowed him to support his now-extended family and keep up house payments and utilities for Rowan Oak.

Even though Maud had had her fill of Hollywood after the first week, Dean loved every minute of his stay. One of my favorite stories about William's time in California took place that fall. Hawks took William and Clark Gable (and perhaps Dean) on a dove shoot in the Imperial Valley. Gable, whom William had never met, brought along his .410 over and under, a shotgun that William coveted on sight.

As they drove into the valley, Hawks began talking about books and authors. Clark Gable listened in silence. At last he said, "Mr. Faulkner, who would you say are the best living writers?" William replied, "Ernest Hemingway, Willa Cather, Thomas Mann, John Dos Passos, and myself."

"Oh," said Gable. "Do you write, Mr. Faulkner?"

"Yes, Mr. Gable," William replied. "What do you do?"

7

The Waco

IN LATE OCTOBER 1932, WILLIAM, MAUD, AND DEAN RE-
turned to Oxford, where William settled, no doubt gratefully,
into the quiet routine of life away from Hollywood.

William and Estelle's daughter Jill was born June 24, 1933,
and he celebrated the happy event by buying a bright red, pow-
erful, luxurious four-seat Waco C cabin cruiser. He took flying
lessons from the top pilot in Memphis—Vernon Omlie—and introduced Dean to him. Dean soon was spending more and more
time flying with William. Sometimes, on the spur of the moment, the always impulsive Dean would invite the adoring boys
loitering on the sidewalk outside the Falkner home to go with
him to Memphis, where William indulged them with flyovers of
the Mississippi River.

Dean was at loose ends. At twenty-five he had finished college and was living at home with his mother. Unfortunately, the
only job he could find—pumping gas at the Gulf Station across
the street from their house—kept him under Maud's nose. Each
day she grew more dependent on him, and he felt more and
more responsible for her. William could see Dean being smoth-
ered by Maud and offered him a means of escape.

Ever since William had bought the Waco, Dean had been
begging him for flying lessons. Now was the time. William asked
Vernon Omlie to take Dean on as a student. The lessons soon

began, but a day in Memphis three times a week was not long enough, or far enough from home, to break Maud's hold on her youngest son.

By the fall William was urging Dean to fly longer trips whenever possible. In November, William, Dean, and Vernon flew to Murfreesboro, Tennessee, then to Washington, and on to New York. They checked into the Algonquin for a week. Dean was a long way from pumping gas and going home for lunch with his mother.

Vernon Omlie knew a gifted student when he saw one. Dean had an instinctive touch at the controls and an athlete's self-confidence and ability to carry out split-second decisions. He adored flying and often remarked that he would rather fly than eat.

Wacos were a popular aircraft at the time. The *Waco Pilot,* a trade journal published by the manufacturer, convinced William to endorse the plane. A black-and-white photograph shows him grinning (he was the only person I've ever known who could grin from ear to ear without showing a single tooth) while standing next to the cockpit of his newly purchased Waco cabin cruiser. Known as "the Cadillac of the air," it had luxurious leather seats that were so comfortable that seasoned passengers often fell asleep. Early in the spring of 1934, William gave the plane to Dean, enabling him to join Vernon Omlie's flying service, Mid-South Airways, as a partner and charter pilot.

In June, Dean moved into Vernon's McLean Avenue apartment in Memphis. He did not move in the normal sense of the word but instead commuted to work between Oxford and Memphis. He by no means had made a complete break with Maud. His clothes and belongings, for the most part, remained at 510 South Lamar. Every three or four days he flew home to spend the night.

In Memphis, Vernon's lifestyle provided a convenient and comfortable arrangement for Dean. His wife, Phoebe, a pilot and wing walker, spent most of her time in Washington, D.C., a hub of charter flight activity. Thus Vernon lived virtually alone in his large two-bedroom apartment. His maid, Exxie Hardiman, came every morning at seven o'clock to fix breakfast and "look after Mr. Vernon." She was, perhaps, the only female who would put up with the constant flow of unexpected guests and late-night parties. Dean fit right in. Soon, Exxie was as fond of him as she was of Vernon.

That same month Dean soloed in an open-cockpit Waco F. Flying was getting to be so routine it was like having a regular job, only better. Also in June, his first cousin Sue Falkner introduced him to my mother, a beautiful twenty-one-year-old brunette with clear blue eyes from Etta, a hamlet out in the county. A year before, Louise Hale and Sue had become friends at "the W," the Mississippi College for Women. Now both were working as secretaries at the Works Project Administration office in Oxford.

Louise was five foot six—almost as tall as Dean—with a willowy figure. She carried herself with the grace and insouciance of a high fashion model. An off-the-rack ten-dollar suit looked like a Coco Chanel on her. This cool outer demeanor contrasted perfectly with the "real" Louise, a fun-loving, uncomplicated woman with an easy laugh. Blessed with an even disposition, she rarely let obnoxious people upset her. She simply ignored unpleasant situations until they went away. She could have been the prototype for Robert Browning's "My Last Duchess": generous to a fault in her approval of mankind. She was game for anything new and exciting. An excellent listener, she drew people to her. Armed with an instinct for reticence, she knew when to keep her pretty mouth shut.

She also was a proud woman, independent-minded, and, like Maud, determined to be self-supporting. Louise held a variety of jobs, from taking photographs of children posing with Santa at a Memphis department store (when she had never taken a picture with any camera except a Brownie) to working as a secretary for an Ole Miss psychology professor (when she could not type or take shorthand). She was hired for her willingness to work and her unfailing charm.

The attraction between Louise and Dean was instantaneous on both sides. Their courtship roared to life. At the end of a week, Louise and Sue hitchhiked to Memphis, and Dean took Louise up for her first flight. The more loops and stalls he put the aircraft through, the better she liked it. From that moment on she loved flying, and Dean loved her all the more for that. They had dinner at the Peabody at Vernon's favorite table near the bandstand. Dean danced with both girls. Louise had never had a better time.

The next week, Dean flew to Oxford to see her. She was in the WPA office when she heard the Waco as it dipped low over town. Maud heard it, too. This was a signal for her to drive to the airfield south of town and pick up Dean. Each of the women in his life thought he had come just for her. Neither had met her rival. Yet.

In my father's logbooks the entries for June 22, 24, and 28 indicate that Dean had recorded flight times of 120 minutes, 120 minutes, and 115 minutes without stating a destination. Two hours was the approximate time of a round-trip flight between Memphis and Oxford. I don't think he was going to see his mother.

He invited Louise to come along for a Fourth of July air show in Sikeston, Missouri. She flew with him in the open cockpit. Vernon flew the Waco cabin. Pilots came from all over the country. It was the biggest show ever. Around midnight, when everyone was still partying, a tremendous storm blew up. The pilots rushed out of the hotel and begged rides to the airport so they could tie the planes down. Louise sat wedged between Dean and Vernon, sharing their concern that a plane might be damaged by the wind. No planes were destroyed, and the next day, the air show drew an enormous crowd. Dean and Vernon made more money than they'd ever earned at a single performance.

In the weeks to come, Dean recorded nine July entries that I am sure represent round trips from Memphis to Oxford. In August, when he had to stay at the hangar and wait for charters, Sue and Louise traveled to Memphis. They would spend afternoons at the airport, just sitting and talking, or maybe helping Dean wash the planes or change the oil. When they got to Vernon's apartment, they would find the place already filled with people and a party in progress. Often, Vernon would be throwing a "solo party" for one of his flying students. Pilots from around the country were his guests whenever they were in town.

On several afternoons that August, William drove to the Memphis airport bringing Estelle and Jill, a little over a year old, and Jill's nurse, Narcissus. "Airports were hot," Louise recalled, "and we would put up chairs in the shade of the hangar. While Dean and Omlie took up passengers, Narcissus nursed and fanned Jill, Estelle and I chatted, and Bill supervised."

One day, Vernon took Art Sowell, Navy's cousin, up for a parachute jump, an added attraction to entertain passengers who paid a dollar or two to fly over Memphis and the Mississippi River. Louise was about to be introduced to the danger that Dean, Vernon, and the jumpers faced all the time. They never talked about it, so there was no way for her to anticipate what it felt like. On this day, Art's chute failed to open. She saw his body growing larger and larger as he fell to earth. When she cried out, Dean put his hand over her eyes. They ran to Art. To their immense relief, he was alive. Louise made up her mind then that nothing bad could ever happen to Dean. He would be like Art and cheat death; he would be safe for her to love.

She trusted him completely. When she flew with him, she was never afraid. This could have come from confidence in his piloting, her natural pluck, or her casual disregard of danger— but it was this fearlessness that hooked Dean. That and her smile. He called her "Swampy." I don't know why.

Despite his gift for flying, Dean had several close calls in 1934. During an air show, as he was flying passengers out of a hay meadow five miles south of Oxford, the windshield suddenly became covered with oil. It was spewing everywhere, coating the plane and trailing onto the field. Dean somehow turned the plane, cleared a fence, and set the Waco down easy. When he got out he was as calm and as confident as ever. The passengers, however, were so scared he had to help them out of the plane. He gave them their money back.

Late that summer, Dean was flying three passengers from Kansas City to Memphis. As he flew over the Mississippi River at approximately one thousand feet altitude, the Waco's seven-cylinder radial engine suddenly burned a valve and lost its power. Dean was too far from the Arkansas shore to glide back to it, and there was no place on the Tennessee side to land. Between him and Memphis was Mud Island, a small, flat peninsula overgrown with reeds and brush. He noticed flags flying in a stiff breeze, which told him the direction of the ground wind, an all-important factor in executing a tight landing on rough terrain. Gliding in silence, his passengers no doubt holding their breath, he banked the plane to approach the little island upwind, then killed the flying speed so that the aircraft was at the point of total stall at the precise second when the undercarriage, with its fixed wheels, touched the mat of soft brush. The

plane came to a safe stop before it reached the far end of the island. No one was hurt, nor had the plane been damaged. Spectators on the Mississippi River bridge and Memphis shoreline
observed the amazing descent. The passengers—whose money
Dean no doubt refunded on the spot—were later escorted off
the island by boat.

Dean now confronted the problem of getting the plane off
Mud Island. The solution was to install a new valve brought out
by Vernon Omlie and a three-man crew, who cut brush and leveled the bumps and dips to make a narrow runway on the island.
This had to be done by ax and shovel since they couldn't get
a bulldozer out on the mud flats. They camped out on the island for two days. To lighten the plane for takeoff, they dumped
everything not essential to flight—including fuel, leaving just
enough to take off and fly to the airport.

When the engine was repaired and the narrow takeoff strip
ready, Dean cranked the motor and warmed it to operating
temperature, then taxied to the north end of the peninsula. He
turned the plane into the wind with the tail wheel just at the
edge of the water. He set the controls for takeoff, held tight on
the brake pedal, and slowly pushed the throttle all the way forward. When the engine was wide open, the plane straining under
the pull of the propeller, he released the brakes and pushed the
control yoke to the dashboard. The Waco lunged forward and
began picking up speed, bumping along the uneven dirt path.
In seconds the speeding plane approached the abrupt drop-off
where land met water. A pilot's normal instinct would have been
to jerk back on the wheel and try to pull the plane into the air.
However, Dean used every available foot of cleared ground to
build up sufficient airspeed. There was very little runway left
when he pulled the control wheel back just enough to set the
wings at a gentle climbing angle. The undercarriage flicked the

muddy river water for a second; then the plane began climbing and Dean was airborne.

On September 29, 1934, Louise wanted to see Dean. She didn't know how to drive and asked Cecile Falkner, Jack's wife, for a ride to Memphis. Cecile was eager to go. When they arrived at Dean's apartment, Exxie told them that Dean and Vernon had gone to Batesville, Mississippi, for an air show. When Louise and Cecile reached Batesville, about fifty miles away, Dean was delighted to see them. He made an instant decision. They would be married that day.

It was nine o'clock before he finished taking passengers for rides and the planes were tied down for the night. He and Louise set out to find a jeweler and a justice of the peace. By 10 p.m. on Sunday, September 30, 1934, they were married.* Then they returned to the hotel, where they spent the night in one large room with Cecile, Vernon, and Navy Sowell. They did not tell anyone.

The next day, Vernon flew the Waco back to Memphis, and Dean drove Cecile and Louise to Oxford. Four days later, while working at the WPA office, Louise heard a plane and recognized it as Dean's. When he walked into her office she was shocked by his serious expression. Had he changed his mind? Did he want to annul the marriage? As he drove back to town, he turned to her and said, "We must tell."

Dean was well aware of Maud's attitude toward her daughters-in-law. Although she tolerated Estelle, she actively disliked Jack's wife, Cecile, and John's wife, Lucille. No woman was good enough for any of her sons. Louise would prove to

---

*Several biographers have given their wedding date as September 30, 1935. If this had been true, it would have made me a "wood colt." I loved the idea and was disappointed to find a copy of their license dated September 30, 1934.

be the exception. He no doubt was terrified of what she would think. A letter from "Auntee," Maud's sister-in-law Holland Falkner Wilkins, had yanked him up and convinced him that he had no choice but to face his mother. If Auntee knew, so did Maud. Auntee was a master of tact and deadly persuasion:

My dear Dean;

I am just sending my love and best wishes to you and your Bride. I hope you will always be very happy together and That the best breaks will all be in your favor.

I am sorry you did not introduce us to Louise on Monday When we drove up near your parked car in front of Herndon's Store, though we did not know then you were married, you Might have told us, and no one would have been more pleased, Nor wished better things for you than I. I am sure Sallie Murry Shares my feelings on the subject, since I have heard both Sallie Murry and Robert [Williams] express themselves that way. So We hope to meet Louise soon and know her as your wife and like Her for the splendid girl she is said to be by all who already know Her well.

Since you love her, and she is your wife, then I'm sure she is a Fine girl. You see Dean, I love you when you are good, and I love You when you are bad, and now I'm adding Louise to my list since She is a part of you. Be a good sport and write to your little mother Sometimes, and just know that I'm always for you. Lots of love And good wishes from

Auntee

Dean did not have a minute to spare. They drove straight to Maud's, where he introduced his wife to his mother. Maud's merciful reaction must have surprised him. "Thank goodness," she said. "I thought you'd never marry."

After visiting with Maud, Dean and Louise drove to Rowan Oak to inform William and Estelle, who were very pleased. Estelle immediately began planning an announcement party to be held the following Sunday night. Only family members would be invited. Then Louise and Dean drove out to Etta to tell her parents. Sanford and Pearl Hale were delighted. Sanford took Dean out back to the toolshed where he kept his whiskey. The Hale farm came to be one of Dean's favorite places, and William's as well. The hunting was good, the people and the old homestead honest and uncomplicated. Its quiet dignity offered relaxation and peace to William. He and Dean often hunted there. As they passed the bottle, Dean talked to Sanford about hosting a deer hunt early on Christmas morning.

That night, they returned to Maud's. The Sunday announcement party was elegant. Before the family was seated for dinner, William proposed a toast: "To the best wife and the best flier I have ever known." On Monday morning, Dean and Louise gathered their belongings and drove to Memphis, where they moved in with Vernon Omlie.

Married life did not change Dean's routine. He and Louise lived as happy transients, either barnstorming or visiting William and Maud in Oxford. They never unpacked their suitcases. When they were in Memphis, the apartment was full of people coming and going. Often William would appear unannounced to spend long weekends with Dean and Louise and Vernon and Phoebe Omlie. On a whim, he flew with them anywhere they wanted, to all parts of the country either for business or pleasure.

At least once every two weeks, Dean and Louise flew to Oxford. Inclement weather did not stop them. If fog covered the ground, Dean would simply fly his red Waco along the railroad tracks and follow the Illinois Central line to Oxford. He would circle Maud's house two blocks south of the town square, and waggle his wings and goose the engine. Then he and Louise would look down and watch Maud rush out of the house and head for her car.

Maud and Auntee soon joined the line of pilgrims to the Memphis airport. Once a month they came to see Dean and Louise. They would drive up in Maud's car and visit during the afternoon. As soon as it was dark, Auntee was ready for dinner at the Peabody, and the Peabody had to be ready for her—with its best table, waiter, food, and wine.

The Peabody sparkled whenever Captain Vernon Omlie joined them for dinner at the Skyway, the hotel's rooftop restaurant. Word spread that "the Pilot" was on his way upstairs for dinner, and when the Omlies and Faulkners appeared in the restaurant, the band played a short fanfare, Vernon was introduced, and a spotlight followed them to their reserved table.

The fall of 1934 was an easy, comfortable time for my father. He made a near-perfect score on his commercial pilot's examination, making but a single error. When asked to list the equipment a pilot should always carry with him on a flight, Dean omitted one item: a watch. This became a running joke in the family. As his cousin-in-law Bob Williams said, "Dean never needed a watch. He lived every day of his life by the sun."

As the year came to a close, Dean was looking forward to 1935. Maud had accepted Louise without reservation. They corresponded weekly whenever Louise was away. Each letter from Maud closed the same way:

> *I love you, Louise.*
> *Mrs. Falkner*

Also, business at Mid-South Airways was steadily increasing. Although Dean had never worried about money, it pleased him to be on his way to becoming financially independent. He was surrounded by people he loved. He still had time for a day in the woods. And he always knew the Waco was waiting for him.

—

CHRISTMAS OF 1934 was the best Christmas of all. At 4 a.m., Dean and Louise were sitting on the front steps of Sanford Hale's farmhouse, drinking coffee and waiting for William to arrive for a deer hunt. Louise was not about to let the men go hunting without her. She was dressed in her brother Edward's hunting jacket and pants. In the predawn stillness, they heard the motor of William's Ford Phaeton coming up the narrow dirt road. They saw the glow of the headlights. The dogs began to bark. Dean was wearing his heavy wool Ole Miss letterman's sweater under a bloodstained hunting jacket, the sleeves of which had been ripped and torn by the thorns of Lafayette County.

When the car stopped in front of the house, out stepped William and his sister-in-law, the sturdy and indefatigable Dorothy "Dot" Oldham, more finely turned out in hunting gear than the men. The dogs barked and raced around the car, then became quiet and sniffed the newcomers. Dot declared that she had talked William into bringing her so that she could try out the new 12-gauge shotgun that "a beau" had given her. William repeated Maud's remark that "It was no 'beau.' Gentlemen don't give ladies shotguns for Christmas." Then he added, "But of course hunting don't make much sense to Mother for you or me anyhow, much less Dot."

Louise's father and brother now joined the group. The Hale men, Sanford and Edward, towered over the short-statured Faulkners. They exchanged quiet greetings. Wood smoke from the house drifted down from the roof. Sanford kenneled the dogs to keep them from spooking the deer. He led the way down a worn path past the barn, through the pasture, and into the bottom. The deeper into the woods they went, the quieter the hunters became, until the only sounds were the cries of morning birds and their footsteps. They were in their stands an hour before daylight: Dean and Louise together, Edward alone, William and Sanford together, and Dot by herself with her new shotgun.

It did not matter that they saw no deer. As the sun rose, Sanford called across the clearing, "Let's go back to the house for some breakfast." Coming up the path they smelled smoke from the woodstove and the mouthwatering aroma of frying ham and boiling coffee. On the front steps they took off their muddy boots and went inside in their heavy wool socks. It took my grandmother Pearl years to get over the fact that Dot Oldham refused to take off her hunting hat at table. Nevertheless, Pearl served up an admirable hunter's breakfast of ham and fried quail, grits and redeye gravy, scrambled eggs, biscuits, molasses, and coffee. After the meal, William drove Dot, Dean, and Louise back into town.

Christmas dinner at Rowan Oak always started at two o'clock. Dean and Louise cleaned up and got dressed at Maud's house— Dean in tweed coat and tie, Louise in her best dress of navy blue silk with white braid at the collar and cuffs. They drove Maud in her Buick roadster the few blocks to Rowan Oak, turning up the curving driveway flanked by tall cedars.

Since William and Estelle rarely placed a wreath on the front door, the first sign of Christmas as Dean, Louise, and Maud entered the house was the smell of roasting turkey. Sage and thyme mingled with the clean, sharp scent of the cedar Christmas tree standing ceiling-high in the parlor. Dean and William had cut it the day before, walking less than two hundred yards into the woods west of the house but spending two hours in the process. They inspected every potential Christmas tree, weighed its merits, debated its good and bad points, and when their pint of bourbon was empty, cut down the next tree they came to. William's theory regarding ornaments was that the beauty of a Christmas tree was "in the tree itself, not the stuff that folks put on it." Hence, the tree was sparsely and randomly decorated.

Soon Jack and Cecile arrived, along with Estelle's parents and Dot. Eggnog was presented in a heavy cut-glass punch bowl on a silver tray. William served.

The table was elegant as always with white linens stiffly starched and glittering crystal wine glasses, silver water goblets, and bread and butter plates reflecting the light of the candles. After everyone was seated and the wine glasses were filled, William proposed the first of many toasts to family members young and old—to deer hunts past and future, to Christmas and to Christmases to come. "If we were aristocrats," he said, "we'd break the glasses in the fireplaces. But we aint, so we won't."

The turkey was brought in and paraded about for all to see. William wielded his carving knife with martial precision, standing over the bird and chatting as he worked. After the turkey, dressing, and gravy had been served and the plates passed, platters of wild rice and vegetables streamed from the kitchen. At dessert time, finger bowls were placed on the table, and then came flaming plum pudding. Everyone applauded Estelle, who had cooked all day since early morning and had, in fact, been putting away the homemade cranberry sauce and various jellies and condiments since summer.

William invited the men to join him in the library for after-dinner drinks. The ladies returned to the parlor. The weather had gotten warmer, and the doors were opened in late afternoon. Narcissus brought eighteen-month-old Jill downstairs for everyone to see and hold. The sun was setting. Afternoon slid into evening. The house was filled with the sounds of soft voices and quiet laughter.

William walked Dean, Louise, and Maud to their car. He put his arm around Dean's shoulder and kissed his mother and sister-in-law. "This Christmas was so good," he said, "let's have one like it next year and all the years after that. Merry Christmas, Mother. Merry Christmas, Louise. Merry Christmas, Dean."

—

IN MARCH 1935, the novel *Pylon* was published—a story about the early days of flying. William had become even more familiar with the world of pilots and barnstormers through Dean's experiences, and some elements made their way into his novel about an unnamed reporter who follows three barnstormers and a child as they make their way from air show to air show, living with reckless abandon. It was the dash and vigor he envied, Dean's fearlessness. "Why doesn't a pilot fear death?" he asked Dean and Vernon Omlie over a bottle of bourbon at the Memphis airport. He knew the answer as well as they: *Because, in effect, he is already dead.*

William's habit after finishing a book was to go on a binge. Louise and Dean would receive the first, urgent phone call from Maud: "William is drinking. He needs you." They would drop what they were doing and fly to Oxford, where Maud would be waiting. She would drive Dean directly to Rowan Oak and take Louise home with her.

William once said about his drinking: "When I have one martini I feel bigger, wiser, taller. When I have a second I feel superlative. After that there's no holding me."

Alcoholism has run through each generation of the Faulkner men like a bad gene. The consensus of William's biographers is that he began drinking at an early age for the same reason most people do: He liked the taste of liquor and the way it made him feel. But as he aged, he came to depend more and more on alcohol, not for pleasure but for relief, an anesthestic for pain both physical and psychological. Drinking himself into oblivion was a sure if temporary escape from reality and responsibility; yet he never allowed his alcoholism to interfere with his work. The binges came after the books were made.

He has been described as a periodic drunk: He could abstain or control the urge to drink for weeks, or even months, at a time, but three or four times a year he was overwhelmed by the craving for alcohol. He would take to his bed, a ready supply of liquor on hand. These bouts could last anywhere from several days to over a month, during which time he avoided eating, becoming weaker and weaker until he was gravely ill. Frequently he would have to be hospitalized, usually at Wright's Sanatorium in Byhalia, Mississippi, his preferred drying-out place.

He was blessed, however, with a constitution as strong as his destructive tendency to drink and a body that responded well and quickly to treatment. Otherwise he surely would have suffered irreversible cirrhosis of the liver, blackouts, and memory loss.

William's drunks were never a subject for family consultations, much less the "interventions" of modern day, any more than my mother discussed Jimmy Meadows's binges with anyone. They were simply ignored. Perhaps if no one talked about them, they never happened.

I never saw William Faulkner drunk.

Dean had his work cut out for him. Of everyone in the family he had the most patience in dealing with his older brother's addiction, though he himself rarely drank to excess. When Dean drank, it was to have fun. Sometimes he would take William for long drives in the country. More often, they would closet themselves in William's upstairs bedroom at Rowan Oak. Dean did not confide in anyone, including Louise or Estelle, about what went on between them. Louise never questioned Dean's time-consuming devotion to his family. Shortly after they were married he told her, "Mother and Bill will always come first." She accepted the situation. She had little choice.

Not all of William's drinking bouts were life threatening. Occasionally, Dean gave up trying to make him quit drinking and simply joined him. One day in the late spring of 1935, William appeared at Vernon Omlie's apartment with a gallon jug of corn whiskey. After an hour of matching drinks, the two brothers decided they must go downtown. William declared that since he was in Memphis, he ought to do some shopping. They put the jug in the car, drove down Union Avenue, and parked near the Peabody. They were both barefoot, their pants rolled up to their knees. With William carrying the jug, they walked around the corner to the hotel entrance. A policeman was directing traffic at Second and Union. William carefully placed the jug behind the officer in the middle of the intersection. Assured that their liquor supply would be taken care of, they proceeded to go shopping. (Family members have sworn to the truth of this story—and that the jug was waiting untouched in the street when they returned two hours later.)

———

DEAN AND LOUISE enjoyed a relaxed schedule of work and play. Dean's flying skills increased with every hour he logged. Vernon was always there to answer his questions and to teach by example. One night they were flying into Memphis after a trip to St. Louis. At five thousand feet, the Waco swallowed a valve, and the aircraft lost power, forcing Dean to shut down the engine completely. Vernon took the controls and executed a difficult dead-stick landing. Dean watched and learned.

In July, he performed his first solo night landing. He had been barnstorming in Oxford that day, entertaining a small crowd with stunts and taking passengers for rides. At dusk people were still waiting to go up. Dean would not allow darkness to deprive him of a few dollars more. The pasture south of town was not lighted. So in between hauls, he called two of his young followers over and sent them to town to get lanterns to mark a runway. He promised to take them flying as a reward. They raced to town on their bikes, rounded up a bunch of friends, and raided cars parked at the Lyric Theatre, detaching the carbide headlamps from Model T Fords. These early automobile lights could be removed and turned on and off like flashlights. Back at the pasture they formed an illuminated runway with the stolen lamps. After the last paying customer had left, Dean gave the boys the ride of their lives. When they landed, Dean asked what he owed for the lanterns. The boys admitted that they had "borrowed" them from cars at the Lyric Theatre. In all likelihood, the car owners never saw their headlamps again.

In August, Dean decided that Louise had to learn how to drive. He gave her brief instructions, then changed places with her behind the steering wheel. This was in Memphis, and in her first lesson she had to drive to the airport in big-city traffic. "You did just fine," he told her as he got out of the car. "I'll call you when I'm ready to come home." She was doing just fine on her way home, too, when the car stalled in the middle of a railroad crossing. Louise heard the bells clanging. A train was coming. She abandoned the car. Two men saw the danger and pushed the car off the tracks just before the train roared by.

Louise drove home and collapsed. When Dean telephoned her to come pick him up, she said that she could not possibly come. He caught a ride home, and when he heard her story, he was sympathetic, up to a point. He could not understand why she was hysterical and shaking now that the crisis was over. He insisted that she see a doctor. The next day, a physical examination told her the cause of her nerves, though she thought she already knew: She was pregnant. When she broke the news to Dean, he was delighted. "Now you don't have to drive anymore," he said. "Before long, I'll have that boy to come pick me up." She continued to fly with him, however, for two more months. After November 1, the doctor warned, she would be grounded.

William came up for a weekend in October. He and Dean decided to fly to Clarksdale and see their brother John. William had had a good amount to drink when he got there, so Dean flew the plane. After they were airborne, he let William take the controls. The flight to Clarksdale was uneventful, but as they approached the airfield, William wanted to land the plane. Dean let him handle the controls. They started to circle the field. They circled and circled and circled for fifteen or twenty minutes. Nobody said anything. William just couldn't set it down. Finally, Dean suggested that he try. William agreed. Dean shifted the dual controls to his side of the aircraft and within minutes he had landed the Waco.

It was typical of the understanding between the brothers that William did not resent Dean's taking over. Nor did Dean judge his brother for losing his nerve. But on Monday when they prepared to take off, Dean was at the controls.

On one of their regular visits to Oxford that month, Dean and Louise told Maud about the baby. Dean called Auntee, and they celebrated with ice cream and cake. On the weekend of November 2, Dean flew to Oxford for the first time without Louise. It was a cold, foggy Saturday morning. He flew low over the railroad tracks, his map to Mississippi.

———

DEAN'S FUNERAL WAS on Armistice Day, November 11, 1935, at two in the afternoon. His casket lay on a bier in Maud's front parlor in the same spot where Murry's casket had lain three years before. William went into Dean's old room to see Louise on the morning of the funeral. "Dean's body is here now," he told her. "But I want you to remember him the way he was." The casket remained closed.

The ceremony was private, as are all Faulkner funerals. The immediate family—William, Estelle, Louise, Maud, and Jack and John, along with their wives and children—sat in Dean's room. The door to the parlor remained open. Several of Dean's closest friends—the pilots Vernon Omlie and Murry Spain among them—stood at the far end of the parlor. There were few flowers and no music. The minister read a short service. Louise slumped in her chair. William gently helped her straighten up. He did not suggest that she leave the room.

As the family left to go to St. Peter's Cemetery, they found that the house was surrounded by an enormous, silent crowd, townspeople of all ages, from their father Murry's contemporaries to small boys brought together by common grief.

After Dean's burial, William moved into Maud's house at 510 South Lamar to care for his mother and his brother's wife. He slept on a folding cot in the dining room, with his Underwood portable on the table next to the galley proofs of *Absalom, Absalom!*

Each night he drew Louise's bath, and before she went to bed he would bring her a glass of warm milk and a sleeping pill. One morning as William and Louise sat at the table waiting for breakfast to be served, Louise said, "I can't eat. I dreamed the whole accident last night." William answered, "I dream it every night."

For three weeks William tended solicitously to Maud and Louise. Then grief and guilt erupted inside him and he began to drink. Louise knew it at once; Maud, however, was unaware of his condition. One afternoon, William and Louise were sitting on the sofa in the front room, talking about Dean, when suddenly William began to cry. "I have ruined your life," he said. "It is my fault." Louise was sobbing, too, when Maud appeared. She looked at both of them and said, "You understand, Louise, he cannot help it. He could not stand it anymore. He had to have some relief." She left the room not in anger but in sorrow for both of her favorite sons.

On December 10, 1935, William departed again for Hollywood. Early in 1936, the small marker he had selected for Dean's grave was placed in St. Peter's Cemetery. The biblical inscription was identical to the one William had written in 1929 for John Sartoris: "I bare him on eagles' wings and brought him unto me." Upon returning to Oxford, William drove Maud and Louise to the cemetery to see the marker. Maud did not like the inscription, not because she objected to the obvious comparison between John Sartoris and Dean Faulkner but because she saw it as a monument to William's grief and guilt.

I've always wondered why he did not choose a verse from *A Shropshire Lad*. "To an Athlete Dying Young" was one of his favorites—and mine.

Years after Dean's death, when *Sartoris* was republished in 1951 and Maud received her copy from William, she told me to read the novel and to remember that whereas young Bayard represented a combination of William, Jack, and John Falkner, John Sartoris was based on my father, who loved people, who

was spontaneous, full of laughter, "warm and ready and generous." She knew well the lines in *Sartoris* that introduced the epi-
taph William had chosen:

> Yet withal there was something else, as though the merry
> wild spirit of him who had laughed away so much of his
> heritage of humorless and fustian vainglory managed
> somehow even yet . . . to soften the arrogant gesture with
> which they bade him farewell.

Although he rarely spoke of his youngest brother, on one occasion he told me, or tried to tell me, how he felt. "Your father
was a rainbow," he said.

"The Old Colonel," William Clark Falkner (1825–1889), of Ripley, Mississippi, great-great-grandfather of Dean Faulkner Wells, a colonel in the Confederate Army, planter, lawyer, and railroad builder.

Sallie Murry Falkner and J. W. T. Falkner, grandparents of William Faulkner, photo taken in 1910, the year that J.W.T. became the founding president of the First National Bank in Oxford.

Lelia Dean Butler, "Damuddy," mother of Maud Butler Falkner and the author's great-grandmother.

Maud Butler Falkner, twenty-five, in 1896, the year she married Murry Cuthbert Falkner.

The four Faulkner brothers:
Dean, three, in front;
standing left to right, Jack,
William, and John (1910).

Maud Falkner with William,
"Billy," as an infant; his first
studio portrait, taken in 1898.

When World War I ended,
William, twenty-one, shown
here in an RAF lieutenant's
uniform, returned to Oxford
in December 1918. For
his rakish airs he soon
became known about town
as "Count No 'Count."

Rare photo of "the Doodlebug," the locomotive on the Old Colonel's Gulf and Chicago Railroad (later named Gulf & Ship Island Railroad), circa 1920.

and he stops against the sky; perhaps his heart also misgives him. He stops, half turned toward her, and for a fleeting second, he is the utter master of his soul; fate and the gods stand aloof watching him, his destiny waits wordless at his side. Will he turn back where she awaits him in her rose bower, or will he go on? He goes on, his eyes ever before him, looking into the implacable future. Perhaps a newer, stronger love has called him away, that he does not return; perhaps he is fallen upon by

Marionettes, William Faulkner's first book, was written, illustrated, and handbound by the author, then a student at Ole Miss. He and his classmate Ben Wasson sold copies on campus for five dollars each.

William Faulkner was living in New Orleans in 1925 when his friend William Spratling made this sketch of him.

Estelle Oldham Franklin, in Shanghai circa 1926, before her divorce from Cornell Franklin and subsequent marriage to William Faulkner.

Estelle Oldham Franklin and her daughter Victoria (Cho Cho) in Shanghai before Estelle's 1927 divorce from her first husband, Cornell Franklin. She married William Faulkner in 1929.

Dean Swift Faulkner at his high school commencement in Oxford in 1926, the same year his brother William's first novel, *Soldiers' Pay*, was published.

Dean Swift Faulkner played baseball at the University of Mississippi from 1927 to 1931.

Dean Swift Faulkner, twenty, SAE fraternity picture at Ole Miss, circa 1927.

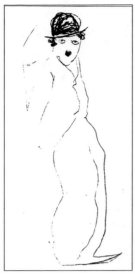

Pen-and-ink study of
Charlie Chaplin by
William Faulkner that
may have been sketched
in Hollywood where
Faulkner worked as an
MGM screenwriter in
1932.

William Faulkner showed off his new Waco C
cabin cruiser in 1933, the plane he gave to his
brother Dean a year later.

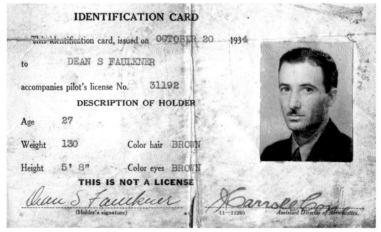

Dean Swift Faulkner, twenty-seven, shown in a photo taken for his
pilot's license.

William selected a biblical inscription for his brother Dean's tombstone: "I bare him on eagles' wings and brought him unto me."

Louise Faulkner took two-year-old Dean to the dedication ceremony of the Dean Faulkner Memorial Airport in 1938. The grass landing strip was located five miles south of Oxford.

Dean Faulkner's fellow pilots and barnstormers at Mid-South Airways in Memphis, Captain Vernon Omlie and his wife, Phoebe Omlie. Vernon was killed in a commercial plane crash in 1936. *(Courtesy of the Mississippi Valley Collection, University of Memphis Library)*

8

World War II

WHILE THE CENTER OF MY FATHER'S WORLD WAS ALWAYS Oxford, when I lived with Wese and Jimmy the moving never seemed to stop. The war years, 1941–45, were great levelers. Suddenly I was not the only one moving away on short notice. Anyone's father could be drafted; thus, everyone was in the same boat, all ready to go wherever we were sent and to pull together in the war effort, all subject to abrupt changes in lifestyle and stuck with the same number of rationing tickets for sugar, coffee, gasoline, chocolate, or eggs.

After the initial shock of leaving Oxford at age five, I adjusted to life on the go, to being the new child in school, exploring new neighborhoods, looking for new playmates. I was a natural-born common denominator, a social little creature who liked people and expected them to like me back. I'm always surprised when somebody hates me. Most of my schoolmates liked me. I was no threat to anyone. The older I got, the more I came to accept, even look forward to, the next move, to a different house in a different town.

When I was in second grade, Jimmy, Wese, my dog Little Bit, and I lived in a white two-bedroom clapboard house in Clarksdale within a few blocks of my grammar school. Jimmy had been hired to run the Clarksdale Chamber of Commerce, though he did not last a year. To save gasoline he rode to work on my bicycle, often with me perched behind him.

Money was short for everyone we knew, and Jimmy didn't have health insurance. Fortunately, I was an abnormally healthy child. When outbreaks of measles (red and German), chicken pox, mumps, or the flu swept through the schools, I caught none of them. Wese would keep sending me off to school every morning, until the day came when I was the only child left in my class. Home I went with the familiar note, *"School closed until further notice due to an epidemic of* _____.*"* I ended up catching all of those diseases from my own children. My natural immunity seemed to have vanished by then, and I was far sicker than they ever were.

In those days, rather than send each child to a doctor's office, nurses came to our school for "Shots Day." We didn't know what we were getting shots for, but we all lined up in the auditorium staring in misery at the table center stage, where two nurses in white starched uniforms sat. The smell of alcohol was all pervasive and we tried not to look at the needles. If I could, I bribed my way with "recess candy" to the head of the line in order to get it over with, and to be able to watch my classmates suffer as I had and guess which one of my friends might start to cry. Tell me children aren't pint-size savages. Or maybe it was just me.

We had a fenced-in backyard with a garage—a natural place, Jimmy said, to raise chickens. The next weekend he came home with two little chicks, still fuzzy yellow, but with the tips of gray and black-and-white feathers beginning to show. They were fun to feed, ate a lot, and grew fast. Jimmy made them nests of straw in the garage. Having gathered eggs with Mama Hale out in the country, I was eager to go into the egg business myself, mentally adding up how much money I'd make when my chickens started laying. I named them Hedy Lamarr and Betty Grable. Betty did fine, actually laying several eggs, but Hedy was a disaster, flying at Little Bit and me whenever we came close. When we had fried chicken for Sunday dinner I didn't ask any questions but ate the pully-bone as I always did.

I spent a great deal of time with my grandmother Maud, Nannie to me, during the war years. She was devoutly, even obsessively patriotic. During WWI, she had placed two stars on a piece of red, white, and blue felt and hung it in her window to show that she had sons serving in the armed forces—one for Jack, a marine who fought in the Argonne Forest in France—and one for William.

In the Second World War her fervor returned. She read a newspaper daily, subscribed to *Time* and *Life*, and listened to H. V. Kaltenborn reporting war news on the CBS Radio Network at six o'clock every evening. A radio console was kept in the parlor. It looked like a wooden cabinet with double doors. Nannie would open it up and turn on the radio and we would gather to listen. As soon as Kaltenborn said "Good night," Nannie turned off the radio and closed the console until 6 p.m. the next day.

After John's son Jimmy Faulkner completed his basic Marine Corps training at Parris Island, South Carolina, he learned to fly Corsairs. Nannie and Aunt Lucille, Jimmy's mother, drove to Cherry Point, North Carolina, to see him off to the Pacific. The family could not believe it. The two women had not exchanged three civil words in a lifetime, yet off they went on a two-day journey in Aunt Lucille's station wagon. Their mutual affection for Jimmy, their tall, blue-eyed, flying Faulkner, had effected a temporary truce.

Early one Sunday morning, when all of us except Nannie were still in bed, we heard a steady knocking at the front door. Nannie didn't have a door knocker much less a bell. We heard bare knuckles on wood growing louder with each rap. I heard Nannie open the door and invite someone into the parlor. When I peeked through a crack in my bedroom door I saw an ancient creature, even older than Nannie and smaller than she, a tiny, gray shriveled figure in a faded housedress, black high-topped lace-up shoes, and a bedraggled sun bonnet. She sat very straight in Nannie's best chair next to the fireplace with her heels together. Their communication was intense, though I could not distinguish from their whispers what was being said. Then I heard Nannie say, "Thank you. But I must say no. Thank you."

The woman stood. Nannie reached for her hand, shook it gently, and steered the visitor by the elbow to the front door. As soon as the woman had left, I raced into the room. "What was that? What did she want?"

Now Nannie sank into her best chair. "Her name is Mrs. Ragland. She grew up out on Pea Ridge Road. She must be close to ninety. I've heard of her all my life. I never thought I'd meet her."

"What did she want? Why did she come?" I asked.

Nannie smiled and pulled me into her lap. "To give me a present." She whispered in my ear, "She's a rainmaker. The last one in the county. She came to offer me the gift."

"Oh, Nannie, that's wonderful. Isn't it? You can do it. Can't you?"

"Yes, Lamb. I might be able to. But I couldn't stand up to that kind of responsibility. What if I made a mistake and our weather patterns turned out all sixes and sevens? She'll find somebody else. But I thanked her for thinking of me. It was an honor." She held me tight.

When Pappy was in town, he came to see Nannie every afternoon. They would visit in her bedroom, the only place she received family members with the exception of the front gallery. In good weather she and Pappy would sit in rocking chairs and watch people go by, remarking if anyone had a new car, its color, make, year, and how much it cost.

The living room was reserved for unexpected guests. Nannie considered it too cold and uninviting, and too large for an intimate get-together. Her room was just the opposite: fifteen by fifteen feet with two large windows overlooking the backyard and a big oak tree. It faced west so the afternoon sunlight streamed in, turning the white walls a soft yellow, sometimes burnt orange. A concrete sidewalk led from the back door beyond the property line to a small gingerbread-trimmed house, part of which had been the kitchen of the Big Place.

Nannie's screen door had a checkerboard metal guard covering the lower half of it. I liked its perfect squares and the simple scrollwork across the top. Rowan Oak had one just like it. Nannie and Pappy may have purchased these "screen savers" at the same place. Her house was under construction in 1930 while his was being repaired and restored. The kitchen sinks in both houses were also identical: white porcelain with double drains on each side of the basin, separate hot and cold taps with "H" and "C" marked in black on the porcelain knobs.

The furnishings were sparse but comfortable: a single bed with a wrought-iron bedstead facing the windows and a night table beside it with a brass crook-necked lamp within easy reach.* A wooden bookcase with glass doors stood against the north wall and was filled with books that she loved: signed first editions of William's and John's works, a set of Rex Stout mysteries, and Joseph Conrad's *Lord Jim*. She had a marble-topped oak dresser with a gilt-framed mirror hanging above it. We all knew that the upper left-hand drawer held her "secret treasures," mementos of the people she loved. There was a postcard that Dean had sent her from Boy Scout camp in Waterford, Mississippi, asking her to bring him his baseball glove; a red rock shaped like a heart that Jimmy had found; a delicate lace handkerchief monogrammed

---

*On the night she died, in 1960 at age eighty-nine, a copy of *Lady Chatterley's Lover* was found on the bedside table.

with Nannie's initials that Auntee had given her; a nickel I once picked up off the street and slipped into her pocket. Years later, in December 1950, soon after Pappy had returned from Stockholm, she would open the left-hand drawer to find a Nobel Prize medallion nestled in a velvet-lined case.

The right-hand drawer held her fans, at least fifteen beautiful ones that folded out to reveal hand-painted scenes on silk or parchment and staves of carved ivory, some inlaid with pearl. They came from all over the world. Everyone knew that the one gift that never failed to please Nannie was yet another folding fan. In warm weather she used them every day, opening them with a flick of her wrist, snapping them shut with a crack, gesturing regally.

Her bedroom had two rocking chairs and it had a small wooden chest that was just right for me to sit on. One wall was lined with her paintings, including three of her sons in profile, each done when the boys were seven. In winter it was the warmest room in the house due in part to its western exposure and because it was located directly over the coal-burning furnace, which she stoked daily. Yet the real warmth radiated from Nannie. This was her nest, her favorite place. There was no painting of Dean.

In support of the war effort we saved tin foil by stripping it off chewing gum wrappers and mashing it into balls (though none of us were allowed to chew gum in the house). We also saved bits and pieces of string that Nannie wound into large balls. Nannie and Auntee were rarely without their knitting needles, making socks and sweaters to send to the troops.

At forty-four, Jack was determined to reenlist in the army. Initially rejected for being too old, he managed through his FBI connections to get a wartime commission as a captain in Military Intelligence. It was supposed to be a desk job, but he wrangled a combat assignment just in time for the invasion of Sicily.

Pappy was jealous of Jack's WWII commission, I think, though he said nothing. He tried to enlist in the navy but was rejected because of his age. So he volunteered for the civil air patrol as an "air raid warden." He put on his official armband every night and patrolled the neighborhood. A blackout was in effect. Any sliver of light could provide a beacon for German or Japanese bombers. The fear of invasion in 1942 and '43 was very real.

Sometimes Pappy allowed me to accompany him on patrol. We began by inspecting Miss Kate Baker's* house, next to Rowan Oak. The night Pappy spotted a bit of light escaping beneath the shade of a window, he knocked. We waited. Miss Kate was not surprised to see us at her door. This happened once a week. She smiled when Pappy dutifully warned her that he saw light at the window. She went to close the shade while he gave instructions from outside. Miss Kate winked at me and said she was glad we had stopped by. Wouldn't we stay for cake and coffee? *No, no,* Pappy replied. We had rounds to make. I shrugged, wishing I could have some cake, yet intensely pleased with myself for serving my country.

War news was a standard feature at the movies. During the summer months Nannie and Auntee took me to the picture show almost every night at Oxford's Lyric Theatre. We would cheerfully watch the same movie three times in a row, or at least I did. Theater owner Bob Williams was mayor of Oxford and Auntee's son-in-law. He let Nannie and Auntee in for free, but I had to buy a ticket, which cost ten cents. Nannie paid. Nannie and Auntee would seat me between them to keep me from fidgeting. They knitted the whole time, needles clacking in the flickering light. One unforgettable night, a newsreel about the invasion of Sicily

---

*It's an old southern tradition for children to call close adult family friends "Miss" or "Mister" with their given names as a sign of familiarity and respect.

came on. Nannie abruptly jumped up and shouted, *"That's my Jackie! Bob, run it back!"* I looked, and sure enough there was my uncle Jack in army uniform, a .45 pistol in his hand, wading ashore with the invading troops. My cousin-in-law Bob—who not only owned the Lyric but ran the ticket booth, made the popcorn, and served as projectionist—dutifully rewound the film by hand, turning the reels so that "my Jackie" walked backward in slow motion to the landing craft, then at great speed invaded Sicily over and over again. *Clack, clack, clack* went Nannie and Auntee's knitting needles, keeping time with the troops and somehow never missing a beat or dropping a stitch. By the third or fourth invasion the audience was on their feet clapping and cheering *"That's our Jackie!"* until finally Nannie had seen enough. As we walked home that night, I felt completely safe and secure. Jack had saved Sicily from the Nazis and Pappy would save us from the Japanese.

Everyone was a patriot in those days. Pappy and Aunt Estelle put in a "Victory Garden" at Rowan Oak—a kitchen garden on the east lawn with tomatoes, okra, and string beans, and a much larger one next to Chrissie Price's cabin with corn, squash, potatoes, black-eyed peas, and butter beans. Neighbors—including professors at Ole Miss—volunteered to hoe and weed. At harvest time they returned to pick the vegetables. Aunt Estelle and Chrissie began canning. They bought mason jars by the case. The snapping, shelling, peeling, and paring went on every day. Steam from boiling pots of water fogged the kitchen. Jellies and jams, pear chutney, and quince preserves were Jill and Estelle's specialties. I liked the feel of a sharp kitchen knife that had been in use so long that the wooden handle was worn down in the middle of the shaft. I could peel tomatoes like an old hand, but my forte was tasting the jelly.

In January 1945, Wese, Jimmy, and I were living in Memphis. I volunteered to lead my third-grade class in a "save dimes and win the war" campaign. I was relentless in persuading first and second graders, and all the third graders smaller than I, to contribute a portion of their lunch money to me for Uncle Sam. My class won the citywide contest and I was chosen to make a sixty-second speech on WREC Radio. Standing on a little platform in front of the school, wearing my favorite Friday dress and speaking into a microphone, I addressed Memphis and vicinity in my best FDR imitation: *"My fellow Americans, our dimes will give us victory overseas."*

As soon as school let out for the summer, Wese and I went to Oxford for several weeks. During that time I practically lived at Rowan Oak with Pappy's daughter Jill and his step-granddaughter, Vicki. Jill's favorite book that summer was *Great Tales of Terror and the Supernatural.* She was bent on scaring Vicki and me senseless, and we were willing victims. Each night she would read horror stories out loud: "The Monkey's Paw" and "Rats in the Walls." When she tired of reading, we begged for more. (Years later I discovered that Pappy's classic horror story, "A Rose for Emily," was included in *Great Tales.* For some reason we did not read that one.)

Before going to sleep every night, Vicki and I chanted a stanza that we'd found on the frontispiece of *Great Tales.*

> *From Ghoulies and Ghosties*
> *And Long-Legged Beasties*
> *And Things that go Bump in the Night,*
> *Good Lord deliver us!*

—

JIMMY MEADOW JOINED the navy in the spring of 1945 and reported to basic training at the Great Lakes Naval Training Center in Waukegan, Illinois. For once, he was not fired but instead was hired—by Uncle Sam. Wese and I joined him in Waukegan. From early June until V-J Day in August 1945, the three of us lived in a single room on the third floor of a Victorian house owned by a Swedish family. It was located on a cul-de-sac bordering a small park with swings and slides, and picnic tables under big old trees. In the center was a small gazebo where an all-female band played sing-along war tunes every Saturday night.

Our small living quarters and close space were not as bad as they might have been. The nightmares brought on by *Great Tales of Terror* made sleeping in the same room with anybody, even Jimmy, a relief. We had an ice chest and a hot plate. I lived on Cheerios, baked beans, and peanut butter sandwiches. Each evening we rode a bus downtown and met Jimmy at a USO center for supper. The food was good, plentiful, and free.

Jimmy was sober all summer, and I had a wonderful time, culminating with the delirium of V-J Day. Jimmy borrowed a car and drove us into Chicago. Wese and I stayed with friends in a fourth-floor hotel room, where we watched the mob below cheering and celebrating the victory over Japan in Chicago's Loop. The next day, Wese took me to breakfast at a diner. We ordered eggs over easy. I ate four. The twelve-hour train ride back to Memphis was happy chaos, with soldiers and sailors laughing, singing, dancing in the aisles, toasting the victory.

Wese and I arrived in Memphis after midnight. Wese somehow got us into a taxi full of people going to the Peabody. I sat on a sailor's lap. When we walked into the lobby, we saw that every chair and couch was occupied by sleeping men in uniform. There were no vacancies. I sensed Wese's nervousness and exhaustion and her obvious relief when we heard a bellboy say, *"Paging the lady with the little girl with braids . . . paging the lady . . ."* He led us upstairs to the mezzanine where one large couch was empty. We curled up together and slept till dawn.

2

Wese and Jimmy

Ｆ ROM 1945 TO 1947, WESE, JIMMY, AND I LIVED IN OXFORD
with Jimmy's mother, Letitia. "You may call me *T,*" was how
she introduced herself to me, forming the letter with her hands.

My bedroom was the back room of the main house with a
doorway that opened into our apartment. It was sparsely fur-
nished with an old wrought-iron bed and a dresser with a mirror
and stool. Hanging over the mantel of the coal-burning fireplace
was a picture of "Lo, the Poor Indian" leaning dolefully on his
lance. He was the last thing I saw every night for three years.

As I would later discover, T was something of a legend in
Oxford. She dressed for her role as one of the town characters:
shapeless housedresses in pastel colors, matching "scuffies"
(bedroom slippers), and "hair bobs," as she called the pink, blue,
or pale green narrow strips of plastic—shower curtain material—
with which she tied her abundant white tresses. Each night after
playing the piano for an hour or so, she would retire with a bottle
of Geritol and the latest issue of the *Upper Room* to her walk-in
closet lit by a naked lightbulb dangling on a cord.

She and her husband, J. T. Meadow, lived two blocks from
Nannie's house on South Lamar. I was taught to call J.T. "Little Father." He was vice president of the Bank of Oxford, a
quiet spoken, gentle man of small stature. He and T were staunch
Presbyterians, so when I was old enough I was enrolled in a

catechism class: a children's study group led by a Sunday school teacher named Mrs. Gathright, who challenged us to memorize the Shorter Catechism before Easter, when we would become members of the church. We met once a week after school at Mrs. Gathright's house. Armed with a near-photographic (trash-bin) memory and a competitive streak, I became an ardent catechism reciter: *What-is-God?-A-spirit-infinite-eternal-unchangeable-in-His-Being-wisdom-power-holiness-justice-and-truth*, I think. With not a clue what the words meant I could repeat them faster than anyone. As soon as the afternoon's lesson was over, Mrs. Gathright would serve a chocolaty dessert with whipped cream topped by cherries and nuts. I did not miss a class.*

Jimmy once told me the story of his mother's having caught him at age eight sneaking a puff of his father's cigar. She wrapped him in a sheet, put a tinsel Christmas wreath around his head, sat him in a chair in their front yard in broad daylight, and made him smoke a cigar until he threw up. As a child I found the story weird and didn't react one way or the other, but now I see that he may have been trying to explain his problems with alcohol, not to mention women.

T did all she could to protect us from Jimmy's abuse. One night I awakened to the sight of her rushing through the French doors like an avenging angel, her long white hair streaming

---

*Before Jimmy and T, I had been a hymn-singing Baptist with Mama and Papa. My predestination phase lasted through high school until I discovered and fell in love with the words of the 1928 Book of Common Prayer ("erred and strayed from Thy ways like lost sheep . . . not fit to pick up the crumbs"). For the next thirty years I was a genuflecting Episcopalian. When the church saw fit to adopt a new prayer book, the music of the language and the profound feeling it generated was lost on me. The services no longer rang true. Language matters too much to some of us. At the same time, the mistakes of a lifetime began to haunt me. I decided my best bet was reincarnation. I'll be starting all over as a black-eyed Susan.

down the back of her pink flannel nightgown. She was barefoot and brandishing a poker. She stood over Jimmy, who was passed out on the floor, saying in a voice from hell, "If you hit Louise again, I'll kill you."

In addition to being our protector, T made the best chow-chow I've ever eaten.

A few times when Jimmy was drunk we went to stay with Mama and Papa Hale in the country while we waited for Wese to heal, physically and emotionally. It could take weeks, or it might take months. And then she would go back to him—or he would come pick her up, with me in tow. The abuse was never physical with me, but the psychological assaults have affected me for a lifetime. Jimmy planted the seed of doubt. What was I worth as a human being? Half of my world, the Faulkners and the Hales, said I was wonderful, while the other half relentlessly told me ("that goddamned Faulkner brat") how much I lacked. The first time I heard the song "Anything You Can Do" from *Annie Get Your Gun,* I couldn't get it out of my head and sang a duet with myself:

> *Anything you can do I can do better*
> *I can do anything better than you.*

We moved thirteen times in twelve years. I lived in Oxford, Clarksdale, Memphis, Little Rock, and Chicago. Frequently we relocated from one house to another in the same town. I was never told why but, of course, knew instinctively that Jimmy had been fired because of alcoholism. Many times I was unaware that we were moving until I came home from school and my bed was gone.

Other times, I had plenty of warning. I would be awakened by drunken brawls in the night, screams and shouts of profanity, the crash of broken glass. I would rush out of my room in my nightgown to be confronted by my mother's beautiful, battered face. In the morning I would be packed and sitting on our front steps ready to go when Pappy drove up. Sometimes Wese left with me, but most of the time she stayed behind to close down the house. The guilt I felt at leaving her would come later, when I was older.

Like all children, I was adaptable. I did not know it then, but I was learning how to "compartmentalize" my life. When we moved to Little Rock, where Jimmy was night editor at the *Arkansas Gazette*, I liked it fine. His work schedule suited our strange little family perfectly because shortly after I came home from school, Jimmy had to go to work. We were together only on weekends.

While we were in Little Rock, Billy Graham's "Crusade for Christ" came to town. Jimmy was assigned to cover the Crusade. Though raised a Presbyterian, he was now a staunch skeptic. He attended two or three Graham services. The story he filed was a scathing critique. After it appeared in the Saturday *Gazette*, we were awakened early Sunday morning by what sounded like the Mormon Tabernacle Choir belting out "Onward Christian Soldiers" in front of our duplex. We peered out through the venetian blinds and saw the yard filled with fifty or sixty cross-bearing Christians. With the final "going on before," their leader—not Graham, I was sorry to see—began to pray long and loud for our poor lost souls. Jimmy told us to dress quickly and get going through the back door to a neighbor's house to wait out the holy storm.

I was actually proud of Jimmy for having the courage to stand by his convictions. I felt the same way when I read another story that he filed on a tornado that ripped through Jonesboro, Arkansas. His focus was the death of a sixteen-year-old girl. Told from a father's point of view, it was a sensitive portrait of grief, so beautifully written that the Associated Press picked it up and ran it on the national wire with his byline.

And yet this was the same man who would not allow Wese and me to turn on the TV except when he was at home (unless we could get away with it), or use the telephone or drive the car. Once, when he was on a drunk, Wese sneaked me out to the Department of Motor Vehicles so I could pass my driving test. We had a tacit agreement. I knew not to ask for the car if Jimmy was sober.

I'm not sure when he joined Alcoholics Anonymous, but the people there sustained us many times over. After one particularly long bout, when he had hauled himself and his jug up the disappearing staircase to the attic—"holed up to die," he bellowed over and over—Wese called her friends in AA. They came immediately and were talking to her in the kitchen when I walked in carrying Jimmy's 12-gauge shotgun. "It's not loaded," I said, "but if you'll show me where the shells are, I'll take them to him."

They quickly defused my bravado, and when the phone rang thirty minutes later, I grabbed it. One of my friends wanted to know if I'd go out with him. Taking advantage of the situation, I asked for and was given Wese's permission to go out on a school night. I left home without a second thought.

I often think how different, yet how similar, Pappy and Jill's relationship was to Jimmy's and mine. Both men were periodic drunks: They could resist drinking for weeks, sometimes months on end, but when the craving struck, Jimmy would drink anything he could get his hands on—cheap bourbon to start with, then when his liquor and money were exhausted he resorted to anything with alcohol content: vanilla extract, cough medicine, mouthwash, paregoric. Pappy had the wherewithal to plan ahead, so that when his supply ran out he could dispatch Andrew Price or one of his drinking buddies to a bootlegger to replenish his stock. We knew the binge was over when we saw him on his knees digging up bitterweeds in the pasture. He used a hand spade and worked steadily to keep the demons at bay. If he was unable to recover on his own, there was always Wright's Sanatorium in Byhalia, sixty miles north of Oxford, where the drying-out treatment sometimes involved tapering off, not going cold turkey. On one occasion he drank cognac until he collapsed on a plane from Paris to Rome. The pilot radioed ahead for an ambulance to carry him to a hospital. And yet Pappy in his later years could drink socially, whereas Jimmy (and Aunt Estelle) could not. One drink led to a bender.

Pappy led two lives quite openly, and yet we at home were the last to know. To us he was the retiring recluse, shy, distant, and difficult to know, stuck in the red clay hills with Aunt Estelle. Needless to say, we were shocked at a photograph of him getting off a plane, drunk and disheveled, in 1955, when he traveled to Japan as a cultural representative for the U.S. State Department. The photograph appeared in the "People" section of *Time* magazine.* (Nannie promptly canceled her subscription.)

In a way I was luckier than Jill. I had a built-in escape hatch in the four-letter word *step*. For me there was always somewhere else to go, another family to love me and take care of me, someone else to bear the shame. Jill had no such option. She had to

---

*I think Pappy drank on airplanes because he was afraid to fly. He told me in the late 1950s that he had come to dread long commercial flights. This surprised me, because he'd been the first Faulkner to embrace flying and encouraged my father in his career as a pilot. I didn't fully understand it until the same thing happened to me. After years of fearless flights, of looking forward to takeoffs and landings, I became terrified almost overnight. Now I fly only when necessary, and only on "Air Vodka" or "Air Ativan," or both.

stay in the only home she had ever known. Pappy was her flesh and blood. Whereas I had only to worry that my friends might find out, Jill had to worry about the rest of the world—newspaper stories, biographies rife with tales of his drinking and depression, rumors of shock treatments. If Pappy or Aunt Estelle or both went on a spree, it reflected on her, or at least she felt that way. Whenever I was packed off to Oxford, everybody sobered up and took care of me. I wonder what my life might have been like if Wese hadn't married Jimmy. But then again, how different might Jimmy's life have been had Wese not had me?

When Jimmy lost his job at the *Gazette,* he and Wese moved to Chicago's Oak Park where they lived in a housing project that looked like a prison compound. Every building in the neighborhood looked just as bad. The first time I came to see them, I thought, "Is this where I live?" The inside of their apartment was worse. It had only one bedroom. By day, *my* bed lived in a broom closet. Perhaps Jimmy hoped that if there was no room at the inn, I wouldn't stick it out for the whole summer.

The apartment building had a security buzzing system installed in the bare, dingy entryway. Each resident's name and apartment number was listed next to the buzzers. When a visitor pushed the buzzer, the resident buzzed back and the door to the stairwell opened. I never figured out why anyone wanted to get past that door.

In spite of this, Chicago became one of my favorite places. I loved riding the Panama Limited from Batesville to Chicago, having lunch in the club car, looking over fences into backyards, seeing the lighted kitchens and screened porches, clotheslines, and doghouses, hearing the porter sing out "Cairo, Illinois," knowing that soon we would pull into Union Station on Canal Street at midnight. Going to Old Comiskey to watch my beloved White Sox was wonderful: Nellie Fox on second; Luis

Apparicio at short; Sherm Lollar behind the plate; and Larry Doby in the field. Jimmy's cousin Boo Ferriss had pitched for the Boston Red Sox in the 1940s and was their pitching coach a decade later. When he came to town, he gave us tickets behind the Red Sox dugout, almost close enough to touch Ted Williams or Jimmy Piersall. After the game sometimes we got to join the team for dinner. Many times over, Boo was a godsend in my life. I loved the Loop, the L, the Palmer House, the jazz clubs. I loved all of it. Still do.

Jimmy Meadow died on skid row in Chicago. In June 1963, the Chicago police phoned Wese in Oxford, having found her name, address, and phone number in Jimmy's otherwise empty wallet. He was discovered dead on the sidewalk and buried in a pauper's grave. He weighed sixty-eight pounds. Wese did not return to claim the body.

10

Jill

PAPPY'S DAUGHTER, JILL, AND I WERE CLOSE IN AGE BUT WE could not have been further apart in temperament. Few photographs exist of us together: Jill's third birthday at Rowan Oak, my fifth at Nannie's. There is only one of Jill and me by ourselves. We are standing in Nannie's front yard. It is cold. Jill's coat is too small. Mine is too big. If we'd traded coats we would have looked better. She is holding a small bouquet of leaves. We look like sad war orphans, possibly hungry.

Though we were brought up by the same people, spent time in the same households and with each other, Jill and I were never close. The distance between us widened as we grew up, perhaps because it was impossible to be best pals with someone I was afraid might be perfect. Even as a little girl Jill had donned her invisible armor, her protection from the pressures she would endure for a lifetime: too much to live up to, too much to live down, and no means of escape. We never shared a secret.

When we were growing up, Rowan Oak was a quiet house with only one radio, in Jill's room, and no TV. Pappy worked at home, of course. We didn't really understand what he did all day long. He never told us to be quiet—or, at most, "Don't thunder through the house!" He was so deep in his own world that often we ceased to exist for him. We could have ridden horses through the library and he would not have noticed. One day at the beginning of the school term, Jill's second grade teacher had the students write down their fathers' occupations. She told us later that, having no idea what Pappy did for a living, she left that part blank.

She was a brilliant horsewoman with a seat that rivaled our grandmother Nannie's who was said to have the best in the county. She and Pappy would ride out on Old Taylor Road, a dirt road in those days and a fine track for a fast horse. Pappy would send Jill ahead to a predetermined spot, then at his shout she would spur her horse and fly down the road, kicking up clumps of earth, racing against the stopwatch Pappy held. For days afterward he would tell people, "Missy rode a two-minute mile Saturday morning out on Old Taylor." My role was to cheer and clap as Jill flew past.

At twelve Jill seemed more like the lady of the house than her mother was. I thought she knew everything. She had a vocabulary an adult would envy, got straight As seemingly effortlessly, could draw, write, and play the piano. She could pronounce Jean-Pierre Aumont's name with a French accent and whip up exotic chutneys. She and her best friend, Mil'Murray* Douglas, ate watercress sandwiches with the crusts cut off, while I was stuck with peanut butter. She was editor of the *Optic*, Oxford High School's newspaper, and she and Mil'Murray starred in *Our Hearts Were Young and Gay* their junior year. Her taste in clothes, thanks to Aunt Estelle, was incredibly chic. I relished getting her hand-me-downs, the last of which was her wedding gown, along with a hand-me-down father to give me away. She even had Rh-negative blood.

---

*When a grade school teacher began to call Mil'Murray "Mildred," which no one had ever done, Jill solved the problem at recess by inserting an apostrophe. She was "Mil'Murray" from then on.

One morning I was in the dining room at Rowan Oak help-ing Jill set the table for lunch. She had taken out all kinds of flatware, several forks and knives for each place setting. This was not for "company" but only for the four of us—Pappy, Aunt Estelle, Jill, and me. After several attempts at placing silver in some kind of order beside the plates, I banged a handful onto the table, scattering some on the floor. *"I'll never learn what goes where! I'll never be a lady!"* I said. Jill glanced at me and said, "You were born one. Now pick that up."

Pappy and Aunt Estelle organized pleasant social schedules for Jill. Vicki and I were always included when we were in Ox-ford. It was fun, if sometimes rather intimidating, to be with the "older crowd." There were hayrides in a mule-drawn wagon in the late summer and fall. Pappy sat up front as Andrew drove the team down Old Taylor Road to a friendly pasture. He'd pull off to the side and we all went looking for firewood before the sun set.

With the fire blazing, full of hot dogs we had roasted on sticks, we stretched out on the cool grass and listened as Pappy pointed out the constellations. "See the Dipper, the big one just overhead, and Orion and his wondrous belt?" Sometimes we'd see a shooting star, and always there was my favorite, Venus, "the morning and the evening star." After Pappy told a chilling ghost story or two, we'd put out the fire and pile back into the hay-filled wagon. Vicki and I sat close to Pappy. Nobody was interested in holding hands with either of us.

Pappy could be a prince charming when he chose. He once saved me from an awkward moment during a tea dance held at the home of Estelle's parents, the Oldhams. There I was, eleven years old, all dressed up in a Jill hand-me-down that I adored—an ankle-length, black watch plaid taffeta skirt with a black velvet top piped in watch plaid, white kid gloves (Jill's), and black patent-leather Mary Janes (*not* hand-me-downs, since my feet were bigger than hers). The tea dance started at four o'clock. I was horrified to see that each girl had been given a dance card as she came in, a folded paper square with a gold twine loop to fit over her wrist, and numbered dances with a blank beside each dance (waltz or polka) to be filled in by a dance partner (a boy).

The wait was long but finally at Pappy's urging I managed to get four or five blanks filled in. About midway through the party, after the Virginia reel—my favorite dance, no partner necessary—Pappy announced that tea was being poured in the dining room. Miss Mary Jenkins, a nurse-friend-companion of the Oldhams, was seated at the head of their long dining room table behind an elaborate silver service. Pappy and I were the last two people in line. Miss Mary smiled at me as she picked up a China cup and saucer so fine that the candlelight shone through them. "Will you take milk or lemon, Dean?" My experience with tea was limited to the drink that came in a tall glass with ice, already sweetened, with a lemon wedge. "Both," I said after a long pause. "Thank you, ma'am." She poured milk, then squeezed lemon. I watched it curdle. Something was terribly wrong. Over my shoulder I heard her say, "Bill, will you take milk or lemon?" And Pappy say, "Thank you, ma'am, Mary. I'll take both."

Pappy's gallantry extended to any lady in distress. Once, at a dinner party with close friends, Pappy was seating his dinner partner, the wife of a friend, who had had one too many cocktails. She missed the chair completely and sat down hard on the floor. Pappy immediately sat beside her and offered her a drink from his glass, saying something like "You know, I've always wondered what it was like to have dinner on the floor."

When Jill was in her early teens, Pappy had a two-wheeled pony cart built as a Christmas present. He bought her a harness horse—which Jill and Mil'Murray named "Lady Patricia"—and taught her how to drive the cart. Two could sit on the seat and two in the rear, legs dangling. Jill went everywhere in her cart. She and Mil'Murray rode up front. Vicki and I rode in the back. Whenever we came to a steep hill, Vicki and I had to hop down and walk, then run fast to catch up.

One Saturday, Jill decided to take us to Taylor, a hamlet six miles south of Oxford. We did not tell anyone where we were going. We were on our own most weekends, and knew that as long as we were home before dark, everything would be fine. When we arrived at Taylor in midafternoon, Jill first watered "Pat" at the trough outside the grocery store, and we all drank from a gourd dipper. Realizing that we were awfully hungry, we searched our pockets. I had five pennies. Jill took my money and disappeared into the store, emerging with five pieces of rock candy. She took three pieces and gave Vicki and me one each. She was the driver, after all. Then we got in the cart and headed back to Oxford. It was past dark when we got home. Pappy, Aunt Estelle, Wese, the neighbors, and the sheriff, furious to a person, were waiting. I had planned to spend the night with Vicki but home I went with Wese and to bed without supper. Vicki and Jill didn't get to eat, either.

Sometime later, when Jill was riding her pony on Old Taylor Road, her dog, Pete, trotted along beside her. Pete raced ahead to Rowan Oak and was killed by a hit-and-run driver. Pappy wrote a letter to the *Oxford Eagle*. Published on August 15, 1946, it read in part:

> *His name was Pete. He was just a dog, a fifteen-months-old pointer, still almost a puppy even though he had spent one hunting season learning to be the dog he would have been in another two or three years if he had lived that long. . . . He was standing*

on the road waiting for his little mistress on the horse to catch up, to squire her safely home. He shouldn't have been in the road. He paid no road tax, held no driver's license, didn't vote. . . . To say he didn't see the car because the car was between him and the late afternoon sun is a bad excuse because that brings the question of vision into it and certainly no one unable with the sun at his back to see a grown pointer dog on a curveless two-lane highway would think of permitting himself to drive a car at all, let alone one without either horn or brakes because next time Pete might be a human child and killing human children with motorcars is against the law.

No, the driver was in a hurry: that was the reason. Perhaps he had several miles to go yet and was already late for supper. . . . But Pete has forgiven him. In his year and a quarter of life he never had anything but kindness from human beings; he would gladly give the other six or eight or ten of it rather than make one late for supper.

It could have been Jill.

Jill's birthday in June was often celebrated with costume parties and dances held on the back gallery when Aunt Estelle's blue and lavender hydrangeas were in full bloom and the cedars along the driveway were aglow with fireflies. The boys sported coats and ties, and the girls wore full-skirted pastel-colored dotted Swiss and organdy dresses. Graceful in the moonlight we danced to music from Jill's record player.

It was magic. But I never knew what happened after the party was over and I went home to Nannie's or T's. Sometimes when it got late I could feel the tension, a sharp edge in Pappy's voice, a slight wobble in Aunt Estelle's step, my mother and Cho Cho's shrill laughter, the familiar smell of bourbon. I knew all the signs; I knew when to run: how to make myself very small and quiet, how to disappear into the night. I did not know if Jill had learned any of this yet. The enchanted scene could have been quickly distorted, the soft aura shattered by an argument between Pappy and Aunt Estelle that escalated into cutting remarks that once spoken could not be forgotten, that could not be taken back, secrets dark, strange, and painful. I never saw it happen but I feel sure that it did. I can only hope that Mil'Murray was with her.

With her silky blond hair, icy hazel eyes, military bearing, and clipped, near-British accent, Jill was a formidable first cousin. She was so formal and distant that when she smiled at something I said or did, I felt that she had given me a present. She and Pappy were very much alike, and she was his pride and joy. In the 1978 television documentary *A Life on Paper,* she told of a time when Pappy was on a binge and she attempted to get him to stop drinking. He turned on her and drunkenly blurted, "Nobody remembers Shakespeare's child." Then she casually remarked to the interviewer, "Pappy didn't care about anybody!" I *screamed* at the TV set, at her as she sat in her garden in Charlottesville, as cool and unruffled as the pale green sleeveless summer dress she wore.

Then I thought about what she had said. Even though I never saw Pappy drunk, I didn't have to. Because of my stepfather, I knew what it was like. Genius cannot alter the stench of an emaciated body drenched in alcohol and sweat, lying in days-old soiled underwear, entangled in stained bed linen, a voice hoarse and rasping, babbling incoherently, cursing the gods one moment and begging for whiskey the next. His alcoholism did not, however, mean that Pappy did not care about anybody. I know how much he loved Jill, his mother, and my father. He loved mankind—even the Snopeses.

Yet there is no doubt that Pappy's fame eased the burden of

his drinking. He could always count on somebody to pick up the pieces.

———

IN 1947, PAPPY's neighbor and friend Colonel Hugh Evans, a retired army officer, began building a houseboat next to his home, a block and a half from Rowan Oak. Evans was assisted in this project by his friends Dr. Ashford Little and Ross Brown, the latter serving as architect and draftsman. Brown's fifteen-year-old son, Billy Ross (Pappy called him "Bill"), was a tireless and strong helper. Pappy worked right alongside him.

Building a boat of this size in one's driveway was an unprecedented event in Oxford, and the project drew many onlookers, some of whom were pressed into service fetching and carrying. It was a forty-four-by-fourteen-foot barge with a seventy-five horsepower Gray marine engine, mahogany paneling, and boarding ladders attached to both sides. It had an ample cabin and the cockpit was aft under a wide canopy that shaded the stern. They planned to launch the boat in Sardis Lake, eleven miles northwest of Oxford. Once launched, the boat would be permanently anchored in the ten-mile-long lake.

Pappy took offense when some job he completed did not meet Colonel Evans's strict standards. He stopped working and stood there glumly, pipe clamped between his teeth. When Evans wasn't looking, however, he resumed working on the boat. Later, Evans took a photograph of him that Pappy liked so much that he declared it his favorite picture of himself (see second photo insert, page 3).

The houseboat was christened *Minmagary*, named for the friends' wives, Minnie Ruth Little, Maggie Brown, and Mary Evans. Aunt Estelle was not included because Pappy did not share in the costs. Besides contributing manual labor, Pappy drew up letters of marque, in which he described the building of the boat: "Out of Confusion by Boundless Hope: Conceived in a Canadian Club bottle She was born A.D. 15th August 1947 by uproarious Caesarian Section in prone position with her bottom upward in Evan's back yard eleven miles from the nearest water deeper than a half inch kitchen tap and waxed and grew daily there beneath the whole town's enrapt cynosure."

When the houseboat was completed, a sizable crowd joined the builders in Colonel Evans's yard to watch the send-off. To me, the *Minmagary* looked like a beached whale. In Pappy's words, "In the gloom of afternoon was raised tenderly in the myriad hands of her conceivers owners & artificers & their friends & well-wishers & dogs & the neighbors & merely curious & their friends & well-wishers & dogs" a three-ton houseboat, towed by a rented truck from Memphis.

Many a bet was on the line as to whether the *Minmagary* could make the first sharp ninety-degree turn onto Old Taylor

> By virtue of whatever authority I may have inherited from my Great Grandfather. William C. Falkner Colonel (PAROLED) Second Mississippi Infantry Provisional Army Confederate States of America I William C Falkner II reposing all trust & confidence in the staunchness & stability of M/S Minmagary & in the courage & fidelity of her officers & crew do by these presents constitute & appoint her to be a Ship of the Line in the Provisional Navy of the Confederate States of America & further direct that all seamen soldiers & civilians recognizing the above authority recognize her as such & accord her all the priviledges respect & consideration of that state & condition.
>
> Given under my Great Grandfather's sword this Twenty Fourth July 1948 at Oxford Mississippi
>
> William C Falkner II

Road. Dollars changed hands and a case of whiskey was wagered. She made the turn and the crowd cheered and applauded as she wound her stately way through the narrow streets and triumphantly circled the Lafayette County Courthouse to the delight of onlookers. Soon the happy entourage turned north toward Sardis.

She was launched in front of a large gathering, a cocktail party for grown-ups only. Miss Mary Evans broke a bottle of champagne on the bow after several tries. The *Minmagary* was officially christened.

The papers that Pappy had drawn up cited "whatever authority I may have inherited from my Great Grandfather William C. Falkner Colonel (paroled) Second Mississippi Infantry Provisional Army Confederate States of America," commissioning the *Minmagary* as a "Ship of the Line in the Confederate Navy given under my Great Grandfather's sword this Twenty Fourth July 1948 at Oxford Mississippi. William C. Falkner II."

When the *Minmagary* was launched, she rode so high that, according to Billy Ross Brown, she "floated like a matchbox" with the propeller well above the water. For the rest of the summer, Billy Ross was hired by his father at twenty-five dollars a week to build concrete blocks to be used for ballast. He can't remember whether he made two thousand or twenty thousand pounds of blocks. At any rate, the boat was soon made seaworthy.

For the next six years the *Minmagary* cruised the waters of Sardis Lake and hosted many festive gatherings. Soon after the launch, Pappy gave a water-skiing party for members of Sigma Alpha Epsilon, his fraternity at Ole Miss. He moored the *Minmagary* next to Sardis Dam and welcomed students aboard. It was a warm day, the sky blue and the lake flat and calm. The *Minmagary* served as mother vessel for a ski boat pulling the water-skiers. The SAEs and their dates watched the skiers and sunbathed, beer and cigarettes in hand. Pappy presided in captain's cap, bathing suit, deck shoes, and blue work shirt with sleeves rolled up. The party was in full swing when the University of Mississippi's dean of women, Estella Hefley, appeared. Sardis Lake was off-limits to coeds while school was in session. Hefley had heard about the SAE skiing party and suspected that "her girls" were involved.

The vigilant Dean Hefley was known far and wide for her vigorous enforcement of university regulations and had added refinements of her own, Victorian by today's standards:

• To leave the campus to attend a football weekend in Jackson, Memphis, or Baton Rouge, a coed had to present a letter from her hostess verifying the invitation and assuming responsibility while the student was staying at her home.

• Coeds could not wear shorts even if going to gym class without covering their exposed legs with a mid-calf-length raincoat. (This meant that even on sunny ninety-degree days, coeds sweltering under their raincoats could be seen crossing the campus.)

• Girls weren't allowed to wear "suggestive clothing" such as angora sweaters. Boys might be tempted to touch them. Patent leather shoes were prohibited because they might reflect underwear.

• Freshmen girls had to be in their dormitory rooms by 8:30 p.m. Sunday–Thursday (11 p.m. on Friday and Saturday) and were required to sign out in the office of the dorm mother when they left and to sign in when they returned.

• Of course drinking was prohibited. As the dorm mother looked on, most second-semester freshmen could hold their breath for well over a minute while signing in. Violators were punished by being "campused," which meant you couldn't go anywhere except class for one to two weeks, depending on the severity of the offense.

The moment Dean Hefley was seen coming up the boarding ladder of the *Minmagary*, beers and cigarettes went over the side. Girls disappeared into the cabin and crouched out of sight. Pappy was amused by their alarm. Hefley and his mother had known each other for years. He went to greet her in his captain's cap and received Dean Hefley with such naval pomp and ceremony he might as well have piped her aboard. "Estella, what a pleasant surprise, please join us." When he chose, Pappy could charm a cobra out of a basket. He seated her in a deck chair and at that moment became a de facto ambassador for Sigma Alpha Epsilon.

Hefley had a built-in radar for coeds and knew they were hiding in the cabin but said only, "How is Maud?" After they chatted about Pappy's mother and passed the time, Hefley began to voice concerns that student regulations were being flouted. The SAE ambassador was fully in sympathy. *How hard it must be to keep up with this impetuous, willful, yet resourceful and inventive younger generation!* He offered her a Coca-Cola and deplored the lack of manners and decorum in the young and wondered what would become of Mississippi and, indeed, the world. Loosening social standards, he agreed, was an unfortunate result of the war. However, he tactfully pointed out, some of the SAEs on board were veterans who, having served their country and put their lives at hazard, felt entitled to relax and enjoy themselves. Still, standards had to be maintained and he promised to take responsibility for the SAEs while they were aboard his craft. He assured Dean Hefley that they would conduct themselves like the gentlemen they were.

The young men looked on, grinning at one another, and when Dean Hefley's car was out of sight they let loose a shrill rebel yell. The coeds immediately came out of hiding, one or two sheepishly shedding raingear stowed below deck.

———

IN 1948, THAT same year, Metro-Goldwyn-Mayer arrived in Oxford to film *Intruder in the Dust* with a budget of $250,000. Pappy's stock shot up. "Count No 'Count," it seemed, was nowhere to be seen and in his place was a benefactor of unimpeachable generosity. I was living in Clarksdale and was eaten up with jealousy that Vicki was living at Rowan Oak, basking in the glitter of Pappy's "sudden fame." (If Hollywood knew who Pappy was, we reasoned, then shouldn't we be famous, too?) We made plans that as soon as I got to Oxford, we would set up a card table in the driveway and charge people a quarter to see Rowan Oak. We were going to be rich. Meanwhile, for every minute that I remained in Clarksdale, I fretted that Vicki was cutting school and going to the movie set. I knew Jill would be a part of it. That was okay. But Vicki . . . *without me*! I could hardly stand it. I figured by the time I got to Oxford, she would have a BIG PART in the picture show. She'd probably get to kiss Claude Jarman, Jr. I was absolutely green with envy after I found out that Vicki had been cast as an extra in a mob scene. Her role was "Little Girl Eating an Ice Cream Cone." It nearly killed me.

Finally, Pappy drove to Clarksdale to get me, promising to show me movie people in action. We returned to Lafayette County where a scene was being filmed at a pond with a wooden bridge. The scene was the one in which veteran character actor Porter Hall, playing the villain Nub Gowrie, was caught in quicksand. We watched for hours, fascinated, as the crew dumped boxes of oatmeal into the pond to simulate quicksand. After each take, Porter Hall would towel off and change into an identical dry outfit for the next take. My interest never flagged. If they had kept shooting I'd still be there.

During the filming Pappy and Aunt Estelle gave a party for Jill and invited members of the cast and crew. The older teens were dancing in the front parlor, but Vicki and I were too intimidated by the sight of Claude Jarman, Jr., to come all the way downstairs. We watched from the landing, goggle-eyed, as Jarman danced with Jill and Mil'Murray and most of the girls at the party. Vicki and I were giddy with excitement but grateful for the safety and anonymity of the staircase. We knew when we were out of our league.

Vicki and I weren't the only family members who were starstruck. The Hollywood bug bit Nannie hard. She met actress Elizabeth Patterson ("Miss Habersham" in the movie) and they became lifelong friends. Since Pappy modeled the fictional Miss Habersham in part on Nannie, I assume that Miss Patterson's interpretation of her role could have come from observing Nannie's speech and carriage. Several days before Miss Patterson was scheduled to fly back to L.A., she came to visit Nannie and purchased one of her paintings: a twelve-by-fifteen-inch oil on canvas of a large, fully opened magnolia blossom with leaves and stem intact, on a brilliant red background, signed "MFalkner" (the *M* overlapping the *F*). Nannie was tickled pink at the sale— thirty-five dollars, Miss Patterson no doubt *insisting* on paying— and was thrilled when Miss Patterson later decided to use the picture as a holiday card illustration. At Christmas, Nannie received several of the printed cards featuring her brilliant magnolia on the cover. She sent one to me with the inscription:

To my granddaughter, Dean
Merry Christmas from
Elizabeth Patterson's friend, Maud Falkner.
Love, Nannie

A year later, the premiere of *Intruder in the Dust* was held at the Lyric Theatre. Wese and I had moved back to Oxford, and I was happily in the thick of things. Vicki and I found out much later that the grown-up world had been in a stew when Pappy threatened not to attend the film debut. If we had known, we'd have died. If Pappy didn't go, nobody, including us, could have gone! Unbeknownst to us, pressure was brought to bear by Nannie and Aunt Bama, who came all the way from Memphis for the occasion. These formidable ladies beat down Pappy's resistance until he agreed to attend the premiere.

The night *Intruder* opened we rode to town in Pappy's station wagon. As we left Rowan Oak, beams were arcing across the sky from klieg lights outside the Lyric Theatre. The Ole Miss band was playing and hundreds of fans had gathered. As we came closer to the square we could hear them cheering and screaming as each car pulled up and a star emerged. The entrance had been cordoned off. Vicki and I were in the backseat, silly with excitement, checking our (first-ever) nylon stockings and smoothing the skirts of our new dresses. Vicki's was iridescent orange taffeta with a wide sash that had been made by Aunt Estelle, and mine was midnight blue velvet, sewn by Wese. We thought we were gorgeous. When a tuxedo-clad attendant opened the door for us, we were sure of it.

With spotlights shining in our faces we entered the Lyric behind Pappy and Aunt Estelle, Jill, Nannie, and Aunt Bama. After being escorted to our seats near the front we saw that some of the stars were already present and being introduced. They gave brief speeches, then Pappy was introduced. He stood up, bowed, and sat back down. The crowd continued applauding. He rose again. I held my breath, hoping that he would say something, anything, so that people would keep looking at *us* in our new dresses. I was far too young to know what a courageous and avant-garde statement on civil rights Pappy had made in *Intruder*. I had not even read it when we went to the premiere. Vicki and I had huge crushes on Chick (Claude Jarman, Jr.). We cheered for Miss Habersham, who reminded us of Nannie. We feared for Lucas Beauchamp (pronounced *Beecham* in Mississippi) and yet like most of the theater audience we were white southerners entrenched in racial division without a trace of irony in our souls. All I knew was that for the first time, Pappy's light was shining on me and I was dazzled. To my dismay he only nodded and sat down again. After the showing of the movie, when the lights came on, the spectators began shouting, *"Author, author!"* Pappy ignored them and quickly ushered us out to the waiting car.

Back home at Rowan Oak, Vicki and I lay awake and whispered and giggled, too excited to sleep. Finally she asked the question we both knew she had to ask. "How did I look in the movie, you know, Little Girl Eating an Ice Cream Cone?" I pretended to be asleep, but she knew me too well. So I yawned and said, "What kind of ice cream was it?" She hit me with a pillow. Then we snuggled down, listened to the grown-ups talking downstairs, and dreamed our Technicolor dreams.

11

Cho Cho and Vicki

E VEN THOUGH VICKI (VICTORIA FRANKLIN FIELDEN) AND I were not related by blood, many people inside and outside the family thought of us as sisters. We were a year apart in age. Vicki had sandy reddish-brown hair and green eyes and freckles; I had dark hair and eyes. But we were both scrawny, wore our hair in French braids, frequently dressed alike, and were inseparable when we were in Oxford. All of our lives we were either best friends or best enemies. We seemed to have known each other forever.

Vicki's mother was Victoria Franklin, my aunt Estelle's daughter by her first husband, Cornell Franklin. Victoria had been born in Honolulu. Her amah called her "Cho Cho," Chinese for butterfly. Cho Cho looked like Vivian Leigh, black hair pulled back into a chignon and green eyes, a stunningly beautiful woman with delicate features and an ample bosom. With her narrow shoulders, small hands and feet, she could have been Asian.

Vicki's father was Claude Selby of Vicksburg. Nobody in the combined families—Franklins, Falkners, and Oldhams—ever mentioned Selby's name out loud. But there were whispers. As much apocrypha surrounds Cho Cho's marriage to Claude Selby and Vicki's birth as surrounds any Faulkner, Pappy included.

My favorite version of the story, because it makes Pappy the hero, is that shortly after Vicki's birth in 1937, Selby abandoned her and Cho Cho and ran off to a logging camp in Canada. Cho Cho was distraught and within days she and baby Vicki were on a bus headed for Quebec. Weeks passed without any word. Pappy and Estelle were frantic. Finally Cho Cho telephoned. She was a desperate, broken woman. She had found Selby. He would have nothing to do with her or their child. Would Pappy come for her? Despite being hard-pressed for money, Pappy took the bus to Canada and brought his stepdaughter and stepgrand-daughter back to Oxford and Rowan Oak. He did everything he could for Cho Cho that awful Christmas. They worked puzzles together and he read to her constantly, offering diversions. "He kept me alive," she once said. Years later she told me, "Never once in my life did Pappy make me feel like a stepchild." He was as tender and solicitous of Cho Cho as he had been of Wese after Dean's death.

Her divorce (or annulment) from Claude Selby was final-ized in 1938. With Pappy's urging and his help, Cho Cho took Vicki and went to Shanghai to live with her father, Judge Cornell Franklin. In a sense she was going home again. There she met Bill Fielden, a handsome executive who ran the Asian headquar-ters of the Reynolds Tobacco Company. Within a year they were married. Two years later they were at Rowan Oak. Pappy man-aged to care for all of us.

As a stepfather, Bill Fielden proved to be more like Pappy than Jimmy Meadow. He was devoted to Vicki and a source of strength and kindness to everyone in the Faulkner family. Vicki assumed the name Fielden with pride and kept it all her life, whereas I dropped Meadow when I was eighteen—becoming Dean Faulkner again as soon as I thought my mother had left Jimmy for good. (She had not, as it turned out.)

Over the years Vicki and I crossed paths often in Oxford.

I would have come back from Clarksdale, Memphis, or Chicago, whereas Vicki would have been returning from Caracas, Manila, or boarding school in Switzerland. The first time that Pappy brought Vicki to Nannie's to play with me, she had already traveled halfway around the world—twice. I had flown in a plane only once. (My uncle Jack had taken Wese and me up in his beautiful black and yellow Aeronca the day that the Dean Faulkner Airport was dedicated in 1938. We took off on the grass strip five miles south of Oxford in a flat field in the Yocona River bottom and flew over Oxford for about thirty minutes. I was two years old.) In 1941, four-year-old Vicki arrived at the Memphis airport, alone, with a note safety-pinned to her coat: "Please get me to William Faulkner in Oxford, Mississippi." The Japanese were about to invade China. Soon, Bill Fielden and Cho Cho followed Vicki to the States.

Vicki and I were both in Oxford the year that she was in the seventh grade and I was in the eighth. She was living at Rowan Oak with Pappy and Aunt Estelle. Cho Cho and Bill Fielden were abroad, I think. During the week, I was living at T's with Wese and Jimmy and spending every weekend with Vicki at Rowan Oak.

Wese and Jimmy did not have a car. By the late 1940s, Pappy had started calling himself our "school bus driver." Monday through Friday he would leave Rowan Oak about 7:45 in his old beat-up wood-paneled Ford station wagon. It had a hole in the floorboard in the back big enough to drop a small book through. We would ride looking down at the pavement rushing under the car and feel cold air blowing through it.

I would stand in front of T's house waiting for Pappy to arrive. My place was next to Vicki in the backseat. At 3 p.m. he would be parked in front of Oxford High School waiting to take us home. Oxford was so small then that grades seven through twelve were housed in the same building. Pappy must have been grateful for that.

I was a Pee Wee cheerleader that year, which added to Pappy's bus-driving schedule. The Pee Wee football team played its home games on Thursdays. I thought I would surely die if I missed one. Vicki wanted to be at the games as well. On the given Thursdays, Pappy would pick us up at school and ferry us home. I'd change into my Pee Wee uniform, have a quick supper, and at 6:45 our "bus driver" would be waiting to take us to the game (which was played on the high school field). I knew where to look for Pappy and Vicki in the stands. They always sat in the same place on the fifty-yard line, halfway up the wood bleachers. They stood out among the other two dozen loyal Pee Wee football fans. Vicki sat next to Pappy, who always wore a hat.

At dinner one Friday night, Vicki looked particularly full of herself. We could read each other like open books. Secrets were impossible. As soon as we were excused from table we headed upstairs and I whispered, "What do you know that I don't? Did Sonny [her prospective boyfriend] call you?"

"Better than that," she said.

"Do I have to guess or are you going to tell me?"

No answer.

"Who knows besides you?"

No answer.

"Okay, *Stick.*" I knew how much she hated that nickname. Maybe if I threatened to call her that she'd give. Or maybe if I said . . . "*Please?*"

"Well," she said, picking up a deck of cards and giving it a professional shuffle, sinking to her knees ready to do Spit battle until the wee hours. "Did you ever hear of a writer named Lewis?"

"Sure, Robert Louis . . . you know."

"No, he's been dead for ages. This man came to the door *today*. And he spells his name different."

"What did he want?"

"To see Pappy. I heard him knock and when I opened the door, there he stood. He had red hair and his face had these pock marks. He told me his name and said he was a writer and asked if Pappy was at home. I told him to wait just a minute and went into the library where Pappy was working.

" 'Who's there, Vicki?' he said.

" 'A man named Lewis. He wants to see you.'

"Pappy didn't even stop typing. He said, 'Tell him I'm busy.' "

"And you did?"

"Yup, and he walked off."

"Who do you think it was?"

"I don't know. But he had a funny first name . . . Sinclair."

We had no idea what books Pappy was writing then. Perhaps by 1948 he was already working on *A Fable*, which would win a Pulitzer Prize in 1955. Two years before I became a Pee Wee cheerleader all of his books were out of print, but we didn't know that, or that his reputation as one of this country's leading novelists was in jeopardy until Malcolm Cowley's *Portable Faulkner* came out in 1946. Cowley was the first to describe in layman's language what Pappy once called "a cosmos of my own," the Yoknapatawpha saga and its class struggle—the aristocratic Compsons, the resourceful and formidable McCaslins, and white-trash Snopeses, and presiding over all, the African American earth-mother, Dilsey. The effect of *The Portable Faulkner* was immediate and far-reaching. New editions of his novels would soon follow. In 1948, Harvard professor Carvel Collins created the first college seminar exclusively devoted to the works of William Faulkner. I had no idea of all this while I was on the ball field doing cheers and cartwheels. All I knew was that Pappy was in the stands watching me and would take me home after the game.

Pappy shielded us from worries. He never discussed money or the lack of it. I knew nothing about his financial straits until I read Joseph Blotner's *William Faulkner: A Biography* in 1974. So it came as a surprise when I learned that he was supporting Nannie, Estelle, and Jill; several of Mammy Callie's kin who lived in the cabin behind Rowan Oak; my mother (until she remarried) and me, the on-again-off-again waif; and sometimes Vicki and Uncle John and his family, who lived rent-free on Pappy's farm and accepted an occasional allowance from Nannie, whose income consisted of ten dollars a week that Pappy deposited in her account, allowing her to pretend that it came from bank dividends. He was, as he later wrote, "the sole, principal and partial support—food, shelter, heat, clothes, medicine, kotex, school fees, toilet paper and picture shows, of my mother, an inept brother and his wife and two sons, another brother's widow and child, a wife of my own and two stepchildren, [and] my own child."

Saturdays were allowance days at Rowan Oak when Vicki and I would be given a quarter apiece. We spent them at the ten o'clock movie at the Ritz—admission for children was a dime, plus popcorn and a small bottle of malted milk tablets from Gathright-Reed's Drugstore to eat on the way home. I think these tablets were marketed as "vitamin supplements," but for Vicki and me they were better than candy. We speculated that they might make us "fill out" sooner. On special Saturdays we got fifty cents, which paid for the movie, popcorn, and a hamburger and Grapette at Mrs. Cook's diner around the corner from the Ritz. Vicki and I roamed the town on weekends, walking anywhere we wanted to go. Our only rule was to be home by dark.

Our favorite playground was Bailey's Woods, the thickly forested area around Rowan Oak where trails wandered over hills and crossed "stink creek," a rain gulley that contained stagnant, festering pools. Behind Pappy's barn were the "sand hills," where erosion had eaten into a slope and exposed colored layers of clay—blue, gray, orange—with a patina of sand that glittered like fool's gold. Here, the neighborhood kids gathered to build forts, or play war or kick the can or capture the flag.

Sometimes Pappy took us on hikes. We knew the paths with our eyes closed, but he taught us to walk in silence, heel to toe, the Indian way, and how to read animal signs or mark a trail for someone to follow.

Early one Saturday at sunup he led Jill, Vicki, and me out of the kitchen, finger to his lips, behind the barn, down through the sandhills, past stink creek—deeper and deeper into the woods. He sat us on a fallen log and spoke in a whisper about the first people who walked the land, the Chickasaws. They walked in silence, he told us. No footfall could be heard, not a sound of a broken twig, no crunch of leaves underfoot. If we respected the silence of the forest, only then could we experience the wilderness.

With the dark forest surrounding us, he knelt and, as we crouched beside him, picked up a handful of dirt and leaves, and said, "Hold this. Smell it. It belongs to no one. This is the way the land should be treated, with respect. The earth is ours to protect as the people who came before us did." We were young then, but I don't think any of us ever forgot what he said that day.

Pappy spent a great deal of time with us. On cold, blustery February days, nobody else in the family would want to go sailing at Sardis Lake on *The Ring Dove*, Pappy's sailboat. He'd say, "Let's go, girls!" And Vicki and I went. When nobody else wanted to walk uptown with him to catch the late movie—Charlie Chan movies were his favorites—Vicki and I went. At that age we'd go anywhere, anytime, with anybody.

When Pappy drove us to Sardis Lake to go sailing—long, slow drives on a gravel road twelve miles to Hurricane Landing—he had to listen to two preteen girls singing at the top of their lungs "Ninety-Nine Bottles of Beer on the Wall" all the way down to one bottle, then all the way back up to ninety-nine.

Poor Pappy. We were a noise machine—and this was a man who refused to own a radio. I'm sure he tuned us out.

There was plenty to do at Rowan Oak when we were not sailing. Pappy set up a Ping-Pong table under the porte cochere. His croquet court stayed in place on the front lawn from early spring to early frost. Our croquet matches were complicated by having dogs constantly underfoot. Pappy had terriers and a Dalmatian, Vicki had a mutt (Cutie), and Andrew and Chrissie Price had a pack of mutts and terriers that patrolled the Rowan Oak grounds at all hours.

Said terriers were immortalized in an Henri Cartier-Bresson photograph (now a popular postcard) of Pappy standing in the east garden with the dogs surrounding him. I think one of them is Kudzu, an offspring of my beloved terrier Little Bit. They all looked alike. After the photograph was published, an interviewer asked Pappy, "What kind of dogs are they, Mr. Faulkner?"

"Cartier-Bressons," said Pappy, and so they were from then on.

The dogs made playing croquet almost impossible. We had to shoo them away before lining up our shots. I remember one mortal croquet game during a thunderstorm when Pappy was playing with Jill, Vicki, and me. We played with silent concentration. Jill was about to knock my ball to kingdom come when there was an ear-splitting clap of thunder. We all jumped and looked at one another in terror. Pappy kept playing like nothing was happening. Lightning was striking all around, so close we could smell it. Everything got dark. We could barely see the balls. Only the dogs had the sense to run for cover. Finally, when the rain came down, Pappy relented. The game was over. The very next morning, he registered Vicki and me at Camp Lake Stephens, a Methodist summer camp not far from Oxford. Everybody needed a breather, Pappy most of all. No Vicki or Dean for fourteen blessed days! It would have been worth any amount of money.

———

THERE WERE NO Halloweens like those at Rowan Oak, nights of magic terror. We grew up believing in our own family ghost, Judith Sheegog, the beautiful girl who had committed suicide by jumping from the second-floor balcony, breaking her neck on the front steps below, all for the love of a Yankee soldier who had abandoned her. Her grave, according to Pappy, was under the huge old magnolia tree at the end of the front walk, and her ghost walked the grounds of Rowan Oak "when the moon was right and foxfire danced in the woods."

Pappy and Aunt Estelle staged elaborate Halloween parties for Jill with Cho Cho dressed as Judith, dead gardenias in her hair and holding real skeletons' hands. Aunt Dot was the hunchbacked grave digger dragging chains behind her. With us children gathered on the front steps, Pappy would tell scary stories and at the supernatural climax we'd hear chains clanking. He would pause so that as we glanced over our shoulders we might see a ghostly white shape flitting in and out of the trees. Sometimes he would invite us to "visit Judith's grave" under the magnolia tree. As twilight gave way to night, the time Pappy called "le temps entre chien et loup" (the time between dog and wolf), he would light a candle and give it to us, saying "If the candle goes out, that means Judith blew it out." Of course, as we took our trembling steps in the pitch dark, heading for the magnolia tree, the candle inevitably went out. At that moment we'd turn in happy terror hoping Pappy would save us, but he'd be gone.

One Halloween he took us trick-or-treating. Vicki and I were determined to "get" an old lady who lived on a street that dead-ended into Bailey's Woods. Rumor had it that this woman was a *dog poisoner* who hated Halloween and would not come to her door *no matter what*. She was leaving herself wide open. Vicki and I went armed with bars of soap, unwrapped and ready for use on her car windows. Pappy knew nothing of this. Staying several front yards ahead of him, we skipped up to her door and began knocking and ringing the doorbell before he caught up. When her porch light finally came on, we shouted "Trick or treat!" and tore around the corner of her house into her garage where the vulnerable car was parked. By that time Pappy had reached her house and was looking for us. We did not see her come out but heard the garden hose being turned on full force. The heavy spray of water missed us but soaked Pappy. The three of us were out of there in nothing flat.

Then Pappy turned the tables. One night we were awakened by the sound of the piano. Someone was playing a Chopin waltz that Vicki had played in a recital. She and I recognized it at once. We sat up in our beds and said *"Judith!"* While the piano continued playing, we crept out of the bedroom in our nightgowns holding on to each other. Pappy came out of his bedroom with a flashlight and led us downstairs. As we reached the bottom steps, the music stopped. Pappy switched on the lights in the hallway and front parlor. We searched every room. No one was there. To this day I don't know how he managed it.

On rainy weekends at Rowan Oak, Vicki and I spent hours playing cards—Spit, Casino, Concentration—sitting cross-legged on the soft gray rug in the front parlor, totally absorbed. We held spend-the-night parties, with six or eight girlfriends crowded into our upstairs bedroom, giggling through the night, raiding the refrigerator, talking about boys, telling ghost stories, playing the Ouija board, and trying on Aunt Estelle's makeup in her black-and-white-tiled bathroom with ceiling-high windows.

Sometimes Jill would recount tales from scary movies such as *Gaslight* and *The Spiral Staircase*. We had seen them more than once, which only stoked our fears. Only I had seen *Black Narcissus*, yet every time I tried to tell the story I would get so scared I couldn't finish. It is a terrifying tale of a nun who goes mad in a convent high in the Himalayas. *Each evening one sister must ring the bell summoning everyone to chapel for vespers. The bell stood at the edge of a precipice. In order to make the huge bell ring, the sister had to swing out over the sheer cliff clinging desperately to the rope, then struggle to regain her footing. The night came when an insane nun waited in the shadows* . . . which was as far as I could get.

One night, Jill and Vicki were worn out with me. Pappy (supposedly asleep in the next room) came in and finished telling the story. "One of the Godden sisters wrote it," he noted. "You'll find reading it is scarier than the movie." He told us to look at Nannie's latest painting: a nun's face and habit done in pastels. The nun's tortured face reminded me of Wese's after a god-awful row with Jimmy.

I hold dear the memories of my childhood with Vicki, the good and the not so good. Sometimes we got into hair-pulling, shin-kicking, name-calling fights. The worst, and I do not remember what it was about, ended with Vicki throwing my clothes and the watch that Pappy had given me for Christmas off the "Judith balcony" onto the steps below. "If you broke it, you're dead!" I shouted as I tore down the stairs. Pappy was sitting on the steps outside, my Swiss wristwatch in his hand. "It's not broken, Dean," he said. "Don't you risk breaking something with Vicki that can't be fixed. You are better than that. And I expect it of you."

Those words had a lasting effect on me. For the rest of my life, every time I gave in to my feelings and behaved badly (and there were many) I would find myself saying, *"You're better than that."* His words rarely altered my behavior until it was too late, but they guaranteed that I would own up to the error of my ways.

When we were older, our sailing excursions continued. Pappy would bring along a bottle of stout, a magnum of champagne, and a silver goblet. When he dropped anchor after thirty or forty minutes' sail time, he would have someone hold the goblet steady while he filled it half and half with stout and champagne (a Black Velvet, which I think he discovered in 1918 in the RAF). In order to drink from Pappy's "grail," we had to play his game. He would recite a line from a poem. The lucky sailor who knew the next line was given a sip. He would start with easy ones: "Red sky at night . . ." Or, "Malt does more than Milton can . . ." Or, "Tiger, tiger burning bright . . ." Working up to some real doozies like "Deer walk upon our mountains . . ." and "April is the cruelest month. . . ." We never tired of playing. Winning made the Black Velvet taste better—plus the winner sometimes got to select the next line of poetry.

Vicki went on to become an accomplished sailor and had her own sailboat in Manila. When Pappy went on a State Department tour and visited the Philippines, she took him sailing in Manila Bay. I like to think of them heading out to sea, Vicki at the tiller, Pappy relaxed and happy, purple sails billowing in the wind.

12

Nobel Prize

I N LATE SUMMER OF 1950, PAPPY WROTE A LETTER TO THE EDI-tor of the *Oxford Eagle* to be published on August 31. In it, he took on the conservatives opposed to the legal sale of beer in Lafayette County. To a man the town's religious leaders were opposed to beer and some weeks before had taken an ad in the *Eagle* proclaiming the evils of drinking. The town had voted down the sale of beer in all previous elections. Oxford had always been dry.

Pappy explained that the first beer referendum had lost because "too many voters who drank beer or didn't object to other people drinking it, were absent in Europe and Asia defending Oxford, where voters who preferred home to war could vote on beer in 1944."

When the *Eagle* appeared without his letter, Pappy went straight to editor Phil "Moon" Mullen for an explanation. Mullen told him he didn't want his newspaper to help "Bill Faulkner in jumping all over the preachers."

Pappy said, "Strike me some circulars," and left. When the flyers entitled "To the Voters of Oxford" were printed, Pappy turned them over to Vicki and me. We were enthusiastic about helping him distribute his broadside promoting the legal sale of beer, even though we were much too young to drink. With help from other family members, we went door to door handing out flyers. Our territory, mine and Vicki's, covered the neighborhoods south of the square. With our best smiles and Sunday manners we delivered broadsides to unsuspecting, often teetotaling, residents. We knocked on the door of the Baptist minister's home on University Avenue, a southern colonial house that resembled Rowan Oak, and proudly presented his wife, Mrs. Purser, with a copy of our flyer. "Hey, Miz Purser," we said when she opened the door. "How you doing?"

TO THE VOTERS OF OXFORD

Correction to paid printed statement of Private Citizens H. E. Finger, Jr., John K. Johnson, and Frank Moody Purser.

1. *'Beer was voted out in 1944 because of its obnoxiousness.'*

Beer was voted out in 1944 because too many voters who drank beer or didn't object to other people drinking it, were absent in Europe and Asia defending Oxford where voters who preferred home to war could vote on beer in 1944.

2. *'A bottle of 4 percent beer contains twice as much alcohol as a jigger of whiskey.'*

A 12 ounce bottle of four percent beer contains forty-eight one hundreths of one ounce of alcohol. A jigger holds one and one-half ounces (see Dictionary). Whiskey ranges from 30 to 45 percent alcohol. A jigger of 30 percent whiskey contains forty-five one hundreths of one ounce of alcohol. A bottle of 4 percent beer doesn't contain twice as much alcohol as a jigger of whiskey. Unless the whiskey is less than 32 percent alcohol, the bottle of beer doesn't even contain as much.

3. *'Money spent for beer should be spent for food, clothing and other essential consumer goods.'*

By this precedent, we will have to hold another election to vote on whether or not the florists, the picture shows, the radio shops and the pleasure car dealers will be permitted in Oxford.

4. *'Starkville and Water Valley voted beer out; why not Oxford?'*

Since Starkville is the home of Mississippi State, and Mississippi State beat the University of Mississippi at football, maybe Oxford, which is the home of the University of Mississippi, is right in taking Starkville for a model. But why must we imitate Water Valley? Our high school team beat theirs, didn't it?

Yours for a freer Oxford, where publicans can be law abiding publicans six days a week, and Ministers of God can be Ministers of God all seven days in the week, as the Founder of their Ministry commanded them to when He ordered them to keep out of temporal politics in His own words: 'Render unto Caesar the things that are Caesar's and to God the things that are God's.'

William Faulkner
Private Citizen

Some weeks later, Vicki and I were beside ourselves with delight when the *Eagle* ran a letter to the editor from an irate citizen horrified at "innocents" being used "to encourage drinking," referring to us by name: "granddaughter, Vicki, and niece, Dean." We were famous.

In spite of our efforts, Pappy and beer lost by a vote of 480 to 313. After the election, which banned beer sales for five more years, Pappy wrote to the *Eagle* again, and this time his letter was published. "Oxford should stay dry," he wrote, because that was far "better than to break up the long and happy marriage between dry voters and illicit sellers for which our fair state supplies one of the last sanctuaries and strongholds." He also objected to any clergyman using his influence from the pulpit to sway a civil election. The letter was so well received that two months after its original publication it appeared in *The New Yorker.*

At about the same time, another issue was coming to a vote in a far-off land whose citizenry loved beer almost as much as they loved to read.

———

ON NOVEMBER 10, 1950, a cold, gray morning, Pappy visited Dean's grave at St. Peter's Cemetery. Fifteen years had scarcely blunted his grief over Dean's death. After he paid his respects he returned to Rowan Oak, went to the pantry where he kept his whiskey, and got out a bottle of bourbon and a shot glass. Then he went into the library to smoke and drink. Aunt Estelle knew not to intrude.

That afternoon, the telephone rang. Aunt Estelle took the call (Pappy never answered the phone) and went to get her husband. "It's for you, Bill. Long distance." He sighed and stood up, staggered by whiskey and sadness. He walked stiffly to the telephone in the pantry and picked up the receiver.

"William Faulkner speaking." A voice from very far away said, "Mr. Faulkner, it is an honor, sir, to inform you that you have won the Nobel Prize in Literature."

The gentleman on the line explained that the award was for 1949, when no prize had been given, and that Bertrand Russell had received the 1950 Nobel Prize in Literature. He expressed hopes of seeing Faulkner and Russell together in Stockholm on December 10 to receive their prizes. Pappy, dreading ceremonies of any kind, especially one where he would be expected to deliver a public address, thanked the caller and hung up. Turning to Aunt Estelle, he said, "That was Stockholm calling. They gave me the Nobel Prize."

Aunt Estelle scarcely had time to express her delight when he declared that he wasn't about to go all the way to Stockholm, even to receive a Nobel Prize. She searched her mind for a winning argument. Jill had never been to Europe. This was *her* chance to fly there courtesy of the Nobel Prize committee. She would go in Aunt Estelle's place. If Pappy refused to think of himself, she argued, the least he could do was to consider his seventeen-year-old daughter's dream of seeing Europe. After putting up fierce resistance, Pappy gave in to Aunt Estelle's suggestion. He didn't have a leg to stand on, but as he told her, "I still have a full month to drink!"

At the end of the first week in December, Aunt Estelle took her husband and daughter to the Memphis airport and bade them good-bye and godspeed. They boarded an American Airlines flight to New York, where they would catch a connecting flight to Sweden. As Pappy and Jill boarded the plane, the captain checked the passenger manifest and chatted with a stewardess. The captain was Pappy's old friend and former Mississippi barnstormer Murry Spain. The last time they had been together was at Dean's funeral.

The two greeted each other warmly, and Murry invited Pappy to join him in the cockpit after the flight was under way. Once the plane was airborne, Murry sent a stewardess for him. The copilot gave Pappy his seat. It was a bittersweet moment for both men. If Dean had lived, he might well have been sitting in Murry's place, a major airline captain. Murry explained the control panel to Pappy, the complicated gauges and radar and electronic flying aids, comparing these marvels to the simple flying machines of old.

When dials and instruments and memories had exhausted themselves as conversation topics, Murry paid his old friend the ultimate compliment. He offered him the controls and invited him to see how it felt to fly a DC-10. After a token refusal, Pappy accepted.* After piloting, or steering, the plane for a few moments, he handed the controls back. Murry put the plane on autopilot and asked what occasion had prompted this trip. Pappy replied simply, "Business." He then returned to his seat next to Jill.

After the plane landed, the passengers exited onto the tarmac. Murry came to say good-bye. As they walked toward the terminal, the captain saw a battery of reporters and photographers waiting just inside the glass doors. He now appreciated the understatement of his friend's "business" in New York. Pappy took Jill by the arm and led her gently but firmly away from the flashing cameras.

With typical Faulkner reticence, none of my kinfolk said a word to me about Pappy winning the Nobel Prize. Wese and Jimmy and I were living in Little Rock that year. The morning that the news broke I was at school. In my Latin class,

---

*I wonder what those passengers would say, now, if they knew that for a few precious minutes they were in the care and keeping of William Faulkner, pilot.

the teacher, Miss Mason, announced at the beginning of class that my uncle had won the Nobel Prize in Literature. I was so surprised I didn't know what to think. Few of my classmates believed he was my uncle.

Thirty-five years later I met Doubleday senior editor Carolyn Blakemore, the only person I know, other than Pappy and Jill, who attended the Nobel Prize ceremony. Carolyn, who was an exchange student in Sweden in 1950, recalled that she and her fellow students were agog at the prospect of seeing William Faulkner, who was "respected at home, but in Europe, and particularly in Sweden, revered. The awards presentation ceremony was held at four p.m. in the Concert Hall, a 1920s building that normally housed the Stockholm Symphony. The laureates were seated in a diagonal row at the front of the stage. Behind them were past winners and the Swedish Academy. Members of the royal family occupied the orchestra seats. Faulkner, in white tie, was ramrod straight, high-arched feet—in blindingly polished shoes—at a military forty-five-degree angle. He clutched and clenched a burgundy-colored handkerchief in both hands—the only visible sign of nervousness."

Dinner was served in the Blue Hall, a vast medieval room that reminded Carolyn of a set for a production of *Hamlet*. The various courses were announced by trumpeters in sixteenth-century costumes. When the dinner was over, a young Swedish friend of Carolyn insisted that since she was an American, she must introduce him to Faulkner.

"Emboldened by unaccustomed wine," she recalled, "I approached the great man. 'Mr. Faulkner, my name is . . . I am an American student . . . a great admirer of your work. . . . These are my Swedish friends who would like to meet . . . ' Then a flock of handsome young men, impeccably dressed, came forward and in turn shook hands, bowed, clicked heels. Faulkner could not have been more gracious and introduced us to his daughter, Jill. Then, soon afterward, he was gone."

When asked the next day about Faulkner's acceptance speech, Carolyn replied that it was "disappointing, because we couldn't hear him. His voice was soft and he didn't speak directly into the mike. Only a phrase here and there came across to the audience: 'the basest of all things is to be afraid . . . I decline to accept the end of man . . . he will endure . . . when the last ding-dong of doom has clanged and faded from the last worthless rock hanging tideless in the last red and dying evening, that even then there will still be one more sound: that of his puny inexhaustible voice, still talking.' And yet, by midday it seemed that all Stockholm—or at least the university world—knew that speech. We had it by heart."

In time, so did the whole world.

———

LIFE SOMEHOW RETURNED to normal. Back home in Oxford, Pappy played the gentleman farmer, determined not to be affected by his unwanted celebrity. Suddenly, however, he had a lot of new friends in town. It didn't matter that most of them hadn't read his work. They wanted to share the international spotlight. From now on they would live in two worlds: Oxford and Lafayette County, cheek by jowl with "Jefferson" and "Yoknapatawpha County." Eudora Welty summed up the state's pride in its native son when she declared, "I'm a Yoknapatawphanatic."

A few months later Pappy made a far less publicized speech. Jill's high school graduation exercises were to be held May 28, 1951. Weeks before the event, while Pappy was in New York, Jill's principal convinced her to ask her father to give the commencement address. When she told him by telephone that her class wanted him to "come talk to them," he agreed. By the time he found out that the "talk" was to be the graduation speech delivered at Fulton Chapel at Ole Miss to the class of 1951 and their parents and friends, it was too late to back out. He would never have disappointed her, anyway.

At the graduation ceremony he was introduced as "Oxford's most distinguished citizen." His speech began by paraphrasing Henri Estienne—"If youth knew, if age could"—and ended with a solemn appeal: "Never be afraid to raise your voice for honesty and truth, and compassion against injustice and lying and greed." If young people came together as one, they could in their lifetime alter the world, freeing it from "tyrants [who] will have vanished from the face of it."

The speech lasted a little over four minutes and was very well received in spite of an early complaint by one of Jill's classmates that they could have chosen a better speaker— "somebody important."

In 1953, Jill graduated summa cum laude from Pine Manor College in Chestnut Hill, Massachusetts. Thereafter she and Aunt Estelle spent several months in Mexico so she could improve her Spanish. I don't know when she met her West Point cadet, Paul Dilwyn Summers, Jr., but when she introduced me to him in 1954 she was as happy as I had ever seen her. Their engagement had been announced in June. About that time, Pappy wrote his Random House editor Saxe Commins, "I will need money, probably a ghastly amount. Jill and her mother seem bent on making a production out of this, and her trousseau wedding stuff, bridesmaids' dresses, champagne, etc., will run to quite a piece of jack I fear."*

---

*I'm sure it did run to quite a piece of jack, but it was worth every penny. And to think that within weeks of the wedding Pappy made the first of many payments to send me to college.

Shortly before Jill and Paul's wedding in August, I was sent along with them to pick up Pappy at the Memphis airport. He was returning from a State Department–sponsored tour of Venezuela. My job was to serve as comic relief and a conversational buffer between Jill and Paul and Pappy. Everything went smoothly. In Memphis, we went out for barbeque and were waiting on the tarmac when Pappy's plane touched down. He was glad to see us, hugged Jill and me, clapped Paul on the back, and chatted all the way home. A good sign.

That summer both Vicki and I were in Oxford for the wedding and the round of parties preceding it. We slept in Pappy's bedroom upstairs. At seventeen, Vicki was far more sophisticated and worldly than I. She had lived all over the world and introduced me to gin and tonics and cigarettes. I had tried, *really tried*—to learn to smoke when I was in high school in Little Rock but could not inhale without getting sick. While the grown-ups were downstairs we closed the bedroom door and opened the windows as wide as they would go. Sitting cross-legged Indian style on Pappy's bed, an ashtray between us, we lit our Pall Malls and puffed away, swinging a wet towel to get rid of the telltale smoke whenever we heard footsteps. I finally learned to smoke that summer of '54. By the time the wedding rolled around I was a pro. Vicki was a good teacher. It took me fifty years to kick the habit.

Our mischief did not end with cigarettes. Left to our own devices, Vicki and I spent many a late night sewing together the hems of Jill's lingerie trousseau—gowns and peignoirs, exquisitely beautiful in every color.

Her white satin wedding gown was trimmed with heavy lace at the neckline and sleeves, and had lace panels inset in the cathedral-length train. It was an elegantly simple, princess-style gown with so many satin-covered buttons at the wrists and from the neckline to below the waistline that Miss Kate Baker had to use an old-fashioned buttonhook to get Jill into the gown, which showed off her eighteen-inch waist to perfection.

Pappy and Paul and Paul's groomsmen were turned out splendidly in gray morning coats, while the bridesmaids, Vicki and Mil'Murray and I among them, wore silvery green tea-length dresses with forest green satin high heels and small wreaths of ivy in our hair. We carried bouquets of gardenias. I know Pappy paid for at least two of the dresses and two pairs of shoes: one for Jill's maid of honor, Vicki, and one for me. I thought we were perfect, but what I didn't realize at the time was that we could have marched down the aisle stark naked and no one would have noticed. All eyes were on Pappy.

The wedding at St. Peter's Episcopal Church was big and beautiful, and the reception at Rowan Oak was even bigger. Champagne flowed long after Jill and Paul left for their honeymoon. Vicki and I sat on the stairs, a magnum of champagne between us, and watched Cho Cho and photographer Bern Keating dance the tango. I barely made it upstairs to bed.

Jill and Paul settled in Charlottesville, Virginia, a happy, comfortable place for them, and for Pappy and Aunt Estelle, too, after Pappy later accepted the position of writer-in-residence at the University of Virginia. Jill became master of fox hounds at the Farmington Hunt in Virginia. Pappy, whose horsemanship could not compare with his daughter's, was thrilled for her and for himself. He rode to hounds every chance he got. When he was invited to wear the Farmington Hunt colors he was delighted. On several hunts, however, he was thrown. One fall in particular was serious and received far too much publicity to suit him. But then again, any publicity was too much. His picture appeared in many newspapers with a wire report that he'd broken his collarbone.

"How painful is it, Mr. Faulkner?" a reporter asked.

"No worse than a hangnail!"

He would return to Oxford full of tales of the excitement and beauty of the hunt, the countryside, the admiration and esteem he felt for Virginians. He loved the formality and ritual of the hunt—from the blessing of the hounds to the splendid blood-lines of the horses and dogs, to the Pinque coat, top hat, and black riding boots. One Christmas he gave away color photographs of himself in his foxhunting attire.

13

Pulitzer Prize

PAPPY SHOULD HAVE WON A PULITZER FOR ANY NUMBER OF HIS earlier novels, but this award came almost six years after he'd won the Nobel Prize. He was awarded the Pulitzer in 1955 for his novel *A Fable*, the one that he outlined on the walls of his "office" at Rowan Oak.* As if storyboarding a movie, he wrote short plot summaries under the headings of days of the week: "MONDAY" through "SUNDAY," with "TOMORROW" hidden behind the door that opened onto Aunt Estelle's music room.

Pappy's "office," a term he borrowed from southern plantation owners, was a bedroom/study with a single bed, a fireplace, and a large oil painting of an angry mule over the mantel. There were bookshelves that held paperback whodunits, the top shelf covered with his bottle-top collection. (Get one out of place while cleaning the room and there would be hell to pay!) His small writing table that Nannie had given him years before held his Underwood portable typewriter and a crooked-neck brass lamp. A ladder-back chair sat at the table in front of a window facing west. Pappy could look out through white cotton sheers at the stables. It was an ideal place to work.

---

*He was posthumously awarded a second Pulitzer Prize for *The Reivers* in 1963.

Two years after Jill married and moved away, Rowan Oak was getting awfully quiet. Aunt Estelle began to complain that they didn't have a lot of friends in Oxford, though over the years they had thoroughly enjoyed the company of Ashford and Minnie Ruth Little, Ross and Maggie Brown, Hugh and Mary Evans, and Ella Somerville. Perhaps Aunt Estelle was already lobbying for them to move to Charlottesville to be close to Jill and Paul. The offer from the University of Virginia for Pappy to be writer-in-residence must have fallen on their ears like the call of the wild.

It was true that Pappy lacked literary companions in Oxford. No doubt his sense of isolation had a lot to do with the fact that he had traveled widely and that he missed his friends and colleagues the world over. He had no one to talk to about contemporary fiction. He and Phil Stone had had what southerners call a "falling out" and were avoiding each other. His mother was the most sophisticated reader in town, but she could only do so much.

This was the man who knew everybody who was anybody, anywhere. He had even had tea with Albert Einstein in Princeton, several years before. When he came home he told Aunt Estelle that after exchanging pleasantries he and Einstein had little to talk about. I could imagine the two men sitting in silence, with absolutely nothing in common but genius. Pappy could hold on to an endless silence with anyone.

What did Oxford have to offer? The square shut down at six. The county was dry. There were no bars. Restaurants stopped serving after nine. *Where could he go?*

There was a single oasis on the square, its lights braving the darkness. Gathright-Reed's Drugstore, on the south side of the square where it had stood for thirty years, stayed open until ten. Here was Pappy's ray of hope, his light in the window. It wasn't exactly a watering hole, but this friendly neighborhood drugstore offered something that bars couldn't: *a lending library.*

Of course, Pappy had his own magnificent library at Rowan Oak, a beautiful room, understated and elegant. Bookshelves lined two walls. He collected everybody from Shakespeare and Henry Fielding to Henry Miller and Dostoyevsky.

A stuffed owl (shot by Pappy's stepson, Malcolm, in the 1940s) perched atop the tallest shelf. Pappy had a leather-padded fender built around the brick hearth so we could sit by the fire. His overstuffed reading chair and floor lamp were to the left of the fireplace. A framed black-and-white drawing of Ahab stood on a shelf. There were four paintings by Maud: a small one of Jill and Mammy Callie taken from a photograph; an oil of William Clark Falkner, the Old Colonel, in his CSA uniform; and, in ironic counterpoint, the elegant and dignified face of a black man known as "Preacher." A twenty-four-by-fifteen-inch oil portrait of Pappy in an antique gilt frame hung over the mantel. In it he is wearing a suit and tie. Nannie painted him in the early '40s when he was forty-four or forty-five. The canvas she stretched was an inch and a half too short for the frame Pappy selected, so, being economical by nature, she added a narrow strip of board and canvas to fill the gap and painted it to match her son's suit.

Having read all the books in his library, he went to Gathright-Reed's Drugstore looking for something new to read but mainly, I think, seeking company.

Pappy had long been friends with the pharmacist Mac Reed, who in the 1930s had functioned as his private mail service, wrapping manuscripts for submission, binding them with string, and mailing them to New York. Reed would not hear of anyone else doing it. After the books were published, he kept copies for sale when they were out of print, stacking them next to the cash register. There was no bookstore in Oxford. Gathright-Reed's was the only place in town to purchase Faulkner first editions—signed when the author was in a good mood.

In 1955, Reed's associate Gerre Hopkins manned the drugstore in the evening hours. This was before Hopkins went to medical school and married Jill's best friend, Mil'Murray Douglas. Reed, perhaps aware of his literary responsibilities, and (rare for a druggist) knowing that books were good medicine, installed a lending library with a rotating stand filled with paperbacks and call cards fitted into the front so that the pharmacy could keep tabs on books that had been checked out.

In Oxford this became the place to be from, say, 9 to 10 p.m. As soon as he heard about the lending library, Pappy was there. The square was a ten-minute walk from Rowan Oak. He could puff his pipe and pretend that he was going somewhere besides Gathright-Reed's and be grateful that at long last there was *somewhere* to go in Oxford after nine at night. He could "drop in" at the drugstore and sort through the paperbacks, greet other regular lending-library patrons, and perhaps exchange an opinion on this mystery or that. Hopkins serenely presided over this burst of nocturnal activity. An avid reader and devoted fan of William Faulkner, he welcomed Pappy to the store night after night.

I don't know if Dr. Hopkins told Pappy about the Case of the Missing Call Cards, but he shared it with me, many years later. One day he noticed that cards were missing in certain paperbacks. He remembered Pappy mentioning that he'd enjoyed this Erle Stanley Gardner or that Dorothy Sayers or Rex Stout. Putting two and two together, Hopkins realized that someone was going through the cards looking for Pappy's signature. That someone possessed the literary acumen to realize that a Nobel Prize winner's signature was valuable. Hopkins's prime suspect was a member of the Ole Miss English Department whose name he would not reveal. (Pharmacist-client privilege may have fig-

ured in.) Anyway, to foil the thief, Hopkins forged Pappy's signature in *all* the library cards. One wonders if any of those call
cards are circulating among collectors as genuine articles.

Then a book went missing. The overdue book was *Murder
in Pastiche; or, Nine Detectives All at Sea*, by Marion Mainwaring
(Macmillan, 1954), checked out by William Faulkner. The time
limit had expired. After several weeks, Hopkins went to Rowan
Oak to pick up the book. I don't know if he went out of his way
to track down every overdue item. Maybe he was caught up in
the art of detection, or maybe he just wanted to visit with Pappy.
When Aunt Estelle came to the door, Hopkins explained why he
had come and she said, "Just a minute, I know right where Bill
put that book." She gave it back to Hopkins and apologized for
it being late. Hopkins thanked her and brought it back to the
drugstore.

A week later, he noticed that the mystery had been checked
out again. He looked at the call card. The book had been signed
out by (the real) William Faulkner.

It's easy to see why Pappy was fascinated with *Murder in
Pastiche*. This sprightly first novel by Mainwaring, a Radcliffe
graduate, has nine famous detectives vying to solve a murder
committed on a ship during a transatlantic crossing. Each chapter is written in the narrative style of one of nine mystery writers,
including Agatha Christie, Dorothy Sayers, Rex Stout, and
Mickey Spillane. No writer could have appreciated Mainwaring's
spoof more than Pappy, who parodied himself in the short story
"Afternoon of a Cow," writing under the pen name of Ernest V.
Trueblood.

After several weeks passed, and Pappy still had not returned
the book, Hopkins had a dilemma. Should he go back to Rowan
Oak again, or should he wait and let the situation resolve itself?
Discretion proved the better part of valor. Hopkins relinquished

Murder in Pastiche to posterity. (I have a hunch that Pappy loaned the book to Nannie. She would have been beside herself to get her hands on it after he mentioned it. And he would have.)

Dr. Hopkins told my husband, Larry, and me this story at the annual Faulkner Conference at the University of Mississippi. Not long afterward, we purchased a copy of the paperback and presented *Murder in Pastiche* to him with an apology ' for having "kept it" so long and, considering that the book was fifty years overdue, with a request for special consideration regarding late fees.

Dean, two, and her cousin Jill, five, dressed for winter in 1938.

Maud; her son Jack Falkner, FBI agent and pilot; and her granddaughter Dean, two, in Oxford in 1938.

Dean with her nurse, Jerry, who taught her to say "Yes, ma'am" and how to say the alphabet backward.

Dean, four, with her mother, Louise;
photo taken at the Lafayette
County farm of her grandparents
Sanford and Pearl Hale.

Dean at age seven in Clarksdale,
Mississippi: "a scruffy little girl
just home from school."

Dean, ten, with her mother,
Louise, and Boo Ferriss,
pitcher for the Boston Red Sox
and cousin of Dean's stepfather,
Jimmy Meadow, circa 1946.

William Faulkner's favorite photo of himself was taken by his neighbor Colonel Hugh Evans in 1947.

The homemade houseboat *Minmagary*, built in 1947 by William Faulkner and his friends Ross Brown, Ashford Little, and Hugh Evans.

William Faulkner relaxing in his library at Rowan Oak. From his weary expression it's likely that this photo was taken just after he had finished "making one of the books."

The premiere of *Intruder in the Dust* was attended by William Faulkner and his family, including Dean Faulkner, thirteen, (not shown). *(News photo by Phil Mullen, the* Oxford Eagle).

Jill Faulkner, twenty-one, shortly before her marriage in 1954 to Paul Summers.

William and daughter Jill boarding a flight to Stockholm, where he would receive the 1949 Nobel Prize in Literature, awarded on December 10, 1950. (*Commercial Appeal photo*)

William Faulkner (center) with son-in-law Bill Fielden and step-granddaughter, Vicki Fielden in Manila, during Faulkner's State Department tour in 1955.
(Courtesy of Gillian Kay)

Dean, twenty, with longtime friend Sandra Baker, nineteen, while studying abroad in 1957 in Aubigny-sur-Nère, France.

William Faulkner, sixty, with niece Dean Faulkner, twenty-two, at Dean's wedding reception at Rowan Oak in 1958.

Dean with her children, left to right: Paige, Jon, and Diane; photo taken in Panama on Mother's Day, 1967.

Larry and Dean Wells, taken
through the window of
Yoknapatawpha Press,
then located over Sneed's
Hardware on the town square
of Oxford, Mississippi.
*(Chip Cooper, courtesy of W. S.
Hoole Special Collections,
University of Alabama Library)*

Faulkner's portable Underwood
typewriter in his "office."

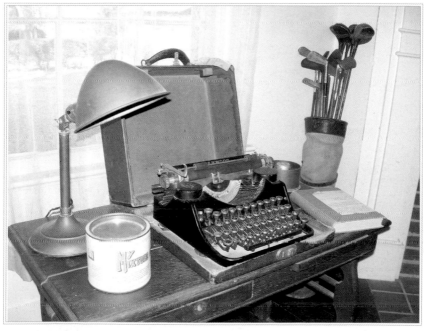

Rowan Oak seen
from the front.
(© Buddy Mays/Corbis)

Falkner family plot at
St. Peter's Cemetery in
Oxford: William Faulkner's
parents, Murry and Maud;
grandparents J.W.T. and
Sallie Falkner; brothers,
Dean and Jack; sister-in-
law Louise; cousin Dorothy
Falkner Dodson, daughter
of Judge John and Sue
Falkner; William's daughter
Alabama Faulkner; and
three infant sons of Judge
John and Sue Falkner.

14

Faulkners and Race

I WAS A STUDENT AT THE UNIVERSITY OF MISSISSIPPI AT THE time of the Hungarian Revolution of 1956, and several Hungarian refugees enrolled at Ole Miss. The administration had a recruiting drive to sign up campus organizations as sponsors of foreign students. My sorority, Chi Omega, declined, so I threw myself into the campaign with a vengeance. In the process I reinvented myself. The Faulkner tendency to play dress-up was alive and well in me. I grew my hair long and pulled it back into a ponytail. I disdained makeup and wore black sweaters with shapeless tweed jumpers, dirty tennis shoes, and a trench coat in all weather. I was obnoxious. When my dorm roommate archly observed that I looked and smelled like a Hungarian refugee, I could not have been more flattered.

That spring, I fell under the influence of Miss Kate, our next-door neighbor at Rowan Oak, and her daughter, Sandra, my childhood friend, who introduced me to a group of students so radical compared to my usual circle that they might have come from the far side of the moon. Fine arts majors in the classics and theater, they were in school to *be* students, to use their minds, to learn how to be better citizens. I wanted to be *them*.

Thanks to Sandra's introductions, my new friends allowed me to help them publish two or three issues of an underground newspaper, a broadside satirizing a nebulous group of white supremacists, Scotch-Irish descendants that we called "the Scottrish." We met in secret on the third floor of the university's YMCA building. Lookouts were posted while we ran off copies of our paper on the mimeograph machine. We had stealthy runners from various dorms, frats, and sororities to distribute the broadside. In the dark of night they would pick up the papers and sneak them into Greek houses and dorms, leaving stacks of them in doorway entrances or on tables to be discovered at breakfast. Afterward the "editorial board members" and contributing writers left the Y one at a time and made our way across campus as casually as our fear would allow.

We thought we were hot stuff, real heroes, riding bicycles around campus, walking to town (in a car-conscious society). We were proud as punch when a carload of students yelled through open windows: "N——r-loving queers!" We sat at an isolated table in the cafeteria with unabashed smugness, certain that no one outside our group of rebels would dare be seen with us. But we were a long way from climbing on a bus with John Siegenthaler or sitting at a lunch counter in North Carolina or walking across a bridge in Selma. Completely safe, we were bush-league liberals.

"Without fear there can be no courage," Pappy once told me. It's easy to be brave when you are very young or very old. The young haven't lived long enough to know any better; and the old have lived too long to care.

We knew that someone was sponsoring our broadside, paying for the mimeograph stencils (which to penniless students were quite expensive) and the paper to run off the broadside, and who, when the mimeograph machine broke, which happened frequently, would pay to have it repaired. We argued cheerfully about the identity of our secret benefactor. It's amazing that we never considered Pappy, even though he had been widely quoted as saying that being against integration was like living in Alaska and being against snow. Pappy and I had not discussed the pending integration of Ole Miss but only whether I would study French Realism or Old English. My peers and I assumed that our mystery patron was the campus archliberal, history professor James Silver, designated by the White Citizens' Council as a "threat to the Mississippi way of life," and our role model and hero. Years later, I was talking to Dr. Silver at a cocktail party and he casually remarked that our anonymous sponsor was none other than Pappy. I was stunned and filled with joy and the hope that Pappy knew that I was a member of the "Third-Floor YMCA Gang."

Pappy, Wese, and I formed a moderate minority in our family of ardent segregationists and racists. One aunt was fond of saying, "I just don't understand why anyone would ever want to go anywhere that they weren't invited, much less wanted. That's like crashing the party. You just don't." In an interview with a local newspaper, another aunt was quoted (accurately, I believe) as saying, "I'm a bigot and proud of it." The Faulkner men, with the exception of Pappy, heartily endorsed this sentiment, using the "n" word, snickering at racist jokes, and openly advocating violence to defend the "Southern Way of Life."

Nannie was as full of bigotry as any of them. Early on a fall afternoon when I was staying with her in Oxford, I came home from school bursting with the Bill of Rights, which I had learned by heart. "Do you want to hear what I learned today?" I called to Nannie, and not pausing for a reply, I began to recite: " 'All men are created equal. They are endowed by their creator with certain inalienable . . .' " She interrupted before I could say another word, her voice soft and firm. "Yes, they are, my lamb, with the exceptions of nigrahs, foreigners, Catholics, and Jews."

Nannie remained steadfast in her prejudice her entire life. Miss Kate, Sandra, Wese, and Pappy saved my soul.

—

WHEN THE FIRST African American student was about to enter Ole Miss, Wese was social director at the campus YMCA and counselor of foreign students. That Sunday evening, she drove out to the Y to go to work as usual, in spite of the growing probability of campus violence. James Meredith was scheduled to be registered at the University of Mississippi the following Monday.

Traffic in Oxford was heavier than for a home football game. Cars and pickups with license plates from every county— Itawamba, Hinds, Choctaw, Yalobusha, Panola—as well as from Tennessee, Alabama, and Louisiana were loaded with men, front and back. I could feel the mounting tension. When the first out-of-state buses rolled in, angry, determined faces staring out the windows, I shuddered and feared for James Meredith, our university, our town, our country.

It was a warm September evening. All the windows in Nannie's house were open, as well as the front door and the French doors. I watched as President Kennedy addressed the nation. He was magnificent, but even as he made his eloquent plea for law and order, we heard the howling of the mob from the campus, a mile away, and the sound of breaking glass. A pall of tear gas hung over the town. The burning smell seeped through the window screens. I closed windows and doors and waited for Wese to come home. She got in around two in the morning, having worked side by side with the Reverend Duncan Gray, our Episcopal priest. The YMCA had been turned into a sanctuary and first-aid station for students and demonstrators overcome by tear gas. Dozens were lying on the floor in the vestibule. Wese brought water to federal marshals and students alike, using the only container she could find, a pencil holder, filling it from a water fountain.

As Wese was tending to the walking wounded, two other relatives of mine were about to confront each other outside the Y. It has been said that the riot at Ole Miss was the last battle in the Civil War, dividing families who fought on both sides. Well, fate brought my uncle John's sons, Chooky and Jimmy, face to face, armed and dangerous, in front of the Lyceum Building. Chooky, a captain in the Mississippi National Guard, was in command of the Oxford company. Jimmy was leading a lynching party (it can't be called anything else) intent on assassinating James Meredith while the mob ruled the campus.

After the Guard was federalized and under government control, U.S. attorney general Nicholas Katzenbach ordered Chooky to move his unit to the campus and take up positions in front of the besieged Lyceum, where thousands of demonstrators, students and rednecks alike, were throwing bricks at the U.S. Marshals who guarded the building. The rumor was that Meredith was inside. Actually, he was in a men's dormitory some two hundred yards away, guarded by a handful of FBI agents.

Jimmy Faulkner was one of the men who commandeered a bulldozer at a building site and drove it toward the Lyceum. Klansmen with shotguns and dynamite followed the bulldozer like infantry behind a tank. Their plan was to storm the Lyceum, drag Meredith out, and kill him. Chooky's arm had been broken when a brick landed in his jeep. He was still in command, his arm in a sling fashioned out of an ammunition belt. Before Jimmy could get to the Lyceum, Chooky stood in the street blocking his path. Jimmy could not bring himself to run over his brother. Instead, he rammed the bulldozer into an oak tree, trying to bring it down so riflemen could use it for cover. The bulldozer's engine stopped. FBI agents swarmed the machine and Jimmy ran. He was not caught. Later, Chooky was awarded the highest military decorations for service outside a theater of war. Two men were killed during the riot, one of them a civilian bystander, the other a Reuters correspondent, and 160 marshals and guardsmen were wounded, 28 by gunfire.

At Nannie's house I could not sleep. I stayed up all night listening as rioters tore through the town like a tornado. There was looting on the square just a few blocks away. I thought Oxford, Mississippi, was going to be wiped off the map. Just before dawn I heard the tramping of feet. Hoping that this was the army, or more National Guard troops, I rushed outside. In the hazy morning sunlight, the air thick with smoke from burning vehicles, I saw soldiers in company formation coming up the hill from the National Guard armory, nine hundred paratroopers from the Eighty-second Airborne, double-timing up University Avenue. In their combat fatigues and helmets, holding rifles with fixed bayonets, they were the most beautiful men I had ever seen. I ran into the street shouting "Thank you, thank you!" The guide-on sergeant ran over from the intersection where he was directing traffic and hollered, "Get back inside, lady, we're shooting live!" The *hut-two-three-four* cadence count and thudding of army boots gave me hope, and I went back into the yard and did as I was told.

The minute the soldiers were out of sight, a moving van stopped in front of our house. Rear doors were thrown open. Thirty or forty white men armed with shotguns and deer rifles poured into the street. A car stopped at the intersection, the driver an elderly black man probably on his way to work. The whites were on him instantly, dragging him from his car, throwing him down on the curb. They smashed the car windows and rocked the vehicle from side to side, then turned it over and set it on fire. Somehow the man got away.

Then the mob overran the Texaco station across the street, attacking the cold-drink machines. They ripped open the machines and emptied the bottles, refilling them with gasoline. They cut up their shirts with pocketknives and used the rags as wicks. Instant Molotov cocktails. Then they headed for the campus.

As the sun rose on that sad, violent day, anyone who dared venture to the square would have witnessed an unforgettable act of valor: Miss Kate Baker, Sandra's mother, Pappy's Rowan Oak neighbor, owner of Baker's Town and Campus, had risen at dawn and gone to her shop on the west side of the square. One of the first people she saw was her store manager, a tall African American woman named Ruth, who had worked with her for many years and who had given her privileged insights into the black community, their attitudes, their fears and hopes. Miss Kate knew that "gone to Chicago" was a euphemism for being killed, and during the civil rights era she helped many African American citizens migrate north in search of a better life.

On their way to work, as usual, Ruth, with three or four of her black assistants, approached the square. Seeing gun-toting rioters stalking the business district, they ran for their lives to Baker's dress shop. Miss Kate motioned them into the alley behind her store and was waiting at the service entrance to let them into the basement. She slammed the heavy door and locked it, and urged them to remain quiet and to open the door for no one. Then she went back to the front of the shop, unfurled a large American flag, and placed it in a stand outside the shop, where Old Faithful waved in its lonely glory all day long.

15

The Women Pappy Loved

IN 1957, AUNT ESTELLE FELT HER MARRIAGE HAD REACHED
the breaking point. She wrote Saxe Commins: "I know, as
you must, that Bill feels some sort of compulsion to be attached
to some young woman at all times—it's Bill. At long last I am
sensible enough to concede him the right to do as he pleases,
and without recrimination. It's not that I don't care—(I wish it
were not so)—but all of a sudden [I] feel sorry for him—wish he
could know without words between us, that it's not very important after all—" She offered Pappy a divorce that year. He did
not accept her offer.

Their marriage had withstood over thirty years of turbulence
and erosion. Their last years together were tender. They shared
a gentle respect for each other, a pleasure in being together, a
tacit closeness that comes only from a lifetime of shared memories. It was a joy to be with them. I cannot imagine either of
them being married to anyone else.

As I met each of Pappy's women over a twenty-year period,
my first reaction was instinctive: I simply hoped they made
him happy. William Faulkner—this man of many faces, literary
genius, desperate alcoholic subject to severe bouts of depression, driven early on by the unassuaged fear of failure—was my
Pappy, not only the sole owner and proprietor of Yoknapatawpha, but the sole means of support, financial and emotional, off

and on, of our family. We took so much and gave so little in return. No wonder he looked elsewhere for solace, and how could one woman have possibly filled the void? My meetings with the women in his life were easy and cordial, accidental in some cases, arranged by mutual friends at other times. Any animosity I might have felt was tempered by feelings of gratitude for what they had meant to him. I wished the same peace and joy for Aunt Estelle in whatever form it took.

I agree with Jill's comment "Pappy liked the ladies." Having personally known five of the women Pappy loved, I must say that he had great taste in women.

Though none of them resembled one another physically—some were dark-haired, others blond—all were graceful, charming conversationalists, sophisticated, quick-witted, and well-read, with a subtle vulnerability that drew people to them. This description also fits Aunt Estelle, who was a consummate hostess, gourmet cook, master gardener, and lady of the house when she chose to be.

The difference was that his mistresses were ambitious, self-supporting, or independently wealthy, and working to establish themselves. Their self-reliance was clearly an attraction to Pappy. None would have swapped places with Aunt Estelle, or buried herself behind closed doors at Rowan Oak. None ever put demands on him, leaving him free to gallivant around the globe, martinis with Lauren Bacall, parties at St. Moritz with Howard Hawks, drinks at the Algonquin with Dorothy Parker and Dashiell Hammett, brunch with Claudette Colbert, dove shoots with Clark Gable. He was a man of the world, while Aunt Estelle was stuck in Oxford, Mississippi, waiting for him to come home to her, until she escaped to Virginia.

It is easy for me to be objective about Pappy's affairs, because as much as I loved him, he was not my father. The fact is,

I have a weakness for writers and tend to forgive them anything. I was not as defensive about Aunt Estelle as I would have been had she been my mother. Being *Mrs. William Faulkner* seemed to be all that mattered to her. As long as she held the title to the throne, though her position might be challenged, no one could take her place. In the meantime, Pappy could do as he pleased. He had his bedroom. She had hers.

After she joined AA, Aunt Estelle became interested in religion, or several religions, from Catholicism to Zen Buddhism. She moved the sewing machine where she had made dresses for Jill and Vicki and me and replaced it with an easel. She painted large Rousseau-like oils on canvas, variations on jungle scenes with dark green backgrounds and splashes of deep reds and purples, often with a stark white long-legged bird standing in a ripple-free pond and, above it, crouched on a massive slab of rock, a panther, coat gleaming, teeth bared, ready to spring.

She had always loved to fish and was very good at it, and now she returned to this wholesome pastime. She would come downstairs at Rowan Oak all turned out in white cotton slacks with cuffs turned up, white middy-blouse style shirt, deck shoes, and straw hat—sometimes with insect netting attached. Off she would go, creel basket and fishing pole in either hand, sometimes with Chrissie, sometimes alone. She would go to the car with a lightness in her step and a smile on her face. I think her favorite fishing spots were on Hickahala Creek or the Tallahatchie River or at Sardis Reservoir. After she returned, the house would be filled with the smell of frying fish, hushpuppies, and homemade tartar sauce.

She either ignored the other women or pretended they did not exist. Distance was her protection, a natural barrier, with Meta Carpenter in L.A., or Jean Stein in Europe or New York. In Memphis, however, Joan Williams would prove too close to home.

When I met Meta Carpenter in Los Angeles, she was eighty-five. Larry and I took her to lunch at Jimmy's Restaurant in Century City. Jerzy Kromolowski, screenwriter and director, joined us. We had met him in Oxford when he was developing *As I Lay Dying* as a film. As we waited for Meta to arrive, Jerzy spoke of her career with awe. She was known in the movie business as a legendary script supervisor. It was said that Mike Nichols would not direct a film without Meta on the set. For years she had been a judge for the Academy Awards. We were having lunch with a Hollywood celebrity. When she entered the restaurant dressed in black with a brilliant red beret, heads turned. Her carriage was regal as she approached our table and we stood to greet her. Her self-confidence was as beautiful as her smile. She was one glamorous lady.

I had read her autobiography, *A Loving Gentleman*, about her romance with Pappy, and my first impression was much as she had described herself: "I was pretty enough, with blonde hair that fell in a straight sweep to my shoulders, with a ninety-two-pound body as lean and as lithe as a ballerina's, and with a waist that was a handspan around."

Pappy met Meta in Hollywood in 1935 when he was writing for MGM and she was Howard Hawks's secretary. His screenwriting period had begun two years earlier when director Hawks had read and admired *Soldiers' Pay* and lured him to Hollywood with promises of seeing his stories and characters on the silver screen. Some of his early work was eventually adapted for film, though not to his liking. In 1933, his sensational *Sanctuary* was adapted as *The Story of Temple Drake*, starring Miriam Hopkins and Jack La Rue. Pappy had submitted a film treatment adapting his *Saturday Evening Post* short story "Turn About." This story was about two WWI officers, a torpedo boat commander and a bomber pilot, who meet in a British pub and invite each other to go on a combat mission. Each is courageous in his own environment—air or water. The navy skipper is terrified during the bombing run and the pilot equally frightened on the torpedo run. Hawks decided the film should revolve around a romance and cast Gary Cooper and Joan Crawford in *Today We Live.**

Meta spoke lovingly of the "Bill" she had known while working at MGM. "I looked up and there he was in a tweed coat, leaning against the doorway. I could see his black eyes all the way across the room."

Once he took her to a bookstore and bought a copy of *Sanctuary* and signed it for her. She recalled wearing low heels so the difference in their heights would not be apparent. What *was* apparent to me was how happy they had made each other.

Our lunch stretched into four hours. I did not want it to end. Meta was a southerner, born in Memphis, brought up in Tunica, Mississippi. That alone would have drawn Pappy to her. She spoke freely, without recrimination, of the heartache of losing him—not to Estelle but to Jill. In a sad, gentle, self-effacing way she observed that Pappy's love for Jill was what kept him from leaving Estelle. She spoke of her only visit to Oxford. She'd been working on the film *The Reivers*, shot in Carrollton, Mississippi, sometime after Pappy died. One afternoon, after being assured that Estelle was in Charlottesville, she and a friend drove

---

*Hawks premiered the film at Oxford's Lyric Theatre, operated by Pappy's cousin-in-law, Bob Williams. Seeing a chance to cash in, Williams raised ticket prices for the debut showing from a quarter to thirty-five cents. He advertised that the author would make an appearance and then got his wife, Sallie Murry, to beg her cousin to show up. The local audience was seated in the little theater, thrilled that the local boy had "made good." Pappy reluctantly appeared. He walked down the aisle to the front. Williams introduced him to wild applause. Pappy faced the expectant audience and said, "This movie bears no relation to the story I wrote," and walked out.

to Oxford and visited St. Peter's Cemetery. She went to Pappy's grave alone and said good-bye.

Because Aunt Estelle treated me always with unfailing kindness I would very much like to believe that Pappy's affairs caused her little if any pain, but I am aware of at least two instances when she was directly affected.

Both involved Joan Williams.

Joan was twenty years old in 1949 when she met Pappy at Rowan Oak. He was fifty-two. She had first fallen in love with *The Sound and the Fury.* Its creator was a literary god to this young woman, whose every dream and ambition was to be a writer. I'm sure she was an attractive girl with her strawberry blond hair, freckles, and green eyes, but that first encounter was abysmally awkward. Pappy got the feeling that he was being used. Joan went home and wrote him a passionate letter of apology, opening the door to an affair that proved more destructive to Pappy and Aunt Estelle's troubled marriage than any other. As his literary "protégé," Joan held a unique position in his life, and her proximity to Oxford was a double threat.

Her affair with Pappy evolved into a stormy on-again, off-again relationship. Both of them suffered periodic bouts of clinical depression, and with Aunt Estelle's awareness of what was going on under her nose, Rowan Oak turned into a war zone.

Aunt Estelle was determined to end the affair. Possibly this one hurt more deeply than the others because so many people in Oxford knew about it. The buffer of distance was gone. One morning, walking through the pantry where the only phone at Rowan Oak was located, Vicki noticed a snapshot of a young, attractive woman placed conspicuously on the shelf beside the phone. Vicki had heard the angry voices, the accusations, and the threats between Aunt Estelle and Pappy for months. Although she had never met Joan, she knew instinctively whose picture it was and who had placed it there and why. She was angry and shocked that Pappy would sink to such depths of intentional cruelty in order to hurt her grandmother. So was I.

That Pappy had placed her picture next to the *phone* made it all the more spiteful. The numbers of Pappy and Aunt Estelle's friends and kinsmen were written in pencil and ink on the pantry walls above the telephone. There sat Joan. He had allowed her to intrude on this intimate family circle.

Aunt Estelle began to intercept Joan's letters and make copies of them. She telephoned Joan's home and spoke to her parents, threatening to go to Memphis and confront them. These threats came to a head on the day that Aunt Estelle asked Miss Kate to drive her to Memphis. My mother went along for support. Determined to save her marriage, Aunt Estelle had arranged a meeting with Joan at the Peabody. The two of them met in a private room while Miss Kate and Wese had lunch in the restaurant. By the time lunch was over, Aunt Estelle returned to the table and said she was ready to leave.

As they drove back to Oxford, Miss Kate asked, "Did it go well?"

Aunt Estelle replied, "She will not destroy my marriage." Nothing else was said.

Among Pappy's mistresses, Joan was the only one who wanted to be a writer. Pappy had helped her with suggestions, close editing, and revisions. Pappy had his agent Harold Ober submit Joan's novel *The Morning and the Evening* to the *Atlantic*, whose fiction editor, Sam Lawrence, excerpted the story as an *Atlantic* "First." Sometime later, Joan contacted Sam and suggested that they meet in New York. She had a "friend" that she wanted to introduce to him. They agreed to meet at the Harvard Club for lunch. Of course, the friend waiting in the mahogany-paneled Grill Room, decorated with the stuffed heads of wild game

bagged by such eminent Harvard alumni as Theodore Roo-
sevelt, was Pappy. He and Sam hit it off, and Sam invited him
back to the Harvard Club on several occasions, offering to let
him charge drinks to his account. Sam told us that one night he
arrived late and apologized to Pappy, who said, "That's all right,
Mr. Lawrence. I've been having a good time pretending I'm
you." On the table was a neat stack of bar chits signed "Seymour
Lawrence" in a small, distinctive hand.

In 1953, Pappy met Jean Stein, the third (I assume) of his
mistresses, at a Christmas party at St. Moritz. She was nineteen,
he was fifty-six. At the time Pappy was working with Howard
Hawks on the script for *The Land of the Pharoahs*. Pappy was infat-
uated right away with Jean's youth and beauty, and drawn to her
when he noticed she was shy around the talkative, self-absorbed
older people at the party. He took her away so they could spend
time alone getting to know each other. This was the beginning
of an affair that would last several years. Pappy wrote Saxe Commins, "She is charming, delightful, completely transparent,
completely trustful. I will not hurt her for any price. She doesn't
want anything of me—only to love me, be in love."

By 1956, their affair had blossomed into a literary collabo-
ration. Jean convinced Pappy to grant her an interview for the
Paris Review. His only condition was that he be allowed to edit
it. This is widely considered the best interview he ever gave,
making Jean Stein the only one of his lovers who added to the
Faulkner legend by drawing out Pappy and getting him to tell
his story in his own words. Several unforgettable lines came from
this interview, such as "Between Scotch and nothing, I'll take
Scotch." When Jean asked if he believed in reincarnation, Pappy
replied that he'd like to come back as a buzzard, because "they
are protected by law and can eat anything."

When she asked if he followed a formula in his writing, Pappy replied, "An artist is a creature driven by demons. He doesn't know why they choose him. . . . He is completely amoral in that he will rob, borrow, beg or steal from anybody and everybody to get the work done."

To which she responded, "Do you mean the writer should be completely ruthless?"

"The writer's only responsibility is to his art," he said. "He will be completely ruthless if he is a good one. . . . If a writer has to rob his mother, he will not hesitate; the 'Ode on a Grecian Urn' is worth any number of old ladies."*

I first met Jean Stein when she visited Willie Morris, then writer-in-residence at the University of Mississippi, and was a guest at his writing class. He asked Larry and me to host a dinner for her. Intrigued by her *Paris Review* interview with Pappy and *Edie*, the biography she coedited with George Plimpton, we were eager to meet her. My daughter Diane and her fiancé, Michael Cawley, joined us for dinner. A biographer had described her at nineteen: "striking, fine-featured with dark hair and eyes," and with a charming, soft, breathless voice. She was still stunningly attractive.

I had recently finished reading *Edie*. When I asked how she put Edie Sedgwick—and Pappy, by implication—at ease, Jean told me she pretended to have trouble starting her tape recorder. I can see Pappy trying to help. *Let's see, why don't we turn it to "record" and push this button. . . .*

We stayed in touch with Jean, at first through Willie, and through the years we contacted her whenever we were in New York. She returned to Oxford for Willie's fiftieth birthday party. One Christmas she sent the children a lovely Italian ice cream maker complete with recipes in English and Italian. It was the

---

*I think Nannie would have agreed completely.

hit of many a dinner party, the first bilingual dessert served in Oxford.

———

THE GREATEST POSSIBLE threat to Estelle's marriage never materialized at all, even though the lady in question was nearer to Rowan Oak than any other, because she loved both Aunt Estelle and Pappy too much to become involved.

The night that I first became aware of the attraction between Pappy and Miss Kate was at a dinner party at Rowan Oak. Aunt Estelle was in Virginia at the time. On this particular evening, Pappy's guests included Wese and me, Tommy Barksdale, a classmate of mine whom Pappy found amusing and called "that redheaded boy," and Jayne Coers, an attractive young widow on whom Pappy had a crush (he always called her "Miz Coers"), and Miss Kate. They were due at seven. Jayne arrived early. She and Pappy were alone in the library when I walked from the kitchen into the front parlor. I started to turn on a light. At that moment Pappy leaned down to kiss Jayne's upturned face. Though he'd long had a crush on her, I think that was all it amounted to. Just then the front door opened silently. Miss Kate entered. She did not see me in the parlor. Instead, through the open door of the library, she could see Pappy and Jayne. I heard a slight gasp. She turned on her heel and left.

Suddenly I knew. Their trips to New York at the same time. Both of them staying at Pappy's favorite hotel. The long horseback rides. Her interest in me. Taking me to New York with her on buying trips to Seventh Avenue. The gift tickets from Pappy to see Paul Newman in *Sweet Bird of Youth*. Tickets to the Met— again from Pappy. Shopping for me "off the models," as it were. Europe. The two of them, Pappy and Miss Kate, shaping my life again and again and again.

I didn't see the tears on her face but I could feel her crying.

Within five minutes there was a knock at the door. "See to it, Dean," called Pappy. "It's Kate, I'm sure."

I opened the door. There she stood in her navy blue silk shantung and pearls, a red fox stole around her shoulders, its beady little eyes glaring at the world, a smile on her lovely face. She hugged me and walked into the library. She offered her cheek to Pappy and her left hand to Jayne. She dropped her fur on the back of her chair and settled in before the fire and said, "Bill, tell us what you think about . . ."

She could have won an Academy Award.

16

Postcard from Paris

AFTER MUCH PLEADING, CAJOLING, AND BEGGING, AND WITH the unflagging support of Nannie and Miss Kate (who planned to be in Europe when I got there), Pappy agreed to send me abroad to study for a year. I had just begun the second semester as a junior at the University of Mississippi when Sandra told me that she and her mother and her brother, William, a handsome thirteen-year-old, would be leaving in April to join their father, an army colonel stationed in Augsburg, Germany.

The Baker family was like that. Here today, gone tomorrow. They weren't like anybody else, but then neither were we. While they were in residence they lived in a two-story brick house next door to Rowan Oak on a three-acre lot with a pasture and a barn and the occasional horse. Miss Kate was an elegant woman, small, dark, and athletic with a beautiful figure. She was a gifted actress. Her stage name was Kathleen Burke. The *Philadelphia Evening Public Ledger* gave a rave review of her performance in the play *The Front Page*, on April 4, 1931.

"Time and again," she said in an interview, "I have been asked by folk who know only the stage from the front whether actors and actresses really live and feel the parts they play. My reply has always been that I do not see how any one can properly act the role unless they actually live it, make themselves a part of it, whether it be a love scene, a dramatic moment, or even the deepest tragedy. Of course I live my part. I live the love scenes . . . and sometimes they affect me so deeply that I am back in my dressing room before I snap back into my normal self." The photograph accompanying the article shows a dark-haired, dark-eyed beauty. Miss Kate was on her way to stardom. In her early twenties, she had a major role in a play in Philadelphia. Bette Davis was her understudy. When Miss Kate's father died before the play opened, she went home to Birmingham, Alabama, to care for her mother, never to return to the stage. Bette Davis went on to become, well, Bette Davis.

I've known the Bakers for as long as I can remember, but I don't know when Miss Kate and Bill Baker were married or how or why she and her three children (Virginia, Sandra, and William) came to be in Oxford. She was well-read, well-bred, and far too sophisticated for this small town. She was a brilliant businesswoman who started her own clothing store at a time when most employed women worked for someone else. She was the boss and a very successful one.

She and "the Colonel" (nobody ever called him anything else—I don't know what he was called before he was "the Colonel") had what might be called a casual marriage. He was some years older, a career army man who had started out in the cavalry. He had been stationed all over the world. Miss Kate joined him when he was posted somewhere that she liked. They had spent two years in Japan shortly after WWII and several months at a post in Maryland. In between, Miss Kate and the children lived in Oxford and the Colonel popped in for visits. They were always exciting times since no one knew when to expect him. Once he arrived in a small airplane he had bought. When he landed he called Miss Kate to come pick him up at the airport. She was unaware that he knew how to fly. The Colonel was brusque but polite, a man of few words, an avid fisherman and poker player extraordinaire. Both Miss Kate and the Colonel were friends and neighbors of Pappy and Aunt Estelle—especially Miss Kate.

Pappy had been helping pay my way for years, but after my graduation from high school he became my sole source of support. He let Miss Kate and me convince him that if I went abroad with Sandra, it would not cost him any more than if I stayed at Ole Miss. When he consented—and I knew that when he said he would take care of the money it would be there—I began making plans for my first trip to Europe. I could never have imagined that I would wind up studying French at the University of Geneva that fall, or that when I deposited the check Pappy sent me, a Swiss bank president would invite me to have tea in his office, or that this distinguished, gray-haired gentleman would say, without a trace of embarrassment, that he was honored to hold a piece of paper with Pappy's signature on it.

I signed up to study French that summer at Aubigny-sur-Nère, the hometown of my French professor's wife, Ginette. Every year Dr. Strickland and Ginette chaperoned a study group in France. We were scheduled to sail on the *Liberté* June 11, 1957, at eleven thirty in the morning. I was deliriously happy.

Recently I found tucked away in a cubbyhole of Nannie's secretary a packet containing my ticket on the *Liberté,* some Western Union telegrams wishing me bon voyage (my favorite is from Billy Ross Brown's wife, Lynn: "Bring home a count for me!"), my Paris hotel bills, and a small, formal note in the unmistakable handwriting of Aunt Estelle addressed to:

Miss Dean Faulkner
Courtesy William Faulkner Esq.

The notepaper was engraved "Mrs. William Faulkner," and the note read:

Mrs. William Faulkner

Miss Dean Faulkner
Courtesy William Faulkner Esq—

Charlottesville
Sunday, 9th —

Dearest Dean —

Enclosed is a tiny going-
away present for you —

I am very happy over this
year in Europe for a most de-
serving little girl, and wish
very good and wonderful things
for you —

Write to us sometime when
you feel as though you want
to, never as a chore —

Give all the Bakers my
love — tell miss Kate twenty
when I go back to Oxford —

Sort of may Pappy getting to
Oxe you this year you said!

Much love from me, and
always remember you are my
little girl too —
Aunt Estelle —

Pappy will cash this for you

Dearest Dean,
> *Enclosed is a tiny going
away present for you.*
> *I am happy over your
year in Europe for a most de-
serving little girl, and wish
every good and wonderful thing
for you.*
> *Write to us sometime when
you feel as though you want
to,* never *as a chore—*
> *Give all the Bakers my
love—will miss Kate terribly
when I go back to Oxford.
Sort of envy Pappy getting to
see you before you sail!*
> *Much love from me, and
always remember you are my
little girl too—*
> *Aunt Estelle*
> *Pappy will cash this for you.*

The check was for a lovely one hundred dollars. Pappy cashed it for me in New York. The note itself is priceless.

Nannie saw me off in Oxford. I held up my key to her front door, while Wese backed the car out of the driveway, as a sign that I'd come home to her. Wese and I spent that night at the Peabody and I caught an early flight to New York the next morning with a classmate from Ole Miss. Her name was Jan. After takeoff, she lost her lunch in an air-sickness bag. I patted her head and looked steadily out the window, smiling inside, certain that I was a natural-born cosmopolite. Immunity to motion sickness was proof positive.

Two notes were waiting for me when I arrived at my hotel in New York. One was from Pappy asking me to call when I checked in; the other was from my Ole Miss classmate and dear friend Bob Garrison, a brilliant classics scholar and member of the "Third Floor YMCA Gang," who would be sailing with me on the *Liberté*. His message said to meet him at some coffeehouse in the Village at three o'clock. Off I went. When I got back to the hotel much, much later there were three telephone messages from Pappy. The last read, "When you come up for air, call your uncle or your grandmother will kill both of us."

The night before I sailed, Pappy and Saxe Commins ("Mr. Saxe," I called him) took Jan and me to dinner. I was absolutely enamored with myself. My idol that year was Françoise Sagan, author of *Bonjour Tristesse*. I wanted to be her. I had my hair cut like hers and had adopted an affinity for black. I wore a little black cotton sheath with tiny tucks from neckline to dropped waistband. With my black stockings and Capezios, I thought I looked stunning. As we walked down Park Avenue on our way to Pappy's favorite restaurant (I wish to the good Lord I could remember which one) I began to notice heads turning. "This is it," I thought. "I am the cutest thing to hit New York. Just wait till I get to Paris!"

Within one block reality set in. They were staring at my distinguished escort Pappy, who continued smiling and chatting, either oblivious or accustomed to the attention. Not since the film premiere of *Intruder in the Dust* had I realized *who* he was, a world-renowned author, but this was New York and there was no marquee with his name on it and these were complete strangers and we were a long way from home.*

---

*Bill Styron once told me that he had a similar experience with Bennett Cerf in 1962 when they arrived in Memphis on the way to Pappy's funeral. As the pair walked through the Memphis airport, Styron noticed heads turning

The restaurant that Mr. Saxe and Pappy took us to was quiet, elegant, and very French, with red leather banquettes, gold sconces, and menus as big as I was, leather-bound with tassels. Pappy ordered escargots and several fine wines. The maître d' and the sommelier were rarely far from our table. I don't remember what we ate, but Mr. Saxe insisted that we order an entrée that we'd never eaten before. We had a very good time.

On the way back to our hotel Pappy and Mr. Saxe decided we must see Bennett Cerf's private office at Random House, which was located in the Villard Houses at 451 Madison Avenue, between Fiftieth and Fifty-first streets. When we got there, we headed straight for Cerf's famous bathroom. Nobody outside of Hollywood had a telephone in his bathroom! But there it was. Pappy immediately began pretending to dial numbers. This was the first time I'd seen him pantomime "black cord fever," that momentary affliction that comes upon solitary folks late at night after a few drinks, when they want to talk to every old friend they ever had. I wondered if he'd ever succumbed to the real thing. Mr. Saxe tuned in a radio station that played dance music. Pappy gave up playing with the phone, climbed fully clothed into the tub, and watched as Mr. Saxe took turns waltzing Jan and me around the office. He was our own Fred Astaire. After each number, Pappy clapped along with the studio audience.

At midnight they hailed a cab for us outside the Random House building. Hugs, kisses on both cheeks, "Bon voyage!" over and over, and a last request from Pappy: "Dean, promise to send me a postcard as soon as you get to Paris. One with a picture of the Eiffel Tower." Mr. Saxe added, "Send me one,

and thought, "They couldn't be looking at me!" And indeed they weren't. Everyone, of course, was staring at Cerf, the celebrity panelist and occasional host of TV's *What's My Line?* Cerf breezed through the airport, Bill recalled with a smile, taking the attention for granted.

too, with the Eiffel Tower." Another hug. Another thank-you. Another good-bye. Pappy gave our driver the hotel address, paid him, and we were driven away. Our gentlemen of distinction stood on the sidewalk waving till we were out of sight.

We headed to the piers early the next morning. It was still dark. Cars had their lights on. Breathless with excitement we boarded the *Liberté*, a mammoth ship. Well-wishers packed the pier elbow to elbow. After checking into our room, we followed the other passengers to the upper deck. In spite of the chilly morning we wriggled to the outside railing for our last view of New York, noisy, dirty, exhilarating, and sad. Then I saw, standing side by side, hats in hand, Mr. Saxe and Pappy. They waved and blew kisses. They raised their hats as we sailed out of New York Harbor.

———

MIDCROSSING, I RECEIVED a note from Ray Bradbury. At the time I had a paperback copy of his *October Country* in my luggage, and I had recently read *Fahrenheit 451*. His note said that he and Mrs. Bradbury had been browsing through the passenger list and had seen my name and were curious as to a possible connection with William Faulkner. Would I join them for tea the following afternoon at four? I nearly fainted. "Tell them yes, thank you," I said to the steward. He held out a tray with a notepad and pen. "If mademoiselle would write a response?" I scribbled an acceptance. When he left, my mind raced over the possibilities to get me out of this invitation. I could get sick. Jump ship. We could hit an iceberg. I could forget to go.

I was a nervous wreck. Ray Bradbury was the first major writer I had ever met (Pappy didn't count, because he was Pappy), and I felt sure I'd make a complete ass of myself if I opened my mouth. What was I to say to him? I had inherited a crippling shyness from the Faulkners. We are natural-born "back-row sitters."

At four the next day I knocked on the door of their first-class stateroom. I wore my favorite navy waffle piqué sheath. It usually made me feel confident and grown up. This time, it didn't help at all. My knees were knocking when Mr. Bradbury opened the door, introduced me to his wife, and offered me a chair.

"Tea?"

"No, thank you, sir."

"Something else? Coffee? A soft drink?"

"No, thank you." *Silence.*

"Well, Miss Faulkner, do you know your famous namesake?"

"Yes, sir, he's my uncle." *Silence.*

"Wonderful. How is he?"

"Fine." *Silence.*

"Is this your first sail?"

"Yes." *Silence.*

And so it went for an endless fifteen or twenty minutes, desperate attempts at conversation from them, monosyllabic replies from me. When I moaned, "I have to go now," there were no demurrals.*

———

THE *LIBERTÉ* DOCKED at Dover. I stayed up all night waiting for my first glimpse of the white cliffs. The next day we took a boat train to Paris and a taxi to the Hotel Cambon, a small hotel just off the rue de Rivoli, close to the Place de l'Opéra and the American Express building.

———

*In 1993, I was invited to judge the International Imitation Hemingway Contest at Harry's American Bar and Grill in Los Angeles. When Larry and I were brought in to meet the other judges, there sat Ray Bradbury. We were introduced. Not a flicker of recognition. After a second glass of wine I asked, "Did you by chance sail for England on the *Liberté* in June of 'fifty-seven?" He nodded and said, "Did you?" *Silence.* Embarrassed to be just as tongue-tied twenty-six years after our first meeting, I murmured, "Yes. Wasn't it a lovely crossing?"

There was a kiosk next to the hotel. I bought two garish postcards of the Eiffel Tower. I took them into the hotel bar, sat at the counter, and spoke my first words in French: *"Puis-je avoir une biere, s'il vous plaît."* The bartender served me with the slightest of condescending smiles. I wrote my postcards at the bar.

Fifty years later a Faulkner collector sent me a page from a catalog listing books and memorabilia from Pappy's personal library at Rowan Oak. Found in a copy of Fyodor Dostoyevsky's *The Brothers Karamazov* was "a color postcard of the Eiffel Tower addressed to William Faulkner from Dean [Faulkner], postmarked Paris, June 19, 1957." The postcard reads,

> *Dear Pappy,*
>   *Here's your postcard—I love Paris! The trip over was grand—wonderful people, food—landed in Le Havre yesterday & came to Paris by train. Went to Notre Dame today & am going back tomorrow & probably the next.*
>   *Thank you sir. Dean.*

Why didn't I sign the postcard "With Love, Dean"?

Bob Garrison came to my hotel late the next day. All smiles, he said, "I have a surprise." We hailed a cab and he told the driver our destination. I couldn't understand what Bob said. Neither could the driver at first. Finally the man nodded and we were off. He pulled up in front of an old theater with a brightly lit marquee. A long line of people stood at the ticket office. Bob had bought tickets in advance. He herded me through the double doors and into the lobby. With its black-and-white tiled floor and French doors it reminded me of the Lyric Theatre in Oxford. I stopped to read a poster with pictures of the cast in the play we were about to see.

"Requiem pour une Nonne"
de
William Faulkner
Adaptation par Albert Camus

I could hardly believe it. I hugged Bob and we walked down the long aisle to our seats: very close to third row center.

When the heavy gold curtains parted, I gasped. There was Rowan Oak, a replica so exact that I could almost smell the cedars.

The play was splendid. The actress who played Nancy Mannigoe looked like Chrissie's daughter; Temple Drake looked like Cho Cho. I knew the story well enough to be caught up in the drama in spite of my bad French.

I was stunned. The performance ended to uproarious applause, and I actually staggered as we left the theater, overcome with emotions I didn't know I had: the joy of seeing a place I loved and knew so well, the pride of knowing this had been created by a man I loved and knew so well, the astonishment that Rowan Oak had come to Paris. It was exquisitely perfect, an act of magic. I felt as if I were in two places at once, two places an ocean apart. It was my Pappy's world and—because he made me a part of it—mine.

17
A Wedding

I N THE FALL OF 1957, SANDRA AND I LIVED ON THE THIRD
floor of the Pension des Bastions, located at 18 rue de Con-
dole, across the street from the University of Geneva, where
we had enrolled as lowly walk-in students. The university also
housed the exclusive Ecole d'Interprêt. Our landlady, Madame
von Steiger, was a White Russian who never went anywhere
without her dog, a nasty little mutt named Fritz. Madame's
establishment had a citywide reputation for offering the best
boardinghouse lunches anywhere. At precisely 11:30 a.m. five
days a week, twenty-odd multinational regulars arrived and took
their places at tables, always the same seats intermingled with
us nine live-in boarders—a Swiss, a German, an Indian, a Scot,
three Italians, and two Americans.

The two young women who ran the kitchen served the soup
course precisely at noon. The third-floor dining room was small
and crowded but aside from the extraordinary food, it was a
wonderful place to be, mainly because it was the only heated
room in the building. (The city of Geneva didn't turn on the
steam-heating system until mid-October.) In the meantime we
huddled around a small, potbellied iron stove until the soup was
poured, then warmed our hands over the steaming bowls.

Most of the regulars were students or instructors at L'Ecole
d'Interprêt, and any given lunch sounded like a combination of

the United Nations and the Tower of Babel with conversations in ten different tongues.

When Sputnik was launched on October 4, we found out exactly where we stood with our fellow diners. Until that point, they had barely spoken to us. Now, in many different languages, only two of which we understood, we heard our country being ridiculed while Russia was hailed literally to the skies, lauded and celebrated. To a person the interpreters and instructors were thrilled that the Russians had been the first to conquer space.

Embarrassed, Sandra and I skipped dessert. We were full of humble pie.

A box of jonquils packed in dry ice arrived at the pension in March 1958. Miss Kate had picked them from her garden and shipped them by air. The minute I saw them I knew it was time to go home. I longed for a Mississippi spring of wisteria and fireflies, thunderstorms and gentle rains. My year-long European odyssey was over. I had sat for exams for only twelve hours of coursework, but I had skied Vevey and Innsbruck and Garmisch. Before leaving I made one more trip to Spain, my last chance to follow in Hemingway's footsteps from La Casa Botin, his favorite restaurant in Madrid, to San Sebastián and Pamplona, where I toasted Papa from the wineskins and Pappy picked up the tab.

A month later my flight from Orly landed midafternoon at La Guardia where I took a cab to 48 East Eighty-third Street to Cho Cho and Vicki's town house. They welcomed me home in fine style: dinner at the Metropolitan Club, tickets to *West Side Story*, brunch or lunch at sidewalk cafés. When we ate in, Cho Cho's Filipino cook served dinner. After a week of super-sophisticated welcome-home celebrations, I caught a flight to Memphis. Miss Kate and Wese met me at the airport and took me to Oxford. First I had to finish my degree as I had promised. I moved into Nannie's front bedroom, enrolled in summer school at the University of Mississippi, and got a job at the university library. The last dime of my year-abroad money went for tuition. Nannie was good for room and board. This was all to the good since my job at the library paid eighteen dollars a week.

Pappy came home from Virginia for a month's visit, primarily to check on Nannie. We had several grand reunions welcoming me back. Pappy picked me up at Nannie's in his new jeep and drove me to Rowan Oak. The motor was noisy and we had to talk loudly to be heard. "Tell me about Europe," he said as he drove.

I thought for a moment and drew one memory out of a year's experiences. "I saw *Bus Stop* in German with English subtitles. I wish you could have heard Marilyn Monroe say—"

"*Guten Tag?*" he interrupted, and we both laughed. Then he said, "And?"

"I fell in love with an Italian in Rome. I may marry him."

"And you'll *live* in Italy!" He seemed shocked. I didn't reply, having no intentions of marrying the boy. I didn't know why I said it. "Marry Italians for love," he said, "and marry Americans for money. Did you meet his mother?"

"No, sir."

"Well, you should have! You'll be a long way from home." I digested this in silence. I was glad to be back in Mississippi and frankly it unnerved me to think about going back to Europe so soon, much less getting married. Pappy made a hand signal and turned onto Garfield. "What happened to your German young man, the one you wrote us about? The one who spoke no English."

"Well, we had to communicate in French. So I ended up speaking French with a German accent and he spoke it with a southern American accent. It was pretty bad. Besides, his mama didn't like me."

He shifted gears with a grin. "Well, neither will your Italian's." I gave him a shifty little look and we burst out laughing. I was glad I had made him laugh.

Pappy was staying by himself at Rowan Oak and took me to dinner at least once a week. I was his logical (only) companion readily available. We usually went to the Mansion, an antebellum house converted into a restaurant by Aubrey Seay, popular with townsfolk and students alike and just up the street from Nannie's.

The steaks and the shrimp rémoulade were good, but the best thing about the Mansion, where Ole Miss students were concerned, was the jukebox, though this machine had been the bane of my existence when I was a coed. To show his respect for Pappy, who hated background music, Seay would unplug the jukebox the moment he entered the restaurant. When I was a freshman and sophomore, I went in with Pappy hoping and praying that I wouldn't see anybody I knew. I felt that every young person in the place hated me. *All those quarters.*

Pappy could never open the cellophane-wrapped packets of crackers. I started out hoping he wouldn't notice them or that he wouldn't want any with his salad, or that if he did he would locate the little red "pull tab" and be able to open a packet by himself. None of this ever happened. Inevitably, he wound up at war with his crackers, twisting and turning the cellophane, becoming more frustrated by the second until *Whamm!* Down came his fist smashing the crackers to smithereens. I stared at the table as other diners glanced at us and Pappy muttered about "the innate perversity of inanimate objects."

He looked healthy and happy that summer, but the same was not true of Nannie. She was eighty-seven and had suffered a series of little strokes that had left her blind in one eye. She still made her own meals, however. Breakfast consisted of intentionally burned toast cut into three slices, no butter or jelly. She still ate at her dining room table, silver sugar bowl and cream pitcher in place even though she never took milk or cream or sugar with her coffee.

She was mobile and as stubborn as ever. She had always paced the house—walking off nervous energy. But now she passed from room to room like a caged animal, anxious and distracted. She played double solitaire for hours on end sitting at the dining room table by herself, chomping on bits of ice that she crushed with a hammer. With her dowager's hump and black eye patch, she didn't look exactly like everyone else's grandmother. A pirate's dagger on her belt would not have seemed untoward.

Pappy told me that the reason for this particular visit was that once again Nannie had fired the nurse-companion he had hired to live with her. He was determined that she not live alone due to her age and fragility, but he couldn't count on me to stay put. Nannie was equally determined that she live exactly the way she pleased—*alone*. This was the third "nice lady" Pappy had hired and Nannie had fired as soon as he left for Virginia. What a battle of wills.

"Have you forgotten, Billy," she said, "the difference between being lonely and being alone?"

Nannie had also lost a great deal more of her hearing since that Sunday twenty years before when she had walked out of the Methodist church muttering to herself about the new minister who "whispered" while he preached. "I'll not waste my time on man or god who won't speak up."* She never went back. She never wore a hearing aid either, even after the day Pappy and I took her for a checkup and, as we sat in Dr. Holley's crowded

---

*This from the mother of a notoriously soft-spoken Nobel laureate.

waiting room, she announced to the world at large, singling out some poor child: "Billy, isn't that the ugliest little girl you ever saw?" He stared at the *Field and Stream* in his lap. "Dean, isn't that the ugliest . . ."

Late one summer afternoon as we sat in her room, Nannie turned to Pappy and said, "Billy, do you think there is a heaven?" Pappy said something like, "I don't know, Mother." Nannie: "Well, if there is, I know those robes will be too long, flapping all around my ankles, and if your father is there, I don't want to see him."

"Believe me, Mother," Pappy said, "you won't have to if you don't want to."

"I want to go wherever Conrad and Shakespeare are," she said.

Pappy chuckled. "And V.K."

Nannie laughed. Pappy's "V. K. Ratliff" was her favorite character from Yoknapatawpha County. The day Pappy created V.K. he hurried to Nannie's and told her. From then on they treated the sewing machine salesman like an old family friend. Nannie never tired of hearing about V.K. and Pappy never tired of the telling. How bad could hell be if V.K. was there? After a while Pappy went on to observe that most people died of boredom. "I'm bored enough and tired enough," Nannie said.

He glanced up. "I won't let you die on me." Before she could reply, he changed the subject to the latest whodunit they had read.

I spent that summer trying to decide what to do with the rest of my life. I had graduated in August with a double major in English and French, a minor in history and a WSI (water safety instructor), which meant I was qualified to teach swimming lessons in French should there be any demand. Pappy had teased me all summer long about my majors and minors, and my being "splendidly" (his word) qualified to do nothing. I needed a three-hour elective to graduate, so my last course at Ole Miss was pottery making.

Pappy was relentless. "All those hours so you'll learn how to throw an ugly pot on a wheel, which you couldn't give away to your own grandmother." But he smiled when he said it.

Once when we were having dinner at a restaurant in Oxford, I noticed a college girl laughing and talking loudly. "Look at her," I whispered to Pappy. "She's had too much to drink and is making a fool of herself." He leveled that dark gaze that could turn you to ice and said, "Don't be supercilious." I didn't know what that meant but it couldn't be good. When I got home that night, the first thing I did was look up *supercilious* in the dictionary. Then I looked in the mirror to see if I could raise my eyebrow. Then I swore to myself not to be guilty of such arrogance again.

Pappy insisted that I would make Nannie happy by participating in graduation exercises. So in August I donned cap and gown and lined up outside the university's Fulton Chapel with the small summer-school graduating class of 1958. It was a rainy afternoon and the chapel was barely half full. As I filed inside with my classmates I could see the chancellor waiting on stage to present our diplomas. I felt too old to be marching in time to "Pomp and Circumstance." Then I noticed two figures, third row center, rising solemnly, so close together they seemed joined at the hip. They stood as straight and tall as they could in the classic European manner of honoring university graduates. The only ones standing, they remained on their feet *the entire ceremony.* Everyone was staring. I hoped in vain—I prayed—that nobody in the auditorium recognized them.

As a graduation gift, Pappy assured me of a job at Random House—starting in the mail room or even lower, as befitted a thrower of bad pots—but I wanted to be just like every other woman in her twenties in the 1950s: married and living happily ever after. There were notable exceptions, no doubt, in Mississippi in the 1950s. I just wasn't one of them.

Underneath this flippant attitude was a desperate young woman who had lived her entire twenty-two years dependent upon, not the kindness of strangers, but the kindness of family members who took care of her financially and emotionally because they felt a moral obligation to do so, not because they had no choice. Nothing as uncomplicated and pure as a father and daughter, he with a blood bond to care for her until she entered an age when she was old enough to take care of herself or find someone else to do it. Very few women in those days looked forward to careers. I was far too full of self-doubt to think I could do anything on my own—certainly not earn a living. I had all the drive and self-confidence, ambition and get-up-and-go of a marshmallow.

But I felt pretty sure I could find a husband, even though at the time nobody had proposed marriage.

Before summer's end I had found a willing candidate. I'd known him for four years, but in all that time we'd scarcely spent thirty days together. After a brief long-distance courtship we were engaged. Aunt Estelle and Pappy planned an announcement party in the east garden at Rowan Oak in late August 1958. My future in-laws were due to arrive midafternoon the day of the party.

I should have known the gods of marriage were up to something. As the time approached, Pappy sat in a rocking chair on the front gallery smoking a Salem cigarette, flicking ashes over the banister.

"Sir," I said from behind his chair, addressing the top of his head, "they'll be here in just a minute."

"So?"

"Well, sir, I sort of thought you might want . . . might think about . . . changing your clothes."

No answer.

"Uh, Pappy, maybe just your pants?"

He turned his face to mine. "What's wrong with these?"

He wore a faded blue wrinkled work shirt frayed at collar and cuffs, muddy brogans with no socks, and a pair of khakis cut off above his knees. The fabric had unraveled so that long fuzzy strings of knotted thread hung down his calves. Before I could reply we heard a car turn into the driveway. I willed myself to vanish into thin air.

He stood, put out his cigarette, stashed the filter in a pocket, squared his shoulders, and walked the few steps to the porte cochere. When the car stopped he opened the door for my future mother-in-law with the flourish of a valet at the Ritz and helped her out. I think she was too shocked to faint.

In spite of this inauspicious welcome by Pappy, Aunt Estelle had done everything to make the party successful. She had handwritten the invitations, planned the dinner, seen to the decorations—large tables with eight place settings and white candles aglow on white linen tablecloths with garlands of pink rosebuds draped to the hems, barely touching the grass. Everything was perfect. The weather was unseasonably cool, and the sounds of the University of Mississippi band rehearsing in the football stadium drifted through Bailey's Woods in muted stereo: "Dixie" inexplicably followed by Copeland's "Fanfare for the Common Man." My husband-to-be should have felt some premonition—if not about the music, then surely when Pappy called us to the east gallery to stand with him as he proposed a toast. I don't remember his exact words but the gist was that my most outstanding character trait was loyalty—unrelenting and unmitigated whether deserved or not. It should have spooked my fiancé but Pappy's allure was too strong.

Before Aunt Estelle returned to Charlottesville, she and I made several trousseau shopping trips to Memphis, spending Pappy's money with abandon and having a fine time doing it.* She was recognized in every store. *Hello, Mrs. Faulkner. Let me find the manager.* In minutes he or she would appear. *It's so good to see you, Mrs. Faulkner. We have a wonderful new line of short coats in your colors. . . .* "Today, we're shopping for my niece," Aunt Estelle said. "She will be married in November." We never had to wait to be waited on.

We spent hours watching models showing suits, cocktail dresses, daytime wear (this was the '50s), kid gloves in short, medium, and opera length with buttons at the wrists, and hats, heels, and handbags to match every costume. Our decisions were lengthy and very pleasant as we sipped coffee. We got to know each other very well on these excursions. Just the two of us.

Aunt Estelle could be an entertaining raconteur with a cutting sense of humor. One afternoon in the shoe department of Goldsmith's, as I took off my heels, rubbing my aching toes and complaining in a whisper how my feet hurt, she corrected my use of the plural. "A lady's *foot* hurts, Dean, perhaps from dancing the night away or turning an ankle as she is helped down from a carriage, but both of them never hurt at the same time," she said. "Remember, there is only one glass slipper."

When the bridesmaid dress model appeared in a royal blue brocade satin cocktail dress with fitted waist, scoop neckline, and three-quarter-length sleeves, I said quickly—before she reached where we were sitting—"That's fine. We need four in

---

*The statute of limitations on Pappy's newspaper ads refusing to assume her debts had long since expired.

these sizes . . ." and I reeled off the dress sizes of my brides-maids. Aunt Estelle looked at me in astonishment. She knew how much I hated royal blue. Not only can I not wear the color, which makes me look jaundiced, it's best that I not be in the same room with someone who does. That's when she knew that the marriage meant nothing to me. She gave me a sympathetic smile. "I think I understand," she said. "I have been there myself."

After Aunt Estelle left for Charlottesville, Wese and I moved into Rowan Oak to give Nannie some much-needed peace and quiet. For months Pappy, Wese, and I did little but prepare for the wedding. Pappy, my wedding planner extraordinaire, threw himself into the arrangements down to the last detail.

It was a happy, peaceful time for everyone. Our schedule did not change from day to day. Pappy fixed his own breakfast and ate in the kitchen. After he read the Ann Landers column in the paper, we met in the library over coffee to plan the dinner menu and our dinner guests.

Each morning he named the same guests: "That redheaded boy" (Tommy Barksdale) and "Miz Coers." Often Miss Kate was included. Then we planned the menu and made grocery lists. I phoned to extend the invitations and we were off to the post office to collect my wedding presents, followed by a trip to the grocery store. Pappy never drank on Monday, in those days, so *nobody* drank on Mondays. In place of alcohol we enjoyed elaborate desserts. It was a beautifully settled routine.

When Pappy was in an exceptionally good mood, usually any day but Monday, he would make up parlor games in the library after guests had arrived. "If you had to be any wife of Henry the Eighth, Miz Coers, which would you be and why?" Or, "Mr. Barksdale," he'd say, watching Tommy squirm. "Which would you rather be, Attila the Hun or Nero? You may need to freshen your drink for that one." From there, he might call on the group to name our favorite horses. Someone always chose Bucephalus or Dan Patch. Trigger and Traveler were banned due to overuse. The games would go on into dinner, and over coffee and nightcaps and more nightcaps, depending on who was playing and how well.

Before bedtime when I came downstairs to say good night, he would be sitting in his favorite chair in his blue pajamas, smoking his pipe and reading Shakespeare or the Bible or Melville or a whodunit. He'd look up and say, "What are you reading?"

Though Pappy and I never talked about his work, I'd begun reading him in high school. I don't remember which year I read which book but over time I grew to love Pappy's Yoknapatawpha and its people, in spite of or because of my closeness to them. I loved their names: Miss Rosa Coldfield, Joe Christmas, Boon Hogganbeck, all of the Snopeses—Montgomery Ward, I.O., Flem—Colonel Sartoris, Jackson and Longstreet Fentry, and, of course, Ikkemotubbe.

He had always directed my coursework at Ole Miss, making sure that I studied "courses that matter," such as the English novel, eighteenth-century lit, the Romantic poets, Old English (so I could translate "Beowulf"), and every semester *one more* Shakespeare course if I could find one I hadn't already taken. He was disappointed that until I went abroad I could not speak French and had not read the Russians. He filled these educational gaps from his library at Rowan Oak.

At his insistence I was reading the Russians that fall: Gogol's *Dead Souls*, Turgenev's *Fathers and Sons*. Just then I happened to be reading Pasternak's *Doctor Zhivago*. I had recently given him J. D. Salinger's *Nine Stories*. His favorite was "For Esmé—With Love and Squalor."

"Where's Salinger going to end up?" I asked, leaning against the door frame.

"Wherever he wants to."

"I guess so. G'night, Pappy."

"Good night, Dean, sleep well."

Before I reached the landing he hurried after me and called, "I've worked out the parking arrangements! We'll have numbered tickets. Hand them out one at a time. So each person will know where his car is—as soon as he matches up the ticket stub with the other half."

"Who's going to hand out the tickets?"

"We'll work that out later. 'Night."

Soon the wedding parties began: showers, teas, dinner parties, cocktail parties, luncheons, and picnic suppers. When we stayed in, we had company. There were few quiet evenings at home, but on the night of October 23, 1958, I set the table for three: Wese, Pappy, and me. The phone rang during dinner. I knew Pappy would ignore it. He always did and expected us to follow his lead. "Please, Pappy, let me get that." I was expecting a call from one of my bridesmaids. He nodded. I walked into the pantry, shutting the door behind me as I picked up the receiver so I wouldn't have to look at Pappy as I chatted.

"Hello," said a famous voice. "This is Edward R. Murrow for William Faulkner. May I speak to him?"

I was speechless. This was one of the most recognizable voices on radio and TV.

Then, "Yes, sir, well, just one minute, sir. I'll see if I can get him to . . . I'll see if I can find him."

"Pappy." Back in the dining room next to his chair, I whispered, "It's Edward R. Murrow. He wants to speak to you."

He sat like a West Point cadet, not an inch of his body touching the back of his chair, his fork firmly in place in his left hand, his knife at the ready in his right. He stared straight ahead. "What does he want?"

Back to the pantry.

"Sir, *Mr. Faulkner*"—it occurred to me that it would serve me well not to be too closely identified with Pappy—"would like to know what your call is about."

"Pasternak has just won the Nobel Prize. I'd like a statement from Faulkner."

Back to the table.

Whispering, *"Doctor Zhivago.* Nobel. What do you think?"

Instantly, "Tell him it is a political hoax."

Back to the pantry.

"Sir, Mr. Faulkner says that I'm to tell you that he thinks it is a political hoax. Sir."

After a slight pause, "Thank you. Good night."

I returned to the table. There was no further mention of the phone call.

The next Friday, our wedding caravan left for a round of parties in Jackson. Pappy, Colonel Baker, and Miss Kate in one car, Jayne Coers, Wese, and me in the other. Pappy was in high spirits from the time we left Oxford until we returned Sunday night. He was surrounded by attentive, near-worshipful young people who clung to him, hanging on every word. At a dinner party Saturday, where whiskey and wine flowed and the food was extraordinarily good, Pappy was caught up in a conversation with a retired general and his attractive wife and daughter about his experiences in WWI. Expecting a repeat of the "silver plate in the head" story, I had moved away from the group surrounding him when they exploded into laughter.

"What a wonderful joke. Tell it again, please, so everyone can hear. Hurry up, y'all." A young man shouted, "Pappy" (as he was to everyone that evening) "is going to tell it again."

A British ladies' club, Pappy began, had invited a WWI flying ace to speak. The officer, who had recently returned from a tour of duty at the front, began talking cautiously, then encouraged by their nods and smiles, warmed to his tale. "I spotted the Fokkers before they saw me, and climbed above them. I dived with one of the Fokkers in my sights. I was just about to fire when bullets ripped through the cockpit, and I saw Fokkers to the left, Fokkers to the right, Fokkers on my tail. . . . " The club president held up her hand and explained that a Fokker was a fighter plane of German manufacture. "Oh, no, ma'am," the pilot said quickly, "those fokkers were *Messerschmitts*."

I don't think it bothered him at all that the state dignitaries in Jackson ignored his visit. Early Sunday morning Colonel Baker drove him around town. Pappy was all turned out in a double-breasted gray suit and black bowler hat later made famous by the Cartier-Bresson photographs at West Point. They toured the old and new capitol buildings then went to the governor's mansion, but they did not venture inside. If Pappy had been expecting an invitation to meet with the governor or the pleasure of turning it down, none was forthcoming. Only Edward R. Murrow, it seemed, wanted to hear from him.

Shortly before my wedding Pappy decided I ought to know more about my family history. One night when we were alone in the library he began to talk of our Scotch-Irish heritage: McAlpine and Murry. He described our tartan and reminded me that he had a skirt made for me from the plaid when I was a child. He repeated our family motto (adding the qualifier, I think): "Fast in battle—especially in retreat." As to our "Falconer" ancestors, he was not content with their having been ordinary falcon handlers. No, they were "keepers of the king's falcons."

This may have been true for the Butler side of our family. As the Earls of Ormond, Butlers were Lords Lieutenant in Ireland down to the time of James II. After he was deposed in 1688, most of the Butlers remained loyal to the Stuarts and thus suffered the loss of their estates. Some became mercenaries and served with distinction in the armies of France, Spain, and Germany. In America, Major General Richard Butler fought in the Revolutionary War, and five of his sons served under Washington. Lafayette was reported to have said, "Whenever I want anything well done, I'll get a Butler to do it."

Pappy was nursing an after-dinner bourbon as he spoke of our ancestry. My mind began to wander when he came to the potato famine that drove our ancestors across the Atlantic. I drifted away from the sound of his voice. I can't say how much I regret this lack of concentration. Cho Cho once said it was a shame all of us did not walk around with a pad and pencil. A tape recorder would have been even better, if we'd known how to make one work.

The days before the wedding flew by. Then it was upon us. All the men in the bridal party were splendidly turned out in their morning coats. My bridesmaids, one from each period in my life—Sheila, Little Rock; Alice, Ole Miss; Cynthia, my new sister-in-law; Sandra, lifelong friend—actually liked the dreaded royal blue dresses because they complemented the rich colors at St. Peter's Episcopal Church. With her magic buttonhook Miss Kate somehow got me into Jill's eighteen-inch wedding dress. Ten days before the wedding I'd gone on a crash diet so my hand-me-down wedding gown would fit.

Pappy gave me away in marriage. As we stood at the back of St. Peter's awaiting our cue from the organist I glanced at him. Eyes shining, the tiny wrinkles in his face smoothed out, he was a happy man. At that moment I realized that I could see over his head even though I had chosen the lowest heels I could find—one-fourth-inch French heels. When we went down the aisle together I slumped until I practically had curvature of the spine, though I needn't have worried. Once again there was no competition for star of the show. Every eye in the church was on Pappy. He was radiant. Yet when I stood in front of the minister and said, "I will," my life as I knew it was over.

Afterward at the champagne reception at Rowan Oak, Pappy stood at the head of the receiving line. One of the few pictures in existence of him smiling shows him tirelessly greeting wedding guests. That photograph now hangs in the entrance hall at Rowan Oak. Once the reception was over, he and Wese and Tommy Barksdale collected flowers from the church, went to the cemetery, and laid them on Dean's grave. Pappy had fulfilled his promise to my father. He looked at the marker he had chosen for Dean and said, "She is married, now. I have done what I thought would please you, my brother. Let us wish her every happiness. Forever." Then he asked Tommy to drive him and Wese back to Rowan Oak.

18

My Last Year at Home

S HORTLY AFTER THE FESTIVITIES, THE WISH I HAD MADE BE-
fore my marriage ("If only we could have the wedding and
then go our separate ways!") came true.

My brand-new husband, a second lieutenant in the air force,
was assigned to duty in Japan. One month after we were married
he left the United States for a year's tour of duty in Sapporo. I
moved in with Nannie, assuming I'd be joining him shortly after
the first of the year. On December 31, 1958, I received his letter
informing me there would be no Japanese sojourn for me. His
year's tour was classified "Remote," meaning no dependents allowed. He'd be returning to the States in twelve months.

I was filled with disappointment, not at the thought of missing my husband, but at missing an opportunity to live somewhere I'd never been.

Uncle Jack had come up from Mobile to check on Nannie
and was staying with us for a few days. Since Pappy was in Virginia, there would be no traditional New Year's Eve champagne
toast at Rowan Oak. At five thirty, the three of us walked up to
the square to Mrs. Winter's diner, Nannie in hat and gloves,
carrying her purse, Jack in his usual coat and tie and braces. Secure in his jacket pocket were his pouch of Bull Durham, cigarette papers, and box matches. You could smoke everywhere in
those days.

The square was deserted and quiet. A rare, lonely firecracker went off somewhere. The combination dry-goods store–diner was the only restaurant open. We had to be there before Mrs. Winter closed at six. Customers could sit at stools at the long counter and watch her cook hamburgers or at one of the few tables placed next to shelves of kitchen matches, mustard, Kleenex and Kotex, boxes of number two pencils and notebook paper, quarts of vinegar and Blue Plate mayonnaise. The tables were covered with cheap oilcloth in floral patterns, all different. We chose a table and sat down. There were paper napkins in a metal holder. We were the only diners in the dimly lighted store. The air smelled of grease. Mrs. Winter's specialties were fried peach pies and cheeseburgers. Actually, that was the entire menu. "I'll have a cheese-boiger!" Nannie declared as if she had a choice.

She and Pappy, as far back as I can remember, always used the same idiosyncratic pronunciation for certain words. For example, in any word containing an *r* preceded by a vowel, such as "word," the *r* vanished, replaced by a diphthong that made "word" sound like *woid* and "verb" become *voib*. "Worth" became *woith*. "Earth" was *oith*. "Purse" was *poise*, and so on. They also consistently, and for their own amusement, used the third person plural "don't" in place of the singular, as in, "He don't care; she don't know." It was their private code or patois, their conversations liberally sprinkled with irregular plural verbs, or *voibs*. I don't know why.

I hadn't said anything about my letter, but as I moped my way through supper, it was obvious that something was wrong. Just as we cut into the peach pies, which Nannie adored, I blurted out my news. The two of them were sympathetic and determined to cheer me up. "What will I do for a whole year?" I complained, relishing my self-pity, imagining my pretty new wedding presents (china and silver and crystal, tablecloths, bed linens and monogrammed towels) packed away for months. Even the thought of practical items such as kitchen utensils lying unused made me sad.

"You'll find something to do," they assured me.

Within a week, Nannie went into high gear. She would see to it that I stayed busy. Under her direction I would hemstitch and monogram all of my linens: twelve sheets, twenty-four pillowcases, twelve guest towels, four sets of dinner napkins. We made a shopping trip to Morgan and Lindsey for embroidery hoops, needles, and skein upon skein of white embroidery thread—whose strands had to be carefully divided—plus many spools of plain white sewing thread. I was in the simple stitchery business for the next year, or maybe for life! I grew to loathe the monogram:

$$\mathscr{DMf}$$

After this, it would be years before I wanted to needlepoint or crochet.

When Pappy made a brief trip home (he was living in Charlottesville then) he joined Nannie's crusade to keep me busy. He offered to celebrate my twenty-third birthday with a dinner party at Rowan Oak. Oxford was still "dry," and Pappy's liquor supply having run out, he dispatched me to Memphis as his rum-runner. I delivered his handwritten list to his favorite liquor store near the Peabody, paid cash, and had cases of wine and booze loaded in the trunk. I also made a fast stop at his tobacco store, where the owner had Pappy's favorite blend of Dunhill tobacco; then at a specialty shop to buy imported orange marmalade and extra-bitter dark chocolate. I drove back to Mississippi like a bootlegger with the rear bumper almost dragging on the ground.

For my birthday Wese had given me a stereo set and a recording of "The 1812 Overture." After dinner, Pappy let me take the stereo out to the front gallery and plug it in with several extension cords. I played the "1812" and turned the volume up full bore. When the cannons began to boom, it sounded like General Whiskey Smith was back in town. The silence at Rowan Oak, rarely sullied by radio or record player, and never by television, resounded for the first and only time to loud music. Pappy smoked his pipe and listened, giving his tacit approval, then went back in the house. I stayed until the last cannon blast, and then my birthday rebellion was over.

The next day was payback for Pappy. I was to work the horses for him.

I like to smell horses. I like to hear them drink. I like the creak of leather saddles. I think riding clothes—jodhpurs and boots and black velvet hard hats and Pinque coats and rat catcher—are sexy. I like to read about horses and learn of their storied history. Pappy saw to it that as children we all knew the annual Derby winner's name, and about the great Dan Patch and Man O' War, and the legendary Traveler and Bucephalus. He told us about his having learned to jump in Canada, when as part of the RAF training all the cadets took the jumps bareback with their arms folded across their chests like Native Americans. Still, despite my family's tradition of horsemanship, I did not share their passion. I was fascinated by horses. I just didn't want to ride them.

Pappy had made a study of the relative intelligence of animals and enjoyed pointing out the disparity between the various species. "Nobody would ever be able to sit a horse if it wasn't broke and dumb," he said. "A creature that big would have his way every time because it can smell fear, but it don't because it don't have any sense." Chickens, he allowed, were one of the few species dumber than horses. "The smartest ones of all—some of them smarter than we are—are the coyotes and the pigs. Pigs, don't leave them out! I know you won't like this part, Dean, but I think dogs are overrated. Their desire to please makes them seem a lot brighter than they are. The best thing about dogs is that you can trust a man who loves one of them."

Pappy believed mules to be the most distinguished four-legged creatures on earth. He often said, "A mule will serve you patiently and without complaint and wait a lifetime for the opportunity to kick you once."

The morning after my noisy birthday celebration, Pappy announced his animal-control plan. He needed help working his horses, Tempy and Ginger. I was the help. Each afternoon at four, when it began to cool off, we headed for the stables. I exhausted my repertoire of prayers to the gods of weather, asking for tornado, hurricane, tsunami, or earthquake. The best I could summon was an occasional thunderstorm. My mother and Miss Kate frequently came to help take the horses through their workouts, with Pappy standing in the center of the paddock, riding crop in hand, putting us through our paces.

Miss Kate had her own mount, a Kentucky trotter named Rex, a big horse that stood over sixteen and a half hands. His coat was bitter chocolate and he had a disposition to match. A few weeks into our daily rides, Miss Kate rode up on Rex all turned out in a gray and salmon tweed riding jacket, soft salmon silk shirt with an ascot, gray jodhpurs, and the most expensive English riding boots to be had from Saks Fifth Avenue. I'd never felt dowdier in my jeans, flannel shirt, and tennis shoes.

I usually rode Ginger, the pretty little blond mare that Pappy had given to Andrew Price. She had a beautiful single-foot, as easy to ride as a rocking horse. Even I could sit her. But she was bad to bite. When she laid those ears back it meant *look out*. I would have done better with a little Dutch courage before the horseback riding. Each afternoon when we finished working the horses, I couldn't wait for our six o'clock cocktail hour on the east gallery.

Ginger and Andrew were town favorites. He rode her to the square every week, Ginger single-footing all the way, dwarfed by Andrew's size. He was very tall, and his long legs dangled below her belly, but he sat her as if a natural extension of the animal. On Saturday afternoons, they made their way from Rowan Oak up South Street, stopping first at Mr. Hall's blacksmith shop, where Ginger stood patiently as Andrew visited with the locals and purchased his weekly pint of Four Roses Bourbon.

Late one Saturday afternoon, we heard a commotion going on at Aunt Sue's house, one block south of Nannie's. I ran down the sidewalk just as a police car and ambulance pulled up. A crowd of neighbors were gathered around Andrew, flat on his back in the middle of the street, alive and well but out cold. Ginger stood next to him, right foreleg cocked, ears flattened, poised to protect her master. A one-man horse, she adored Andrew. The consensus was that Four Roses had caused him to lose his seat. Pappy was summoned. The ambulance took Andrew home to Rowan Oak. Pappy followed on Ginger. Andrew showed no ill effects and was in the paddock the next day getting Ginger ready for the Lions Club Horse Show.

One afternoon, I drove down to Rowan Oak to find Pappy waiting for me, along with Gerald, an Ole Miss student, an experienced rider who worked the horses for the sheer pleasure of it. When I got out of my car, Pappy motioned for me to follow him and Gerald to his jeep. He'd told me to dress for riding. I wore my usual jeans and tennis shoes, thinking I'd be sitting Ginger as usual. Instead, Pappy told me, "We're heading for Charlie Hathorne's farm. He's offered me a horse. I can't refuse. It's not a hunter or jumper, but Charlie says it *could be*. His name is Duke, and he likes to take jumps. He'll clear a tall blade of grass like it was a three-foot gate, Charlie said."

"How do you know when he's going to take off?" I asked.

"You don't." Pappy snorted. "That's what will make it interesting. I want you and Gerald to bring him in for me."

We pulled into Hathorne's drive. He had Duke tethered to the front gate next to a mounting block. There was a bridle on him but no saddle. The closer we got to him, the more skittish he became, and the bigger he seemed to get, sixteen to eighteen hands easy. Before we could mount, Pappy said, "See y'all at home in a bit." And he was gone.

The horse was dancing like crazy. He hadn't been ridden all winter. Gerald somehow got hold of an ear, bent it double, and clamped it between his teeth. Duke went to his knees. Instantly Gerald was on him. He reached out a hand for me and yanked me up behind him. I held on for dear life for the wild ride home. We galloped through Hathorne's woods, then the Ole Miss golf course, where more than one golfer saluted us with raised club, and then we plunged into Bailey's Woods, which were thick with vines, low branches, and treacherous thorns and thickets. *"Duck!"* Gerald shouted again and again. We flattened ourselves against Duke's back, as close as we could get. He was going at a ragged canter when we came up the driveway at Rowan Oak.

Pappy sat on the front steps, puffing his pipe, with the cheerful expression of a man who's getting a free horse. I, who had read Pappy's short story "Spotted Horses," knew that this horse wasn't *free*. Just as we rounded the curve before the stable, Duke began to crow-hop sideways, hoof crossing over hoof, twisting and turning like some kind of crazed merry-go-round creature. I held on as long as I could, then found myself sailing through the air. I landed on my backside in the thick grass with Pappy's *"Ride 'im, cowgirl!"* ringing in my ears.

He took his time walking over to check on me and also, I think, to get his merriment under control. "You're not even bleeding," he said. "Here, I'll give you a leg up and you can help Gerald get him to the barn and cool him down. He's a little the worse for wear."

What about *me*! I thought, but didn't say a thing. Gerald and I took turns riding Duke, this time with a saddle. It helped a little bit, but I would soon discover that Mr. Hathorne wasn't kidding when he said that Duke would jump a tall blade of grass.

Pappy cleared a riding trail through Bailey's Woods that summer. We rode it daily until the afternoon Miss Kate's horse stumbled and fell on her. She was not hurt but Pappy was terrified. We did not ride the trail again.

———

ONE AFTERNOON PAPPY appeared at Nannie's house with several yards of bandanna material. Red was his favorite color. I innocently asked what it was for.

"So you"—meaning Nannie and me—"can make me some kerchiefs to stuff up my sleeve to wipe off the blood when I'm riding," he said, severely pleased. He looked like a little boy. We did not share his enthusiasm, but we set about the cutting and hemming, and then hemstitched every handkerchief. From then on, he had one with him every time he came to call. I suspect that our sewing marathon was one of his projects to keep Nannie active and involved in his life.

Not long after this, we had plenty to do. Hollywood returned to Oxford. Vincente Minnelli was directing *Home from the Hill*, with Robert Mitchum, Eleanor Parker, George Hamilton, and George Peppard. The town went star-crazy, everybody young and old lining up to be extras. I became an extra in a christening scene and was thrilled to be earning minimum wage. We uncomplaining extras would walk around courthouse, church, or other locations for eight hours at a stretch.

They filmed "my scene" at our church, St. Peter's Episcopal. My instructions were to "wear something you'd wear to church plus a big straw hat," and to be at the church by 9 a.m. Saturday morning. I borrowed a hat from Nannie and presented myself to the clipboard lady who was sitting on a tall stool at the door, checking off the names of extras and advising us which pew to sit in. I was told to take my seat in the middle of the pew three rows from the rear.

I sat down in my pew and glanced at the altar. There stood our priest, Duncan Gray, talking with director Minnelli and Miss Kate. She was all decked out in a stunning burnt orange linen sheath and matching pillbox, looking like a million dollars. We were about to film the ending of the christening scene, when people left the church. Minnelli called for silence on the set, then "Action!" Miss Kate stood up in her pew, second from the front. She moved into the aisle, genuflected to the altar, and then turned and walked slowly down the aisle to the back of the church straight into the camera. Because she had told them she'd acted professionally, they'd made her an "extra extraordinaire." Miss Kate was on camera for what seemed at least two minutes. She loved it.

Minnelli himself went a little nuts trying to meet the reclusive Pappy. We heard that he spent hours traipsing through Bailey's Woods hoping to catch a glimpse of "The Man." If asked I would have told him that Pappy had gone back to Virginia for a few weeks. But when Parker and Peppard came calling on Nannie, perhaps hoping Pappy might be there, I wasn't about to tell. They delivered an invitation to her from Minnelli asking her to join him on the set.

The next day they were shooting in the cemetery, not far

from the Falkner family plot with its distinctive obelisk in the center. They sent a car for Nannie. By the time I got there, on foot, a large crowd had gathered. I stood with everyone else behind a barrier watching from a distance. There she sat, my grandmother, in the director's chair, the one with "Minnelli" printed on the back, chatting away with her fellow celebrities. One of her favorite poems was "Requiem," by Robert Louis Stevenson.

> *Here he lies where he long'd to be;*
> *Home is the sailor, home from the sea,*
> *And the hunter home from the hill.*

I wondered if she were quoting the poem to Minnelli, who seemed to hang on her every word. She looked glamorous in the black eye patch she wore tied around her head. I clung to the fence trying to get her attention. All to no avail.

After the shoot was over and the film crew and actors were gone, Oxford settled back into its quiet rhythms of small-town living. For Pappy, the highlight of the summer, however, was the annual Lions Club Horse Show. People brought fine horses from all over Mississippi, from Memphis and Germantown, and a few from Kentucky.

Pappy decided not to enter Tempy in the competition, saying she was "too green." I suspect this was because he had been spoiled by riding to hounds in Virginia. There were two days of competition and many classes: junior and senior equitation, in which owners and some professional riders showed their horses; Tennessee walkers; gaited; walking; hunters and jumpers; pacers; even Shetland ponies pulling lavishly decorated four- and two-wheeled carts; and the finale, the grooms' class.

The shows were held in a large pasture south of town where

horse and cattle barns were located. An arena was set up under portable streetlights, ringed by makeshift box seats, divided into separate areas by rope barriers. Each box held eight or ten seats. Pappy reserved one every year next to Miss Kate's box. We went early and stayed late, fortified by Pappy's gin and tonics and Aunt Estelle's picnic suppers.

The children's classes showed early in the day. In late afternoon came the costume classes. Riders, mostly female, all riding sidesaddle, showed their beautiful horses and elaborate period costumes: plumed hats with ostrich feathers, velvet riding habits. "It aint easy to sit a horse sidesaddle," Pappy said. They were elegance in motion. Only the jumpers and hunters could match them, Pappy said.

We pored over the programs listing riders and mounts, and predicted who would win. Pappy made sure I filled out score sheets for each event and checked my scores against his. Each participant was announced by the emcee over a loudspeaker. All eyes were on the judges' box as the winners were named. Pappy always had definite opinions on the judges' selections. He was partial to the jumpers and hunters, paying serious attention to possible "tics," and vented his frustration quietly in our box when the judges did not award a top prize to his favorite. The trophies included loving cups, silver trays, or blue ribbons.

The box seats were always full. Friends visited from box to box. We saw everybody we wanted to see.

Though Andrew and Ginger never won the grooms' class, they were crowd favorites. Pappy, Aunt Estelle, and I could hardly wait for Andrew to enter the ring. Here came that pretty little horse ridden by the big man in starched overalls and work shirt with a brightly colored bow tie. That night Andrew sported a pair of brand-new size thirteen white high-top tennis shoes. We stood and clapped when he rode by.

Pappy invited his mother to have dinner at Rowan Oak at least once every week. Occasionally she would go. One afternoon late that summer she accepted his invitation. Wese was in town and Pappy had invited Tommy Barksdale, who was also one of Nannie's favorites.

Tommy drove us down to Rowan Oak at twilight. Pappy led us around the house to the east garden where he had placed wrought-iron lawn chairs around his white wheeled tea cart. There was enough breeze to make the evening pleasant. Birds were having a free-for-all in the birdbath in the garden. Pappy began mixing drinks in a large glass pitcher. To placate Nannie, who disapproved of alcohol, he announced that he was making lemonade. He worked off to the side, his body turned so as to shield the ingredients from us. Shortly he produced a second pitcher from underneath the tea cart. "Lemonade?" He poured the second pitcher into tumblers filled with ice. In four of them, he squeezed a suspicious wedge of lime. The fifth and last glass he handed to Nannie, limeless and noticeably murky compared to our see-through gin and tonics. Of course, she knew the difference.

After dinner, I invited Pappy to join us at the drive-in movie. "What's on?" he said, moderately interested. With a straight face, Tommy said, "A movie I think you'd like, sir. It's a rerun. I missed it the first time it came to town. It's called *The Long Hot Summer*."

Pappy said, without a hint of a smile, "Thank you, Mr. Barksdale. Perhaps next time it comes round."

In early September, I went out to my old sorority house to watch the Miss America pageant. One of my sorority sisters, Mary Ann Mobley, was Miss Mississippi, an attractive, smart, talented girl who had already won some preliminary competitions. We felt that she had a very good chance of winning. I wanted to share in the excitement with friends, and besides, neither Pappy nor Nannie owned a TV set.*

Mary Ann made the top ten, then the top five, while we, her sorority sisters, went wild. We shrilled like banshees when she was crowned Miss America, 1959.

The next morning I could hardly wait to get to Rowan Oak to share the good news with Pappy. Nannie hadn't seemed too impressed when I told her at breakfast. I burst into the library. "Pappy, Pappy, where are you?"

He came out of his office. "What is it, Dean?"

"My sorority sister Mary Ann Mobley won the Miss America contest last night. Can you believe it!"

"So," he said, puffing the word out. It was his standard ejaculation, which could have meant "I see," or "All right," or "Well now," or "Who gives a rat's?" Then he said, "Well, it's nice to know somebody has finally done something to put Mississippi on the map."

He went back to his typewriter. I went home to Nannie. The Miss America pageant was never mentioned again.

Later that fall I took up hunting. I'd inherited my grandfather's single-shot .22 rifle and a .410 over-and-under shotgun. For some reason Wese bought me a .218 Bee varmint rifle with a scope. I spent many predawn hours at Pappy's farm,

---

*Pappy had no use for television except for the sitcom *Car 54, Where Are You?* I couldn't understand why he liked it, except possibly that to a cosmopolite like Pappy it came across as theater of the absurd. Every Sunday night you could find him at Professor Jim Silver's house on Faculty Row, watching *Car 54*. I've often wondered if Jim and his wife, Dutch, liked the show, or if they were just being good hosts. Of course, they may have been highly amused at Pappy's continual chuckling. When he laughed, it was through his nose in subdued snorts.

"Greenfield," which was ten miles from Papa Hale's farm. I was comfortable being in the woods where I'd roamed as a child. Like my father, I hunted whatever was in season: dove, quail, deer. Squirrels were always fair game. Chrissie would clean and cook any game we brought in—with one exception. She would not allow us to bring a dove into her kitchen. She believed mourning doves held the dead souls of human beings. To kill one was a desecration. I never saw a dove in the kitchen and certainly never ate one at Rowan Oak. Chrissie made a profound impression on me, and apparently on Pappy as well, for I never saw him eat a dove, at least not when he was at home. The fact is, though, I didn't really want to kill anything and am proud to say I never bagged my limit in any season. My single trophy was a large black spider that sat in the middle of a huge web begging to be a bull's-eye. I got him with my .22 from a respectable distance. Pappy allowed that it was a terrific shot.

After the hunt Pappy taught me to break down my guns and clean them. We worked side by side in the kitchen at Rowan Oak. I found unexpected pleasure in learning which part went where and how to use a cleaning rod and swabs, and I enjoyed sharing the companionable silence, scented by the sharp, clean smell of gun solvent mixed with Pappy's pipe smoke.

Before deer season was over, my husband came home from Japan and we moved to South Carolina. Looking back, I realize that the year I had dreaded turned out to be one of my most cherished, for it was my last year at home with Nannie and Pappy.

A year later, when my first child, Diane, was born at Shaw Air Force Base, Nannie wrote saying she was ecstatically happy and assured me that my baby girl's blue eyes and blond hair would turn brown ("like all the Faulkner babies") before she was three months old. This letter was Nannie's last. A few weeks later Wese telephoned to tell me she was dead. She'd had a massive stroke and lived only a few days in the hospital. She made Pappy promise not to let the doctors put her on life support and left instructions to be buried in a plain pine box right after her death so that she could "return to earth as soon as possible." Pappy obeyed her wishes. Her funeral was small and private, held in her living room, the casket placed next to the French doors just as Murry's and Dean's had been. She was buried in the Falkner family plot. I was unable to attend the funeral. She had lived as long as she could. She had the comfort of knowing my child and I were safe and sound. I live with the ache of knowing she had never held my baby.

Earlier that summer Nannie had copied down three inscriptions from memory and left them on my dresser without explanation: one from Goethe, another from Robert Louis Stevenson, and an old Irish blessing. I didn't know why she wanted me to have them. I think I do now.

> *May the wind be at your back,*
> *May the road rise up to meet you,*
> *May God hold you in the palm of his hand.*

19

Pappy's Funeral

THE TELEPHONE RANG SHORTLY BEFORE DAWN JUST AS MY baby was waking up for the day. It was Friday, July 6, 1962. I was staying with my mother at Nannie's. I heard the urgency in her voice. "No," she said. "No. We'll come right away."

She sat on the edge of the bed, patting my shoulder, looking away from me. "Pappy died. Last night. We need to go down home." I could barely hear her over the whirr of the oscillating floor fans. I did not want to hear. Not Pappy. I dressed hurriedly, awkward in my sixth month of pregnancy, and called a babysitter for my eighteen-month-old daughter. I was as ready to go as I could be. The thought came to me that July 6 was the Old Colonel's birthday.

We drove down South Street and turned onto Garfield. There were few cars. As we approached the gate at Rowan Oak, a single police car blocked the entrance. This was the first time the gate was closed and we weren't allowed to use the driveway. We had to park at Miss Kate's. Other than the single police car, nothing seemed to be out of the ordinary. It would be just as hot as it had been the day before and the day before that. Yet the whole world had changed.

We met my cousin Jimmy Faulkner halfway up the driveway and I shed the first of many tears to come. He told us that Jill was coming on a chartered flight from Charlottesville. Cho

Cho and her husband Bill were flying from Caracas. Jack was driving up from Mobile. Jimmy's father, John, was in the library working out funeral arrangements. The Faulkners were coming together again.

As we walked up the driveway I looked at the house that had known so much joy and sorrow. If the walls could speak what tales they could tell. The sand crunched under my sandals. In the dry heat of summer the heavy scent of cedars and honeysuckle was stronger than usual. Brambles and wild blackberries had grown up along the drive. In the garden off the east gallery Aunt Estelle's spring flowers had bloomed out, the iris and peonies along with the six-foot-tall Cape Jasmines.

Pappy was gone, and I felt like a stranger in his house. I went upstairs to see Aunt Estelle. She sat on the bed in her room, more fragile than ever. She opened her arms to me. "He loved you dearly," she said. We held each other and wept.

The hearse from the funeral home delivered Pappy's body in a plain wooden casket almost identical to the one in which Nannie had been buried, and one that he would have chosen for himself. For some members of the family, mainly Aunt Estelle's sister Dot Oldham, it was not good enough. It "just didn't look right." The funeral home employees had barely placed Pappy on a bier in front of the fireplace in the parlor when Dot, ignoring anybody else's opinion, ordered Pappy returned to the funeral home where she would select a "proper" casket for him.

I was just coming downstairs when I looked out the screen door and saw Miss Emily and Mr. Phil Stone walking slowly up the brick walk to pay their condolences to Aunt Estelle. At that very moment the offending casket was wheeled out the front door to the waiting hearse, which then drove away at an unseemly speed. As I watched, the Stones froze, whispered to each other, turned their backs, and walked at a steady pace to their car.

No one would have appreciated this Addie Bundren moment more than Pappy. Dot went to the funeral home and selected a "proper" casket. She and Pappy were back at Rowan Oak within the hour.

We Faulkners usually bury our dead quickly and with little fanfare, so that we are able, as Nannie said, to return to earth as soon as possible. This was different.

By midafternoon Friday the word had spread all over Oxford. Friends appeared in swarms bearing casseroles, fried chicken, hams, baskets of biscuits, deviled eggs, potato salad, cherry tomatoes stuffed with crab meat, cakes, pies, cobblers. I stood like a statue amid this flow of visitors. I had retreated to a sad, lonely place all my own. I was beyond reach. Dot, Wese, and Chrissie manned the kitchen and dining room, setting out a funeral buffet on the dining table and sideboard.

Pappy made the six o'clock news. The gate to the driveway now held back journalists and photographers representing national and international publications. They camped out within yards of Pappy's "Private Keep Out" sign. William Styron, on assignment for *Life*, was one of the few invited into the house. We recognized him as a writer, not a journalist. He had flown down from New York with Pappy's publisher, Bennett Cerf.

A dozen policemen with walkie-talkies stood at the front gate while others walked the perimeter of Bailey's Woods. To get past the police barricade your name had to be on a list sanctioned by Aunt Estelle and Dot. If the police didn't recognize you, they radioed the house and a family member walked down to verify your identity. Such an assault on the family's privacy in a place as graceful, tranquil, and ordered as Rowan Oak was surreal. As I left the house to go see about my baby, I looked back. It was a circus. Too many lights, too many cars, too many voices, too many people.

Friday night had been so hectic that Jimmy, John, and Jack agreed to meet with representatives of the media at the Mansion restaurant to answer questions about funeral plans. They made it clear that no member of the press would be allowed inside the house at any time. Then they amended the statement that Pappy had died at Rowan Oak and admitted that he'd died of coronary thrombosis at Wright's Sanatorium in Byhalia. Since this was where Pappy had often gone to dry out, the first statement had been issued to counter rumors that he'd been drinking heavily. They were learning on the fly to be spokesmen for William Faulkner. Then they read Aunt Estelle's statement pleading for privacy: "Until he is buried he belongs to the family. After that he belongs to the world."

Night and day the phone calls, wires, cables, and flowers poured in, an overwhelming display of grief at the loss of this man whom I loved so very much. My hands shook as I held the telegram from the White House containing President and Mrs. John F. Kennedy's condolences.

The funeral service was held at Rowan Oak in the front parlor at two o'clock Saturday afternoon. About fifty people packed the room, spilling over into the front hall and the dining room. The heat was intense. Women in summer dresses were fanning themselves, patting their faces with lace handkerchiefs, not merely perspiring—sweating. Besides family members there were close friends, like Miss Kate Baker and Jayne Coers. The Reverend Duncan Gray read from the Book of Common Prayer and Psalm 46: *God is our refuge and our strength, a very present help in trouble.* At the conclusion of the service we recited the Lord's Prayer.

The funeral cortege formed and began its slow, measured journey to the square, then north to St. Peter's Cemetery. Tar oozed through cracks in the asphalt. As the motorcade passed the courthouse, townspeople and university students silently lined the streets. Every store along the funeral route was temporarily closed. The *Oxford Eagle* had distributed leaflets early that morning:

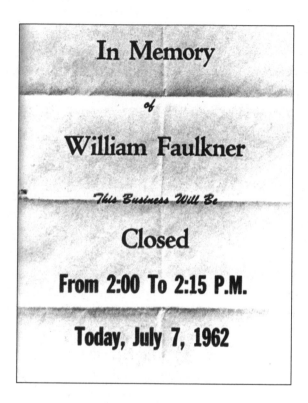

In Memory

of

William Faulkner

This Business Will Be

Closed

From 2:00 To 2:15 P.M.

Today, July 7, 1962

Pappy was the first Faulkner to be buried in the newly opened section of St. Peter's. He lies under a fine oak tree, just below the hill where his ancestors are buried. The inscription on his tombstone reads "Beloved, go with God."

After a brief graveside ceremony, family and friends returned to the house, where Chrissie and I were waiting. I had intended to go to the ceremony but as I walked to Wese's car, I realized that I could not control my grief. I stayed home and wept. Faulkners do not cry in public. Before anyone returned we had emptied all the ashtrays and cleaned up the silverware, plates, bowls, and glasses. Chrissie washed and I dried. Then we replenished the buffet. Doing something with my hands was reassuring, and my salvation. I went back to check the library. A wooden statue of Don Quixote on the large table presided over the room. All was silence.

I was remembering the last times Pappy and I were together, before July 4. My first husband was on a tour of duty in Southeast Asia and I had moved temporarily to Oxford from Shaw Air Force Base with my baby girl, Diane, and my eighty-pound boxer, Beauregard. I was expecting my second child that fall.

We spent many an afternoon at Rowan Oak that summer of '62. Pappy and Aunt Estelle were in residence and it was the perfect place for my toddler to explore. One afternoon, Pappy had Andrew bring around one of his gentlest horses. He wanted Diane to see a horse up close. He picked her up so she could pat him and feel his mane. On another visit, Pappy was waiting for us on the gallery holding a small American flag for Diane. He took her down to the paddock to see his horses. They walked hand in hand, Diane turning to wave the little flag at me.

A few days later, toward the end of June, when we went down home to plan our July 4 celebration, we found Pappy in bed, downstairs in his office. He had suffered a wicked fall that morning while riding his jumper, Stonewall. He was in great pain. Wese was holding Di, and as he reached up to take her, he winced and eased back on the pillows. He was hurting too much to hold her. "Let's have the picnic at Kate's," he said. "I'll be better by then."

When we left, he waved a gentle good-bye. I never saw him again.

After the funeral, Aunt Estelle and Jill came home and went

straight upstairs. I went out on the east gallery to cool off. The hundred-degree heat was stifling. It was hard to breathe. Pregnant women are hotter than any other people on earth. Rowan Oak had no air-conditioning downstairs, and fans did little more than move the air around. One of the first to take Dot's suggestion that the men remove their coats was William Styron. I had read *Lie Down in Darkness* and was pleased to meet him and tell him how much I admired his work. There were perhaps fifty people in the house but conversations were muted and respectful. It was very quiet. Joining me on the gallery was Shelby Foote, who had wandered out to smoke. "It's so hot in there," he observed, "you have to walk sideways." I introduced myself and we sat in comfortable silence. I noticed that his pipe smoke smelled like Pappy's Dunhill tobacco. And like Pappy, Foote was first and foremost a courtly gentleman. His hoarse, whispery voice with southern rhythms was familiar and reassuring. It was as if Pappy had sent him. I would have said anything to keep him talking.

We were joined on the gallery by a young man who attended Ole Miss and who regularly helped Pappy work his horses. Shelby had removed his seersucker jacket and tie but the young man was still suited up. I offered him a chair and the opportunity to remove his coat. "No, thank you," he replied. "I want to ask Mr. Foote some questions about the war."

"Southeast Asia?" I asked.

"No, ma'am, *The War.*" He launched into a lecture on the Lost Cause, so pro-Confederacy, pro-slavery, and pro–Old South that he could have been mourning the Confederate dead at Vicksburg or Shiloh. I was stunned. Foote, the greatest Civil War historian I ever knew, walked over to the brick wall and knocked the ashes out of his pipe. Turning to the young man, he was a study in controlled fury. "Sir," he said, "I have always believed that the young should be liberal, and the very young like you should be the most liberal of all. You, sir, are so conservative that I'm surprised you don't walk backward. Come, Dean, let us repair to the dining room." And we went inside leaving the young man speechless.

It was the likes of Foote and Styron who got me through that awful day. I went upstairs to say good-bye to Jill and Aunt Estelle. They planned to fly back to Charlottesville on Sunday. Aunt Estelle was sleeping. Jill was dressed for bed. She looked like a little girl in her pink seersucker robe and bare feet. "I wasn't at the graveside because . . . ," I began.

"I know," she said. "It's harder to keep from crying when you're pregnant. I got through it because I was seated directly in front of the most garish wreath I've ever seen. Ever. Gold and purple plastic grapes sprinkled with gold glitter and tied together with yards and yards of gold ribbon. Pappy would have found it patently absurd. I don't know who sent it, but I should find out and write a personal thank-you note."

"Jilly," I said. "Think about what you want from Nannie's. You should have the Butler portraits, especially the one of the little blond-haired girl that looks like you."

"I'll be in touch soon," she said gently. "Now go. We all need sleep. Pappy's worn us out again. Take care of you and your babies. G'night."

———

PAPPY WOULD HAVE been one hundred on September 25, 1997. Plans for celebrating his centennial were well under way two years in advance. William Beckwith, the sculptor from Taylor, Mississippi, was hired to render a likeness in bronze. Here the problems started. What would Pappy wear? Hatted or bare-headed? Seated or standing? A bust or full figure? And the biggest question of all: Where would they put him? On the courthouse square or at Rowan Oak? A whole lot of people had a whole lot of very strong opinions.

Most of the family agreed that if there had to be a statue—many preferring none at all—it should be placed at Rowan Oak to set Pappy's likeness amid the surroundings where he had lived in privacy and harmony. The men who proposed and paid for the statue—John Leslie, the former mayor, and Dr. Chester McLarty, Faulkner family physician and friend—wanted the statue placed in front of city hall for all the world to see. The board of aldermen was in general agreement. The statue would be good for tourism and bring people to the square where they would shop and buy souvenirs.

In August, as the centennial celebration neared, tempers heated up. Environmentalists learned that a healthy young magnolia growing at the south end of city hall was to be felled to make room for the statue. The *Oxford Eagle* was flooded with letters of protest, which doubled when the magnolia was unceremoniously cut down. Even Jill wrote from Charlottesville. She was opposed to the statue, as she felt sure Pappy would be, and the felling of the magnolia was "the crowning blow."

All to no avail.

On September 24, 1997, the day before the dedication of the statue, Beckwith invited Larry and me to a private viewing. Pappy had been stored in the basement of city hall for a week along with the city's Christmas decorations. We met Beckwith in the parking lot. It had been raining all day. He led us into a darkened storage area. The statue was draped under a tarpaulin, completely covered except for one rather arrogant bronze foot that poked out.

Beckwith carefully removed the canvas and the three of us stood in silence. In an inexplicable way it was like saying good-bye again. The bronze eyes under the rigid hat brim seemed to stare out over the ramparts of infinity—as Pappy had written of the Old Colonel's statue at Ripley. I wasn't prepared for what I was feeling. My spine tingled and I was short of breath. We spoke in whispers until the physical plant manager came into the storage room, keys jangling, to report that the rain had let up. He barked orders into a cell phone. "We're moving him now. Let's go!"

Three inmates from the city jail appeared in bright orange prison uniforms with "Property of Oxford—Lafayette County" stenciled on them. They pushed the bronze statue onto its trolley. Pappy weighed five hundred pounds and the bench five hundred. I agreed with one of the inmates' observations that Pappy was one heavy mother. With the sculptor himself helping push the trolley, the statue moved up the sidewalk, massive, majestic, as if they were hauling not Pappy but all his people— Compsons, Snopeses, De Spains—maybe even the fyce and the bear. The sun had come out.

As we rounded the corner a small crowd gathered to watch the statue, still hidden under canvas, being hauled into place. A shopkeeper, thinking to get a laugh, shouted, "What's the matter? Is he drunk?" Then seeing family members, he began to mumble apologies. Some things never change. (In high school my daughter Paige listened to an English teacher describe her great-uncle William as "just an old drunk who staggered around town with his pants unbuttoned." Paige didn't cry until she got home.)

The statue was positioned over bolts set in concrete in front of city hall, then lowered into place. The inmates were given a cigarette break. The sculptor accepted congratulations from well-wishers. A TV crew began filming. Standing on the sidewalk during all this activity, looking over the wrought-iron fence at the statue, I thought, Aunt Estelle was right, he belongs to the world.

The dedication of the statue took place the next afternoon. Out of family loyalty, Larry and I did not attend but gave a small cocktail party at our home for Shelby Foote, Willie Morris, and other guest speakers. The university was hosting its own party, a black-tie affair. All of our guests except one rushed off to attend. Foote settled into the bentwood rocker in the living room, tamped down the tobacco in his pipe, and asked for a bit more scotch. He said, "Have I told you about the first time I met your uncle?"

In 1938, Foote and his friend Walker Percy, both twenty-two, drove to Oxford for the express purpose of stopping at Rowan Oak. For some time Foote had wanted to meet William Faulkner, whom he admired and wanted to emulate. Percy, though a fan of Pappy's work, worried about barging in. What reason could they give for knocking on Faulkner's door? Could they claim to be lost? Foote decided he would ask Pappy where he could buy a copy of *The Marble Faun*, published in 1924 and long out of print. This excuse seemed awfully flimsy to Percy, who said he would wait in the car. Foote walked up the driveway of Rowan Oak and was met by the roaring pack of terriers, mutts, and hunting dogs. He "waded through them" and knocked on the door. To Foote's delight, "Mr. Faulkner" came outside and they walked the grounds talking together. The fact that Foote was from the Mississippi delta was a happy coincidence. Pappy had just completed a book "about your country down there" (*The Wild Palms*) and was in the mood to talk about his work. After a couple of exhilarating hours, Foote remembered Percy and asked Pappy to come to the car and meet him. Pappy obliged and was cordial to Percy and wished him and Foote good luck on their trip. The future literary lions went on their way energized and inspired. "We not only had spoken to your uncle," Foote fondly recalled, "he wished us well!"

Later that night we joined the main group at the Sizzler, a weathered, brown-bag catfish and steak house six miles east of Oxford. The restaurant overlooked a duck pond, a litter of puppies lived under the front stoop, and the interior was decorated with bowling trophies. I walked in on Shelby Foote's arm and liked it when people turned to look at the star of Ken Burns's Civil War series. He liked it, too.

Willie Morris had reserved a long table for our group of about two dozen, which included Judge Neal Biggers, baseball coach Jake Gibbs and his wife, Tricia, and Faulkner family friend Billy Ross Brown and his wife, Lynn. Shelby, a man who knew his trivia, sat by Jake, a former catcher for the New York Yankees, and began talking baseball.

After dinner the wine flowed and we sang "Happy Birthday" to Pappy, then someone started a WWI song and we launched a songfest that would do an Irish pub proud. When "Bye, Bye Blackbird" gave way to "Let the Rest of the World Go By" we sang romantic songs from World War II, honoring Pappy in a spontaneous, schmaltzy way. Shelby and I knew all the words. The Sizzler resounded with our finale, "Good Night, Sweetheart," as unseen diners sitting in other rooms joined in.

It's a shame that Bill Styron was not among the guest speakers at the centennial celebration. His voice would have added dignity and grace to the proceedings, and he and his beautiful wife, Rose, would have enjoyed our songfest. He had been a longtime admirer of Pappy's work, but they never met. When *Lie Down in Darkness* was published in 1951, Styron's work was compared to that of Faulkner. When Pappy died, Styron was the ideal choice to cover the funeral for *Life*. His article, "As He

Lay Dead: A Bitter Grief, " published on July 20, 1962, was the finest of all the tributes to Pappy, a haunting evocation of the grinding July heat, the town's outpouring of grief, and finally his own sense of loss, hard and unexpected, as the funeral cortege circled the courthouse and sweat-soaked policemen stood at attention with hats over their hearts. Oxford was a "stiller town" that afternoon. The courthouse and Confederate statue had loomed over so much of Faulkner's work, Styron wrote, "and now, for the first time this day, I am stricken by the realization that Faulkner is really gone. And I am deep in memory, as if summoned there by a trumpet blast."

———

I STILL MISS Pappy. The bond between us that began with the accident of my birth remains strong and unbroken. He and the gods still smile on me. I know that in the grand scheme of things his words will live forever. In writing this book I am sending him one last postcard.

Thank you, sir.
With love,
Dean

Epilogue

THE OLD FAULKNER CEMETERY PLOT AT ST. PETER'S IS FULL now: J.W.T. and Sallie Murry; the three tiny graves of the infant sons of Judge John and Aunt Sue; Pappy and Aunt Estelle's baby girl Alabama; Murry and Maud; Dean; Jack; my mother, Wese; and most recently, Dorothy "Dot" Falkner Dodson.

The early Oxford settlers buried their dead on the high ground at St. Peter's around a circle of cedars planted nearly two centuries ago. My family's twelve-grave plot surrounded by a wrought-iron fence lies close to the cemetery entrance next to one of the narrow lanes that wind past carefully marked family grave sites. Four marble steps set in a grassy incline lead down to a rusted gate. At the center of the plot a thirty-foot Italian marble obelisk bears the images of J.W.T. and Sallie in bas-relief on the north and south sides, marked "Father" and "Mother." "FALKNER" is engraved at the base of the pedestal.

The graves have identical twelve-by-twelve-inch headstones with names and dates. Only Dean's has an inscription. Instead of slabs, a five-inch-thick marble oblong covers each grave, joined at the bottom by footstones bearing the individual's initials. Formal, elegant, and meant to last. A row of dogwood trees stretches along the western boundary of the cemetery.

—

When I came back to Oxford in 1970, divorced and ready to start a new life, I moved into Nannie's house and enrolled in graduate school. The next year, Vicki's husband, Jim Black, died. They had lived in his native Caracas for several years, and Vicki had a daughter, Gillian, whom I had never seen. Wese and I met them at the Memphis airport, with Larry Wells, who would soon be my second husband. They were bringing Jim Black's body to be buried in St. Peter's Cemetery not far from Pappy's grave. Vicki and Cho Cho moved into Rowan Oak. At that time the house was overseen by the university and open to the public, but family members were allowed to stay there for short visits. It was October, my favorite month, when zinnias were still in bloom but it was chilly enough for the first fire of the season. Larry scavenged for wood; we had drinks in the library in front of the fire and Cho Cho's favorite meal—chicken livers on toast and fried bananas—in the dining room, the first dinner we'd had there in a very long time. We were all at home again. My children—Diane, twelve, Paige, ten, and Jon, six—were taken with their new little "cousin," Gillian. The sounds of their voices and laughter brought the old house back to life, upstairs and down, inside and out, from the stables and Mammy's cabin to Judith's magnolia out front. For a brief moment Rowan Oak was again a house of children.

I don't go to Rowan Oak very often anymore. For me, it is no longer a familiar and private place for Faulkners but a well-kept museum. Once I overheard a tourist, upon seeing Pappy's little portable Underwood, observe, "Think what he could have written if he had a computer!"

The university has taken great care to maintain the house, but the last time I walked into the library I glanced at the waist-high top shelf of the bookcase on the north wall and remembered that once upon a time there were three black-and-white photographs all in a row, unframed, each in a studio holder. The first was of Vicki taken at Pine Manor; the second was Jill's engagement photo; the third was mine. They've not been there in a great while. I wonder where we are.

Vicki and Jill died within four months of each other. In the fall of 2006, Jill suffered a massive stroke. She was incapacitated for seventeen months. She died on April 21, 2008. A self-contained woman of impeccable good manners and indomitable courage, she was Pappy's child.

Vicki's death on December 10, 2007, was the result of inoperable lung cancer. The loss of these two, the last surviving relatives of my generation, nearly wrecked me. Vicki was buried at St. Peter's Cemetery. Her grave is within several yards of Pappy's and Aunt Estelle's.

My mother, Wese, survived Dean's death, an abusive marriage, a car wreck in which she was thrown through the windshield, cancer, more broken bones than she could count (ankles and clavicles, ribs and back, arms, wrists, and legs, some more than once), and many surgeries. I spent many hours with her in the hospital. I never saw her afraid.

William and Jack adored her—as did I, in spite of my difficulties in understanding, or accepting, her tormented relationship with Jimmy Meadow. Whenever she dined at Rowan Oak, Pappy seated her on his right, the place of honor. She maintained close ties with both the Faulkners and Jimmy, without explanation or apology to anyone, literally until death did them part. She had an endless capacity for giving of herself, spending hours as a volunteer in the children's cancer ward of a local hospital and taking many a "wounded bird" under her wing when she worked with foreign students at Ole Miss.

Wese fought a four-year battle with Alzheimer's. She died of pneumonia at home.

At her graveside service, I was surprised at the number of people who came to honor her. She had been sick for such a long time; but the people who loved her, and they were many, did not forget. In the eulogy, her Presbyterian minister recalled how often she spoke of her life with Dean, of their flying days, as if it had all happened but a short while ago, as if their marriage, the happiest days of her life, had lasted a very long time. At the close of the brief ceremony, a small single-engine pale blue Cessna flew low over the cemetery in its landing approach to the Oxford airport. To me it was a blessed assurance that Wese would spend eternity with her beloved Dean.

They are all there now, in St. Peter's Cemetery, but some of them come back to us at 510 South Lamar, Nannie's home. On beautiful rare occasions, when we enter the house, I will stop and remark to Larry, "Pappy's been here." The smell of him— pipe smoke, cedars, tweed, leather, horses—permeates the hall-way. I know I'm not making it up because Larry can smell it, too. Other days, in the back of the house, close to Nannie's room, a presence of lilac sachet along with the scent of dried paper, as if she had just opened one of her fans, or perhaps a book, tells me that she is with me.

I always know Wese is back when I smell fresh air in the dead of winter when doors and windows are closed tight against the cold.

I don't know the scent of Dean. The closest I ever came to him was the first time I held his pilot's license, something that he had touched, that had been warmed by his hands. From the cockpit of the Waco, across time, he reached out to me.

Not long ago, Larry, my son, Jon, and I drove out to the hamlet of Thaxton, twenty miles east of Oxford, to see the field where Dean's plane went down. The crash site is on the Graham farm. The present owners told us that every spring when they plow the field they turn up pieces of Dean's plane. The old barnstormers believe that when a pilot's luck runs out there is a place on earth waiting for him, that in the split second before he crashes, he will recognize it as his own. This field was Dean's place.

Then we drove to Sand Springs Cemetery, where the three young men who died with Dean are buried. Only a mile or so from the Graham farm, the rural church cemetery lies west of Hurricane, Mississippi. The Graham markers were easy to find. Each stands about four feet tall with embossed black-and-white photographs of the deceased. They look happy and very young. We could not find Bud Warren's grave. We will try again.

Acknowledgments

FIRST, I APOLOGIZE to those who are not pleased that they *are* included in these pages as well as to those who *aren't* but feel they should have been.

When I went beyond personal experience and sought biographical facts and general background about William Faulkner's life and work, I relied on Faulkner biographer Joseph Blotner and historian Joel Williamson, whose scholarship I gratefully acknowledge. I appreciate also the close reading and suggestions of Jay Watson, president of the William Faulkner Society.

Thanks also to Bill Griffith, curator of Rowan Oak, and to Robert Hamblin, director of the Center for Faulkner Studies at Southeast Missouri State University.

My sincere thanks to those who knew my family and shared their memories and offered encouragement: Carolyn Butler Cherry, John Cherry, Sandra Baker Moore, Billy Ross Brown, Clair Smith Gurley, Gerre Hopkins, and Mil'Murray Hopkins.

For information regarding my great-grandfather Charles E. Butler and Laura and Lou Poindexter, I would like to thank Tom Freeland, the Fort Smith Public Library, and the Fort Smith National Historical Site.

I am especially grateful for the encouragement and support of my friends and fellow writers Cathie Pelletier, Neil White, and Lee Durkee, and of my editor at Crown Publishing, John Glusman, and my agent, Jeff Kleinman.

Finally, I would like to thank my children—Diane, Paige, and Jon—who heard this story and lived with it all their lives before I began to write it and who believed that their mama could write the book, and my husband, Larry, without whom the book would never have been written.

Index

About the Author

DEAN FAULKNER WELLS lives in Oxford, Mississippi, with her husband, Larry, and two good dogs, Shakespeare and Lizzie.